IN DEBT TO C. S. LEWIS

For

MIRIAM

and in memory of

KEITH
STEPHEN
DONALD
MARGARET
and
Others who had to leave before the Story ended.

IN DEBT TO C. S. LEWIS

by

PATRICIA BATSTONE

"Child," said the Lion, "I am telling you your story, not hers. No one is told any story but their own."[A]

A COTTAGE BOOKS

Special Edition

Dunkeswell, Devon 1999

ISBN 1-899601-15-5

A Catalogue record for this book is available from the British Library.

A COTTAGE BOOKS Special Edition
from Dunkeswell, Devon.
EX15 0QE

Typeset by the Author
Printed and bound by

MASLANDS LIMITED
TIVERTON, DEVON EX16 5HW

Headington Quarry Church with the grave of C. S. and Warren Lewis in the foreground [second from front marked by a simple cross] - 26th January 1998
Author's photograph

ACKNOWLEDGMENTS

Thanks are expressed to the Editors of the following publications [listed alphabetically] in which research letters referred to have been published.*

Act Now
Areopagus
Aware [formerly *Harvester*, ceased publication]
Baptist Times
Bulletin of The New York C. S. Lewis Society
Canadian C. S. Lewis Journal
Catholic Herald
Choice
Christian Family [now incorporated into *Woman Alive*]
Christian Herald, The
Christian Newsworld [ceased publication]
Christian Woman [now *Woman Alive*]
Christianity and Literature
Chronicle of The C. S. Lewis Society
Church of England Newspaper, The
C. S. Lewis Journal
Dial 174
Epworth Review
Family Life
Fellowship of Christian Writers' [FCW] Newsletter [now *Candle and Keyboard,* the Journal of the Association of Christian Writers]
Friend, The
Good Stories [ceased publication]
Gradlink
Lady, The
Literary Review, The
Local Preacher's Magazine, The
Me [ceased publication]
Methodist Recorder, The
Miscellany
One
Reform
Renewal
Success [ceased publication, succeeded by *Springboard*]
Swansea Evening Post
Universe, The
Woman and Home
Writers' News
Yours

* A number of respondents did not state source.

Thanks are also extended to:

Walter Hooper, Trustee of the C. S. Lewis Estate for assistance with information;

Harper Collins, Publishers, for permission to quote from The Chronicles of Narnia.

Faber and Faber, Publishers, to whom application has been made for permission to quote from *A Grief Observed.*

Sally Scott, The Vicar and Churchwardens of **Headington Quarry Parish Church,** and **Gordon Flanagan** of **Photographic Heritage** for permission to reproduce the drawing of the Narnia Window used on the cover of this book.

To the **Good News Bookshop, Taunton** for assistance in updating the bibliography.

And, since the book actually begins in his study, to **Dr. Jack Priestley** formerly of St. Luke's College, University of Exeter, for his infinite patience and forbearance in taking on one of his Hull colleague's 'more interesting' students.

Special thanks to

Daphne Ayles for her helpful advice and conscientious checking of the draft manuscript;

my husband, **Geoffrey**, for his assistance with some of the appendices and for the practical input which has made this publication possible;

and to my sons, **Martin** and **Noel**, for encouraging me to persevere - and for their Chronicles of Narnia!

Most of all, my thanks are due to those 218 respondents who have to remain anonymous, without whose contributions this book would not have been possible. I am only sad that the passage of time has meant that several people have died and in the case of some of these I have broken my own rules and included them in the Dedication: these were people whose own earthly stories I shared in some small way; those stories are now over and new ones have begun. The small number of respondents who have kept in touch and chivvied me along from time to time has been an added bonus.

NOTE ON THE TEXT

Statements rendered in bold type followed by * indicate the author's emphasis not that of the respondent.

CONTENTS

INTRODUCTION

From Shadows to Substance – A Personal Encounter

> Suddenly, at a given point, I was face to face with myself:
> I was Orual; she was me. I began to learn some uncomfortable lessons about myself.

It is not the 'done thing' to write personal experiences into academic theses, but having written my encounter with Orual well into the rough draft, I waited with a certain deference for my supervisor's reaction.

It was swift and unexpected.

"After all you've written you wait till page 1308 to tell me what this is really about. Get that into the introduction." 'That' was my encounter with Orual.

At that point, I subsequently wrote in my doctoral thesis, 'the goal of this research revealed itself: man's search for identity could not be divorced from his image of God.'[1]

For Orual, the ugly Queen of Glome, arch-protagonist in *Till We Have Faces*, was a seeker after truth - in this case, a seeker after her half-sister Psyche, one of C. S. Lewis' 'Christ-figures' - and her own journey of self-discovery, what she portrayed, not so much on paper but to the reader's mind and senses, was important. Following that dramatic encounter, as I snuggled up to a warm radiator in my small study, I engaged in some intensive psychotherapeutic study which, as I wrote then, 'has shed light on the study of Orual and her inter-relationship with the deity and with others, and on her understanding of herself in the context of Love.'[2]

Orual's external experience of deity was, in fact, no more than a block of granite in a pagan temple, but her intense need to find her lost half-sister led her into the spiritual encounter that eventually rid her of all that was ugly and transformed her.

THE SYMPOSIUM

It was, of course, a lovely story, and for me the most moving of all Lewis' fiction. The original plot was not his own but that of the second century Greek mythologist, Lucius Apuleius Platonicus, who wrote the legend of Cupid and Psyche into *The Golden Ass.* Lewis, while retaining every vestige of a barbarian kingdom, had subtly 'Christianised' it by putting Love and a living encounter with deity at the centre of it.

Long after the thesis was written that encounter stayed with me. So did something else I read - 'Sincerity Personified' by Kathryn Lindskoog[3] in which she gave examples of three people who 'liked to read, liked ideas, and had no conscious intention of becoming Christian believers' - but through encounters with Lewis' fiction that's exactly what happened. I had marked that passage as significant, and as time went on it began to seem even more significant.

The main thrust of my research had involved the way in which readers identified with the characters about whom they read: not a surface understanding only, but a real 'in shoes' experience. This was at the heart of a small survey I conducted which eventually became the basis for a workshop submission to the committee organising a Symposium at Mercer University, Atlanta, in October 1988, to mark the Twenty-fifth anniversary of Lewis' death.[4]

It was at that workshop that the most stunning example of responsive reading presented itself. I had handed out questionnaires about the influence of the books and character identification, which members were invited, first to complete, and then, if they felt able, to share, after which I planned to share my encounter with Orual.

During the discussion a man told the very personal story of how he and his wife were at a low ebb in their marriage. They had read all the 'right' books, sought all available help, but to no avail. Then his wife had happened to see a copy of Lewis' *The Great Divorce* in a bookshop window. Thinking it to be a book about marriage and divorce, she had bought it and taken it home, where she devoured it avidly. Like Eve, she then 'gave to her husband and he, too, did eat.' That first encounter with Lewis saved their marriage. Something - I don't know what, and neither, really, did they - had so involved them that it caused them to see their relationship, one another and the spiritual dimension in a new light. The book had transformed their lives, and, at the same time, introduced them to C. S. Lewis.

THE QUESTION

When the questionnaires were returned I was disappointed to find no reference to that account written down and only some of the respondents had identified themselves, yet it was unforgettable and gave rise to a question: if this had 'worked' for me and for this couple and for those people Kathryn Lindskoog cited, how many more people were there out there with stories to tell? So much had been written on Lewis' theology, philosophy and literary studies, yet little more than academic theses and scholarly books emanating from them had appeared on the fiction. At that particular time, and over the next two years, in fact, the emphasis was to be on guidebooks and biographies, including the controversial volume by A. N. Wilson.[5] The only book with any reference to the fiction was Brian Sibley's *Shadowlands*[6] the television film of which seemed to bear no reference whatsoever and to be full of chronological inaccuracies.

Clearly, at that stage, the matter still seemed to hinge on identity with the characters, so as a small pilot study I circulated copies of my workshop questionnaire among other delegates and twenty-six were returned, a surprisingly low number bearing in mind the enthusiasm for Lewis. That was explained by the fact that most participants were devotees of either the man or his theology. As ever, his fiction rated way down the line.

Some of those first respondents, themselves long-standing authorities on Lewis, were more than generous with their comments, confidences, range of thought and in one case, an additional unpublished paper. I was encouraged. Reading them pointed to the direction of future enquiries. It needed, not an involved or loaded questionnaire, but an invitation to share, in confidence, any way at all in which the reading of Lewis' fiction had influenced the lives of his readers.

Over the next nine to twelve months the invitation was published in virtually all the denominational newspapers and a great number of religious magazines, followed by another mailing to mass-market and other secular and literary magazines. Some appeared almost immediately so that by January 1989 I was already receiving responses. The fact that some took so much longer was due to publishing agendas and when asked by one if the following autumn would be too late, I said no, realising then that this was to be no short-term study. The point at which it would cease would be when a specific number of responses was received. I took counsel, and set the figure at two hundred. In fact, including the pilot survey, in one way or another just short of two hundred and fifty people participated. The conduct of this survey is outlined in Part I.

SHADOWS INTO SUBSTANCE

My initial use of the cryptic phrase 'Shadow into Substance' arose out of the early stages of my doctoral studies and was originally intended as the title to this book. It was brought to my attention through reading Gunnar Urang's study *Shadows of Heaven*[7] in which he discusses Lewis' contrast between shadow and substance as derived from Plato's Myth of the Cave, a graphic illustration of how the idea and the reality can both support and distort one's concepts of material and spiritual entities. The distorted shadow image breeds fear and misunderstanding. It may also so cloud the vision of the onlooker as to undermine the true nature of glory - in tandem with the Gnostic notion of the insubstantial Christ.

It was this line of thought that caused Lewis to write of a 'shadow of an image of God' before which people may be as fearful as they are of their own shadow, because they have an insubstantial picture of what God is like.[8] He also suggested that modern Christianity tended to confuse substance and shadow[9] and so undersell its own message.

Lewis was determined not to undersell his message, and whether overtly so or not, it lies at the heart of all his fiction. Yet it is possible for people to read him at their own stage or level. The Christian will see God while the non-Christian will see Goodness, and in both the desire is the same. Another major reason for choosing Lewis (along with

Tolkien) was his ability to bridge the gulf between childhood and adulthood - and one respondent summarised this very clearly.

'I think Lewis' books supplied a very real lack when I was about ten years old as they bridged the gap between "fairytales" and "baby books" which children of that age were too proud to be interested in, and books written exclusively for adults, with only adults as heroes or heroines. That was what made me enjoy them - the fact that the heroes/heroines were both male and female and they were my age. I could identify with them and the stories were not too incredible.'

My original study had embarked from the simple premise, founded on another statement by Plato[10] that in order fully to know ourselves we must first know God, and that our own self-image rested on our formulation of an image of God. The fiction of Lewis was seen as one of the vehicles whereby the readers could so identify with the characters in the book as to gain full self-understanding. This is epitomised in the little experience recorded at the beginning of the chapter.

Lewis was, of course, no unique phenomenon, but one of a breed of writers of 'Christian religious fiction' who see the human species as a mere shadow without the transforming presence of Christ, which alone gives substance. This view, expressed by Robert Detweiler,[11] assumes the necessity of 'knowing God' in order to 'know oneself.'

THE RESPONDENTS

That was the theoretical side. How it worked out in practice became the substance of this research, which went beyond the religious and out into the world in an interesting way, for not only were nearly 50% of the targeted periodicals wholly secular, the readership was also very widely spread, so that a response to a Christian magazine did not pre-suppose the reader was a Christian. Lewis was indeed 'a man for all people.'

I asked no details of age, sex, education or social or religious status, assuming that a good cross-section of publications would guarantee all I needed and not, at the same time, detract anyone from my main purpose or put them off by asking too many personal details. I just wanted to hear from people who had actually **read** Lewis' fiction (not necessarily all of it) and retained some lasting influence from it. In the event, very few did not tell me something about themselves because in most cases it was relevant to their answer. That was how it should be. Had I restricted my target I would have missed out on the elderly **now** whose lives were changed **then** (as student or young soldier, for instance). What mattered above all were their stories.

All but one correspondent gave me full details of name and geographical location, and this information is, of course, regarded with strict confidence. In the case of geographical information, references to Oxford and Cambridge have remained, as have some country references but otherwise only a very minimal number of places far enough in the past as to be unrecognisable. A gap in the response indicates a missing reference.

In the first instance, everyone began as a number followed by 'F' or 'M' but given the nature of the enquiry, I found this to be too clinical and impersonal. Consequently, despite the necessary though cumbersome repetition of the term 'respondent,' each person quoted has been given a new name as a device for identification - as far as possible avoiding the real names of anyone who wrote (and indicated in square brackets after most quotations, together with the publication read and country if outside the British Isles). Thus, whether famous or infamous, rich or poor, old or young, from actor to academic, barrister to barmaid, nurse to nurseryman, priest to porter, all become equal and nothing should be read into any of the names assigned. I readily acknowledge the assistance of the *Penguin Dictionary of Saints* and *The Wordsworth Dictionary of First Names*! An index of respondents is included for the benefit of those who wish to make cross-references.

THE OTHER SIDE

One unexpected side of this exercise was the interest shown in who I was and what I was actually doing. Among respondents from publications which had not rendered my name in full was the grand assumption that, above all else, I was a **man** - 'a very busy man' it was suggested, while another went so far as to enquire, not as one did who was adamant that she didn't 'unlike some - assume that all doctors are male,' but, 'Are you a born-again believer, or just a man with an analytical mind ...?' as though it were not possible to be both.

Then there was the matter of denomination. Most assumed that I was a member of the denomination represented by the publication - a reasonable assumption, though one man wasn't sure.

'I am writing this in ignorance of whether you are an R.C. or not; I am inclined to think not, but your Christian name suggests otherwise. I have never known a Protestant called Patrick [sic], though no doubt there are many. Whatever the case, I hope nothing I have written gives offence.'

Just occasionally I detected a flippant note in follow-up letters, but this was better ignored. However, one second letter is worth quoting for the criteria it set in my mind as I faced the mammoth task of bringing order out of chaos and drawing some kind of coherent conclusion from it.

'Well, you certainly have the ability in your writing to bring out something in people's minds so I hope you are a teacher as that is one of the most important roles in life.'

But the second question remained - **what** was I doing? While some treated the matter lightly others wanted to know for reasons of their own (not least editors of Lewis journals). Was I essaying, researching a doctorate or writing a book? Just one saw, as I soon began to, the enormity of the task.

'Well, you are embarking on a difficult task. I could not do that, although I think research is fascinating - but one thing leads to another. I often find it a help to think on things and let them lie a bit ...'

Regrettably, this book certainly gives the impression of having been allowed to 'lie' more than 'a bit' though it was never my intention.

Or was I merely undertaking 'an exciting journey' or 'having a fascinating time'? 'Infinite work for you! Very interesting, I would predict!' One even plied me with questions, hoping for immediate answers, but realistically acknowledging that it might not be like that.

And indeed it was not. Beyond the surface of such enquiries came the spur to action I most needed.

'How gratifying to know that someone has thought of researching the influence of C.S.L.'s fiction on the lives of individuals! ... I am excited about your project ...'

I began to perceive the weight of responsibility which grew heavier as each attempt to form some cohesive document was begun, continued and ultimately discarded. As with page 1308 of my original thesis, there had to be a point of departure - and as it transpired, it was not to be in the place I had first thought of.

I
SETTING THE SCENE

C. S. Lewis - Saint in the Making?

"Oh, Aslan," said she, "it was kind of you to come."
"I have been here all the time," said he, "but you have just made me visible."[B]

THE RESEARCH LETTER

Between 1989 and 1993, around fifty letters were despatched to editors of magazines and a number of Lewis scholars in membership with the Conference of Christianity and Literature. In addition some were directly approached or offered to contribute when the subject of my research was known. Although requested to, not everyone who wrote stipulated their source, but analysis would suggest that responses were received via thirty-eight of the magazines contacted. A small number had kindly let me know they did not publish such letters. For the rest I assumed that silence meant that, surprisingly, no readers had responded.

The publications contacted fell into five groups - 1] religious (denominational and others); 2] literary and small press publications; 3] academic; 4] general (women's, etc.); 5] specialist (C. S. Lewis journals); plus miscellaneous contacts. Most came within groups [1] and [4] as outlined in Appendix 2B. These were sent out in four phases - religious/literary, women's/general, overseas academic and C. S. Lewis specialist publications. Group [5] produced the most disappointing response.

The initial letter read ...

'I am in the process of gathering material for research into the influence of the writings of C. S. Lewis (particularly his fiction) on the lives of individual readers.

I would, therefore, be interested to hear from anyone for whom the reading of any one (or more) of Lewis' books has been of particular significance at any time of their lives.

All information received will be treated in the strictest confidence, and all letters will, in due course, be acknowledged. Please mention [*The Journal, etc.*] when replying.'

I subsequently modified this to iron out repetition and to endeavour to discourage people from writing about anything but fiction (an abortive effort, as it turned out), so paragraph one then read ...

'I am in the process of gathering material for research into the influence of the fiction (including allegory) of C. S. Lewis on the lives of individual readers.'

When I came to the more general magazines, especially those aimed at older people, I expanded the requirement a little ...

'I wonder if any of your readers remember their youthful enjoyment of C. S. Lewis' The Chronicles of Narnia - or maybe in later years they have read his Space Trilogy, *Till We Have Faces* or short stories - or even allegories such as *The Pilgrim's Regress, The Great Divorce* and *The Screwtape Letters?'*

In several cases the letter was re-worked into a notice or 'filler' by an editor. Sometimes it was shortened and vital clauses, not least that on confidentiality, were omitted. One magazine had insisted that all responses went to them which both infringed the 'confidentiality' clause and lost me the address of one respondent.

The letter to entrants in the Conference of Christianity and Literature Directory was slightly different since it was a direct approach ...

'I am in receipt of a copy of the 1992 Directory of the Conference on Christianity and Literature and note your interest in the works of C. S. Lewis.

I am currently undertaking research into the influence of his fiction on the lives of individuals and would welcome hearing from anyone who feels they have anything to offer. Perhaps you could make this known among your students or colleagues.

If you feel unable to assist for any reason, please ignore this letter. However, should you be in a position to respond I shall welcome hearing from you. Reply coupons will be sent with any future correspondence.'

THE INITIAL RESPONSES

From these outlets plus a few personal contacts, 218 responses were received, mostly, though not all, enthusiastic about C. S. Lewis. The request itself provoked some interest - and some wrote simply to let me know. Typical of these was the following from a Jesuit priest who styled himself 'an admirer of Lewis' and wrote ...

'I can't point to any influence of his writings on my life such as a conversion to the Christian faith or some new direction taken, but they have made an indelible impression on me and become part of my mental furniture. I suppose I simply found his outlook congenial.

Leaving aside non-fiction such as *The Problem of Pain* and *They Asked for a Paper,* you may like to know the chief writings in the order in which I met them: *The Screwtape Letters* (the 1940s), *The Great Divorce* (if a nightmare can be called fiction - late 1940s or 1950s), his space trilogy, especially *Perelandra* (1950), *Till We Have Faces* (1960, re-read 20 years later). I have not read his stories for children.

I have written only to show that your letter aroused interest ... ' [JACK, *The Universe*]

Another was expressed more vividly ...

'Your letter in the *Reform* jumped out of the page. C. S. Lewis has been an invisible influence in my life for many years, so I was very interested in your request for reactions to his books ...'

After some personal information she continued,

'I first "discovered" C. S. Lewis many years ago when I read a book of his which was answers to letters from an American correspondent. I don't think he ever met her but the way he dealt with her problems impressed me. I forget the title, it was something like "Letters from C. S. Lewis to an American Lady." It wasn't the Joy he later married.

Then I discovered *The Screwtape Letters* but wasn't so taken by that. Later *Surprised by Joy* and *The Problem of Pain* I bought and often re-read. However, the book which has meant most to me is *Letters to Malcolm* on prayer. So much in that book has been an inspiration.' [WINIFRED, *Reform]*

For some the letter had offered stimulus to 'return to the book;' others expressed 'enjoyment' at writing lengthy responses, even 'pleasure in responding' because it recalled the great debt they felt they owed to Lewis - whatever form that debt took.

For one or two the request was turned to their own advantage ...

' ... I feel ... that I should write to you ... if I am to disentangle the threads of something I have up to now accepted without question.' [SIMON, *The Literary Review*]

'I ... would have been deeply gratified to have been able, at some stage in my life, to embark upon such a study of C. S. Lewis as you propose. I write very readily, therefore, to acknowledge my considerable debt to that great writer and Christian for his books (both fiction and non-fiction) and for his life' [PATRICK, *Reform]*

'It feels good to have written all this down; thank you for the opportunity.' [JACKSON, USA]

One respondent wrote to tell me about his own studies and made no secret of the fact that he was actually more interested in receiving help than in giving it. He was looking for a theological correspondence to help make up for local difficulties, since, as he put it, his letter was being written 'on a machine that turns Braille into print.'

Then, too, there were the simple expressions of gratitude ...

'Thank you ... for your solicitation which has given me the opportunity to share this brief expression of gratitude to a man who has so richly blessed my life (or rather opened it to the blessings of God).' [TED, *Reform]*

' ... I could go on and on about this book ... Thank you for the opportunity to express my thoughts.' [RAYMOND, *Baptist Times*]

One respondent appeared to have conducted some personal research in order to write:

' ... it has been good to reappraise *A Grief Observed* to find out more about C. S. Lewis in order to write this letter!' [MORGAN, *The Friend*]

For others there was simply the desire to write and the difficulty of doing so, for one reason and another. Some asked for questions to help them along but clearly expected something more simplistic than my one basic question.

Even the passage of time between the letter appearing and the respondent reading it did not deter the 'addict' ...

'... I wonder if you are still interested in hearing from people? I discovered C. S. Lewis' genius as a child, and have found that everything I have read is deeply profound and relevant to personal understanding and spiritual growth in the Christian faith. I would very much enjoy sharing more with you ... (I am an enthusiast and an addict!).' [NOREEN, *Woman and Home*]

'SAINT' LEWIS?

The freely expressed delight of some was tempered in other quarters by a very big question - **why**?

'If you are trying to get our mutual friend canonised, I think you will fail! There are too many faults in his theology for that! However, I am sure he is in heaven, and is praying that his books will sell here below (though perhaps for different reasons from when he was still here on earth!).' [DESMOND, *The Universe*]

Any cryptic question thrown into the market place will undoubtedly attract comment and questions. The line between 'What are you doing?' and 'Why?' is very narrow here. To some the fact that I was engaged in study of the 'message' rather than the 'messenger' seemed hard to grasp.

But 'Saint' Lewis? One respondent had hinted at the cult of 'Saint Lewis' in America ...

'I would be interested to know what form of project it will be. Is it in connection with studies, for a book, or your own personal interest? I was glad to read of someone who seems to enjoy reading C. S. Lewis too. I have a number of American friends, and they appear to be better acquainted with his writings than the British!' [JANCY, Belgium, *Woman and Home*]

Yet here, even amongst the most ardent supporters, there seemed to be doubts.

'I have not the slightest doubt that C. S. Lewis has been one of the most effective Christian apologists of modern times. He never professed to be a theologian but had great God-given skills in commending the truth of "mere Christianity" winsomely, clearly and persuasively. He was not a perfect saint, but I have not met many of those!' [PERCY, *Harvester*]

Nevertheless, one person believed that there was hope for Lewis in the hereafter ...

'Just as the old explorers - Magellan, Cabot, Raleigh, Scott and many others slowly revealed new and exciting truths about our physical world, and, in the process, overturning many firmly held "beliefs," so Jack Lewis has been the messenger who has brought to this generation a new, exciting insight into spiritual truths. I'm sure at the end of his earthly journey there was a special blast of welcome on the trumpets on the "other side."' [NIGEL, *Reform*]

'At present I am in the third year of my doctoral research into Lewis' theology, as it is expressed in his seven Chronicles of Narnia. I chose this topic because, having done a masters degree on the theology in John Bunyan's *The Pilgrim's Progress*, I wanted to stay in the same area of literature and theology, but looking at a more contemporary Christian writer. When the idea first came to me I was somewhat hesitant. For although I had read a couple of the fairy tales in childhood, *Out of the Silent Planet* in my teens and *The Four Loves* as an undergraduate, I felt I knew very little about him. But then I listened to "Shadowlands" on television, and this convinced me that he was a deeply spiritual man and a worthwhile subject of research. Since then I have not looked back ... ' [CONRAD, *Baptist Times*]

'... it seems to me that he [Lewis] has answered brilliantly and incisively every one of the 20th century's stock of favourite objections to orthodox Christian belief. Yet they can still be heard trotted out as though they were unanswerable! The world carries on as though it hasn't heard. I suppose it hasn't. As he said himself the only way Christian teaching can be imparted to today's hardened and cynical world is to smuggle it in disguised as something else. This, happily, he has also done with his fiction.

... C. S. Lewis is the only writer I have come to feel an intense love for without ever having met him. I really thank God for this great and joyful defender of the faith, whose works are now part of my daily reading alongside the Bible.' [BERNARD: *The Universe*]

That respondent had begun in curiosity ...

'I wonder what your object is, but am only too happy to pay tribute to the greatest literary discovery of my life.'

There was speculation, too, as to how I was viewing the response to my question. One respondent, having just recounted a very traumatic episode in her life, put it in a postscript:

'I imagine you are having an exciting journey with your research.' [UNITY, *The Friend*]

And again,

'I wonder how much variety you have received.' [VERITY, *The Friend*]

PROBLEM PEOPLE - PROBLEM BOOKS

Lewis' popularity posed a problem for one respondent and this in turn led to the danger of his books deliberately being used to influence - or maybe even manipulate - people. The following is part of a very long testimony.

'Finding the Way Alone'

'I was introduced to the Narnia Chronicles in just the way I think C. S. Lewis would have wanted. At the age of nine, our class teacher chose *The Lion, the Witch and the Wardrobe* as the Friday afternoon book to read to the class. Most of us adored it. Several of us descended on the Narnia books in the class library shelves and passed them round avidly until we had devoured the lot. I then spent all my birthday and Christmas book tokens on them until I had the set at home. I read and re-read them, and they were my favourite books of all time, with the *Swallows and Amazons* series a close second.

I am convinced that to label the books as "Christian" or of good "Christian" influence will prevent children from being led past those "watchful dragons"[12] ... Children should simply be given the books, and allowed to enjoy them at whatever level they can take them, and any influence will work in its own way.* The worst thing is that a child should think it is being given the books for their own good, or for some Christian or church end. That will detract from their working. I am most concerned about the evangelical popularity of the books, simply because they are becoming associated with churchy things and religion in a way that may detract from their subtle and gentle effect.

What of that effect? What actually do the books do to the young reader? I have thought a great deal about this, and I think they introduce concepts, ideas, feelings and types of personalities to which a child responds instinctively, and which are recognised at a deep level as true. These relate to Christian truths, morals, and the personality of Christ and God, which are then more likely to be recognised, loved and accepted later on. It sounds rather trite and over-simplistic, but I think it is almost as though, in later discovering Christianity, it was as though I discovered Narnia really existed, with its heroisms and traitors, good and bad, Great Emperor over the Sea, Aslan and the lot. Real, adult life is of course less simple, less concrete than a child's fantasy world, but it is worth remembering that Lewis did not baulk at introducing less concrete elements. *The Last Battle* deals with the phenomenon of those who seemed to love Aslan, but did not, and those who seemed not to, but did, and those who don't seem able to see what is obvious. It is not quite all neat and clean.

Lewis is only a human being, and not perfect, and the trouble with his popularity in the evangelical world is that he is put on a pedestal, then liable to be pushed off. I like him enormously, even though I do not always like all his ideas, but that makes him properly human. If we disagree with some of his apologetics, or find him too neat or particular in his explanations of difficult things, I still believe no one could question his transcendent gift of expressing the heavenly in human terms. This he does par excellence in the Narnia books - touching those chords deep in a child which know Christ because that is who we are made to know, even if we are not aware of it. Not all children who read and love Narnia will come to know and love Christ, for there is an element of acceptance needed, and one can choose not to trust that which requires a childlike response in us in Christianity. A bit like Susan turning against Narnia and saying it was just all kids' stuff, games they used to play. In rejecting Christ, an adult is almost saying the same - not daring or wanting to trust that the "kids' stuff" of good and bad, truth and lie, love and hate, compassion and selfishness are real, grown-up truths. In fact they are. A child introduced to those truths in Narnia needs to recognise and accept those truths in the real world. Not all will, but I was certainly prepared to do so by loving Narnia, and most importantly, by not knowing what was happening to me.

I am sure our teacher hoped and perhaps even prayed that many of us would be influenced by her reading the books towards Christianity. Wisely, she never hinted as such. However, of that class of nine-year-olds, most of us went through to the sixth form together. In the fifth and sixth form a large number were converted to Christianity at a local church youth group. Then there was me, finding a way alone and joining them in the largest C.U. the school had had for a long time. I think at least half a dozen of us were prepared for Christianity back in those young days, and in my case, the link with the Narnia books is particularly clear to trace.' [CHARLOTTE, *Church of England Newspaper*]

Another problem raised was that of distinguishing between fiction and non-fiction ...

'I don't know if I would limit myself to the influence of Lewis' fiction. His non-fiction and fiction are woven from the same cloth, and his non-fiction so laced with metaphor, and his fiction done in an essayist's narrative voice, that we might have a hard time strictly dividing the two.' [NYALL, USA, *Christianity and Literature*]

Though not specifically defined, this seemed to be a recurring problem throughout the responses since inevitably fact and fiction did impinge on one another in people's minds and experiences.

'A Yawning Gulf'

One respondent, a practising Catholic, had read 'mountains of pious Catholic literature,' but while some of it was 'inspiring and helpful,' he found it created

' ... a yawning gulf between itself and the reality of people's ordinary everyday lives in the world we are actually living in.' [BERNARD, *The Universe*]

C. S. Lewis, he added, had, though not a Catholic, 'put the bridge across the gulf firmly into place.' He concluded the statement vehemently, 'Thanks be to God!'

This idea was taken further by those who found that reading one Lewis book, for whatever reason, tended to lead them to others, e.g.

'*Mere Christianity* served to explain the basics to me and confront me with the challenge at a time when I was tempted to throw the whole Christian thing over. The various Screwtape books always rang true.' [ADAM, *Family Life*]

Occasionally the gap appeared from the 'other side,' as it were - the side of ambivalence towards anything and everything to do with Lewis.

'I will try now to break this fence between Lewis and me and read something. I can't remember the illustrations of "Screwtape" (horrible title) but did not care at all for the illustration on the cover. It is four years since I had it but it has really put me off the Christian Book Shop at which I bought it. I do feel though that one tries to read someone who has **found** God. Yet you write as though Lewis has. I am thinking of people who say, Mahler is searching for God, and Bruckner has found him! I believe **that** also, but how can one explain it? ... ' [YOLANDE, *Reform*]

LEWIS UNDER SCRUTINY

Fourteen respondents produced full-scale analyses, which was not what I had envisaged. In addition, several provided very lengthy life histories while others tended to combine experience and analysis. Some respondents wrote an initial letter and then followed it up with the analysis. These varied; a few stand out.

'The edge between Time and Space'

One respondent describes herself as 'a foreign woman,' an 'alien' in a foreign land. Her sheer enthusiasm for "Narnia" is infectious - and speaks for itself.

'I read - I thought - almost anything, from Herodotus, passing along the Greeks, Julius Caesar and Marco Polo, D. Quixote, Shakespeare, French classics and good translations of Arabic and Celtic and Russian works. Anything from philosophy to science-fiction.

Then, twelve years ago, I came to live in [Wales] and one day, I had the shock - the best, sweetest loveliest, "fulfillingest" shock surprise of my life - The Chronicles of Narnia! I saw it again and again in video - and the more I see it the more it enthuses me! I adore every moment of it.

I thought to let you know [how] I feel when I saw your request in *Woman and Home.*

I could tell you the main reasons I love it, but it will take too long ...'

A few months later the following list of 'approaches' arrived.

'FIRST APPROACH - I love Narnia so much because there is nothing "irreal" about it. It is a plain day to day living, but an extensive and exhaustive one, from the beginning of Time, up to now and beyond. Suddenly I realised that I am speaking about Narnia, but I have not read the books, only seen it on television. So I stopped writing to you and went to the local library and borrowed the lot. Back home I read, and read, and read ...

SECOND APPROACH - I was surprised to learn that the story "came about [with] an imaginary faun carrying an umbrella and some parcels"! - To me, in the story, the faun is obviously the author himself. He is the little-boy nature loving that finds himself carrying an umbrella and parcels in a cold world having to repress his love for free spaces and nature to go to school and become "a man." C. S. Lewis loved everybody, he couldn't be nasty or horrible to anyone or any animated creature and he never forgot his childhood and kept all his life the magic touch - to be able to go back in time to any age. I explain: he could be five, or eleven or seventeen years old - but he never was able to find out - as I am not - "When a lovely, clever child becomes a stupid ambitious adult!"

In his books the adults are of no importance; he feels that the organisation of the animal world (O.A.W.) is certainly more efficient and fair - or that the simple people with little knowledge do better.

THIRD APPROACH - In the Tales of Narnia the author gets most if not all of the magic "bits" from his profound knowledge of the classics, the Ancient Greek myths, the 1001 nights, the old stories of Persia and India - all books related to so ancient times that for the average reader around 1945 everything seemed absolutely original. FOURTH APPROACH - going on reading all the voyages across the sea, the strange habits, the different cultures, the deserts, I realised that, probably, the Chronicles of Narnia are the British equivalents of Homer's *Odyssey* - or the *Lusiadas* by Camoes - the Portuguese poet.

I do not know enough of the recent history of British expansionism - but I can find very many "points" of Imperialism approval in the Chronicles of Narnia.

C. S. Lewis, in the whole, after having said about his happy childhood in Ireland, tells us about his travel across the Irish Sea to an unknown land, and beyond, having to say goodbye to everything he loves.

Then he suggests that "you" can be sent away from home for a valid reason (the war is a good reason to send children to the country and men to the battlefields of life) but you can always hope to be back. In fact, sooner or later you will be back.

Back could mean "after death," back to the Kingdom of God, where you will be in peace, after a troubled stay on human soil.

His Christianity appears everywhere, not least in the slaughter of the Lion to save the naughty boy. I love that "bit" because personally I believe that one should give his life for the truth. C. S. Lewis did realise how complex is human nature and how hopeless and hard it is to try to change it, in any way.

The eternal fight between light and darkness, good and evil, knowledge and ignorance, and the thin edge between them is shown in the title of the first book - the lion - justice and strength; the witch - nasty and selfish; - and the wardrobe - the edge between time and space, eternal and ephemerous, the known and the unknown! Beautiful! Beautiful!

The main reason why I love it so much is because I "kind" identify with C. S. Lewis' way of seeing the world and its inhabitants - understanding that the man is really the child that needs guidance and if he does not get guidance, goes astray.

I still feel that C. S. Lewis would have understood me. That makes me happy!' [THURZA, *Woman and Home*]

This seems to be a clear demonstration of Narnia's ability to capture an imagination and Lewis' ability to portray the numinous in unexpected places.

Veiled Realities

Another respondent used a series of key words/phrases ...

'There are ... a number of ideas worth mentioning which run through a large number of his works (his non-fiction as well) which have gone home to my mind.
REALITY: I had cause to write a letter to a friend of mine only a few weeks ago ...

who said that he sometimes wondered if he ought really [to] be working in the "real" world. On thinking about it, I quoted from *The Silver Chair* (my favourite) where one of the children tells one of the Underworld dwellers that "our play world can lick your real world hollow" - doesn't it make you laugh to see such a profound and yet simple statement on the lips of a child and in a children's book! - mentioned *The Voyage of the "Dawn Treader"* and also wrote a fair bit about an article called 'Learning in War-time' in *Fernseed and Elephants* ... In all I think Mr. Lewis had a fair bit to say about where the "real" country was. I could have gone on to talk of his "yearning" for something else (or for his real home) which he talks about in *The Pilgrim's Regress* and of course in *Surprised by Joy*.
MASKS: Another of his themes which I have lodged onto is that of masks. We so often try to hide what we really are and think behind masks. Thus we have the priest masked in *The Pilgrim's Regress* and I remember that it said that the man was quite an ordinary person until he put his mask on. We have the priest masked in *Till We Have Faces* and Orual's veil. I consider the main idea brought home in that book to be that not only did she hide herself from others behind that veil but she didn't know herself either until the veil was taken away.
IN THE BEGINNING: C. S. Lewis seems to have had a picture of creation which he painted so vividly in *The Magician's Nephew* ... and which he wrote of in the beautiful world of Mars (I've forgotten his name for it[13]) in *Out of the Silent Planet*. I refer to his account of its moral beauty - as well as physical - where intelligent creatures could live together peacefully without war. *Perelandra* looks at the Creation again from a different angle - that of the introduction of evil. ...
INDIVIDUALS: I was touched very much by C. S. Lewis' understanding of the individualness of people ... The theme is also brought home by his treatment of Edmund in *The Lion, the Witch and the Wardrobe*, of Eustace in *The Voyage of the "Dawn Treader"* and of the slave boy in *The Horse and His Boy*. I don't have access to the book at present and my recollection is faint but on the last stages of their flight, being chased by lions, they find shelter in some walled gardens ... and the gardener (?) relates (in a manner reminiscent of Jesus' talk to Peter about John - John's Gospel, chapter 21) to the boy that Aslan won't talk of somebody else's shortcomings.

... If you will allow me to speak on a more personal basis, I think that God uses this sort of book quite a lot (!) when He wants to tell me something. I have also read the *Dragon King* trilogy by Stephen Lawhead. That also made me think twice about a few things. I think God speaks to me very much through my imagination. These books seem to get through my emotions and I don't laugh them off as make believe as I think other people might do. I remember that C. S. Lewis said ... that he was drawn towards Christianity by Tolkien's (or Barfield's) comment that it was God that gave the imagination to the novelist and so every novel has its root in God ...

I am also reminded often that C. S. Lewis said that more than half of the initial commentators to *Perelandra* thought he had made the whole idea up himself and that the novel was thereby another means of getting Biblical ideas read by people who wouldn't go near a church (I can't remember where I read that and might have it a bit wrong).' [RAYMOND, *Baptist Times*]

This was just one part of a lengthy continuing correspondence.

For the most part, however, these tended to be critical in the bald sense of the word.

One response comprised a full-scale somewhat negative piece on Lewis lumped with three other writers (F. R. Leavis, Robert Graves, Edgar Lustgarten). This and a similar response are considered further in Chapter IV.

The Real Thing

Occasionally, however, they threw up some brighter moments. One man, having done a Cook's tour of most of the books, nevertheless made it clear that the Trilogy had made an impression on him.

'I am most fond of *That Hideous Strength* which they adapted very well on the radio recently. The other two Science Fiction stories I found rather dated. For example, the lack of space-suits on Mars and Venus! Also, in *Perelandra* I felt the message dominated the story too much. I liked *That Hideous Strength* because I found it so compelling. His very original way of looking at gender, advancement, technology was ahead of its time, I feel. I think he was also better there because the tale was rooted in a tradition he understood well, mediaeval ideas.

... Perhaps the thing I like best ... is discovering some of the ideas behind the fiction. In the published lectures he seems to repeat certain ideas again and again, but in the stories they are given flesh and bones. Such as the idea of the Inner Ring.' [FINLAY, FCW Newsletter]

In a second letter he returned to *That Hideous Strength.*

'I think it is the most rounded book of Lewis'. There is a perfect denouement and an ending which really is an ending. Both the other two science fiction books fell flat on me. They seemed at once contrived, too concerned with a moral message, and, in the case of the first one particularly, rather dull. ... Of course, it doesn't help that his staple food in Science Fiction reading was already rather out of date; I mean Jules Verne, H. G. Wells and the like. So Lewis is quite happy to ignore space helmets, rocket development and many similar things, that even the most gullible SF reader nowadays would expect. I was mainly disappointed at my mentor Lewis' amateur attempts.

Then when I came to *That Hideous Strength* (having read the three systematically, being rather a prig), I was immediately gripped. This was the real thing. Yes, the College image struck me even then as rather 1950s but the story was powerful, profound and timeless. Add to that a powerful use of legend and myth and I am not surprised that I was quickly intoxicated, not to mention converted to the merits of the trilogy ...

... I also very much liked *The Dark Tower.* I think it is rather a pity that he did not finish it but instead wrote the much duller *Perelandra.*'

Another view of *That Hideous Strength* was much more succinct.

' ... a burst of sunshine on a black winter's scene.' [MARILYN]

'Completing the Person'

There were, of course, exceptions among the critical approaches, e.g.

'I have read several times and enjoyed: *The Pilgrim's Regress* [and] *The Dark Tower.* I read often, as old friends whom one needs to meet: *Till We have Faces,* The Narnia Series, the Science Fiction Trilogy.

1. I find Lewis' style of English of a seeming simplicity, that must be supremely "sophisticated" to allow it to flow into one's mind without any effort. His narrative gives the impression that you are walking alongside the characters and both narrative and description show no edges of "contrivance" which so often irritate in fantasy writing. (Despite C. S. Lewis' own recommendation I could never really enjoy Tolkien for this reason.)
2. He has made me very aware of my own ignorance of history, literature and especially religious/symbolic imagery!
3. Personally, with specific regard to the content of these stories, I think I come back to the same point. By direct and indirect means all these works are concerned with re-birth and the "completing of the person." "Traditional Christianity" is incredibly shallow, unless one really delves, on this subject. I have understood far more about the great complexity of the universe, and great differences between people which results in a much deeper awareness of the importance of individual responsibility and response. Through real humility without self deception we can "have a face." - Importantly we are **part** of the total Creation - as all the people in the stories need each other so do we.
4. With regard to the "Brute Creation," it is enormously helpful to find a Christian who includes the rest of Creation in the Universal plan! Traditional attitudes dismiss all but people in Salvation, which feels quite lopsided. He puts into words much that one feels about animals without drippy sentiment.

... I believe C. S. Lewis is a unique storyteller whose work stands alongside other "real storytellers;" I wish his work had been even more prolific!' [NOREEN, *Woman and Home*]

With this letter was a page of notes made as she thought the matter through. Here she expands on a number of the points made above.

'SPECIAL STORYTELLERS - have an added dimension of sorts - "soul stories." Seem to have genuineness, no feeling of contrivance ... **natural** stories, in fact ... The stories have a psychological/spiritual wholeness giving feeling of satisfaction when read. As a Christian - created universe has in it deepest moral truth, despite fall. Storytelling reflects unconscious moral pattern (philosophers trying to get to grips with this!!).

As a committed Christian, one finds its practice often very narrow and very dull, very "traditional." C. S. Lewis expands the vision showing [we] cannot cut off mythology (in broadest sense - **history**), therefore it is part of us, and needs "Baptism" to become whole once more (especially, e.g. Jane in *That Hideous Strength,* Orual in *Till We Have Faces*).

The unconscious is overwhelmingly larger than the tiny portion with which we think - do we still possess a "Creator's blueprint" which enacts the response to "real" stories because of the recognition?

PROGRESSION - all things are part of bigger patterns; fiction Trilogy: consequences of actions progress in unforeseen ways ... Not a question of "goodies" win, "baddies" lose - really points to questions of choice, which have results for personal destiny ...

Children reject **religion**, mere fact of using this word is a turn off, but all children seem to find deep satisfaction in Narnia books - **feeding** on the story.

EMOTIONAL - "yearning for mother" - again can identify a soul yearning feeling of nostalgia for lost paradise - longing for Venus; Revulsion - Belbury.'

Narnia: An 'added dimension'?

One respondent conducted an academic enquiry into The Chronicles of Narnia as part of her degree course prior to an in-depth study on children's reading habits. She made a detailed comparison with the Biblical texts and incidents, including the miracles, from the Bible - some original, e.g. *The Last Battle* and Noah's Ark. There is also comparison with other well-known texts, such as Tolkien's *The Silmarillion* and Coleridge's *The Ancient Mariner.* She highlights the different time dimensions, and also details the reason behind Lewis' 'attack on "civilisation".' She firmly refutes any suggestion that the Chronicles are allegorical.

In questioning children she found no interest in the religious side, and

'... when I asked them about this, they were either confused, or uninterested. They saw The Chronicles of Narnia purely as a world of magic and fantasy.' [PEARL, *Me*]

She sees this element embodied in a number of themes used by Lewis, the most significant of which seems to be the 'dream-like' one. Children, she said, looked for adventure, a good story, lots of action and magic and fantasy. Some children like a book if it is funny - but there was little if any humour to be found in Narnia as far as she could see. It is 'the adult reader [who] finds an added dimension and additional enjoyment.'

II
IN REVERENCE AND AWE

'The Lewis Nuts'

'Far away, and down near the horizon, the sky began to turn grey. A light wind, very fresh, began to stir. The sky, in that one place, grew slowly and steadily paler. You could see shapes of hills standing up dark against it. All the time the Voice went on singing.[C]

'Patricia, I am one of the "Lewis nuts" who could go on and on and on. And, I reflect on what Prof. Lewis said on occasion that he himself did not want the adulation he received. He continually attempted to point to Another.' [DEAN, USA, *Bulletin of the New York C. S. Lewis Society]*

What is it about C. S. Lewis that attracts readers and draws from people such an aura of reverence that few if any other modern writers can equal? Even set alongside Tolkien and other contemporary greats, Lewis stands out as one adored above most - not the man so much as the fruit of his pen. Even when I first approached Lewis and Tolkien in the course of doctoral research, it became apparent that with Tolkien one either loved him or hated him, and with no half measures, but that with C. S. Lewis all things really are possible and one might love him for one book alone and hate him for all else, yet still be able to write volumes in his defence. Needless to say, the opposite is also true ...

'I found the matter thought-provoking despite what even then seemed a mannered, supercilious style. In the course of the next five or six years, at odd times in varied places and situations, I digested *The Problem of Pain, The Abolition of Man* and *Miracles* (the last as soon as it was published), consistently discovering valuable material but put off by the condescending, even sneering style. I sympathised with one critic of *Miracles* who considered that it ran into too many subtle channels and that the author would have been better employed on more everyday Christian problems of life.'

[OSWALD, *The Friend*]

It became easy to see the battle that was being fought in his mind as to how he should 'vote' on Lewis. He goes on to give some outline of his religious background against the over-reaction to 'silly emotional and eschatological obsessions' on the one hand and anti-evangelical on the other. He subsequently read widely, from Stephen Neill to Julian Huxley, and then

'I read *The Lion, the Witch and the Wardrobe* in 1971 after a television performance of it which badly upset some children who were our guests, and resolved not to bother with any sequels. However, in '85 I was having supper with an old family friend ... a very intelligent person of scientific training, and noticed on her shelves a box containing all seven paperbacks. Curious, I asked her what she thought of them, and was told rather shamefacedly that they were a present on her last birthday which she had not so far got around to reading. I asked leave to borrow them for a month ... and worked my way through the lot. The charm ... was lost on me.'

A 'Tumbling Enthusiasm'

Sometimes a response came in the form of what I can only describe as 'a tumbling enthusiasm' for everything Lewis wrote. For instance ...

'I have always found Lewis' books stimulating and deeply inspiring. I watched the two televised Narnia serials, but it is his religious writings that I have found so wonderfully helpful. I thought *The Screwtape Letters* was really clever and wise and witty; I gave it to one of my grandsons at his confirmation. I was impressed by *Miracles* and *The Problem of Pain,* also *Mere Christianity*, to which I believe I listened as *Broadcast Talks* some years ago.' [EUNICE, *The Universe*]

The term 'tumbling enthusiasm' well may be likened to notes falling on to the page like a class of five-year-olds sent out to play.

What are the marks of an enthusiast? Books dog-eared from constant reading? ...

' ... In the past, my copies [of the Chronicles of Narnia] have been so well thumbed that it has been necessary to replace them at least once, and I am probably on my fourth copy of *The Lion, the Witch and the Wardrobe.*' [ZANETTA, *Me*]

One who sees little or no wrong and makes allowances or hotly defends when tackled?

'Why do I love *Perelandra* so much? Well the content interests me greatly - the fact that the story is parallel with the story of Adam and Eve, triumph of good over evil. I am interested in astronomy and have always believed that there must be parallel creations of "soul-bearing" creatures. I love the language Lewis uses, and I find particularly beautiful the dialogue between Ransom and The Lady. I like the idea of the Lady's innocence combined with wisdom and closeness to her creator. I love his descriptions of the creatures, the floating mats of vegetation, the rolling seas, the Fixed Island (and its underlying symbolism). I love the eldila, especially the description and explanation in the early chapter of the eldil at the cottage.' [BEATRICE, *Woman and Home*]

Accepts almost blindly?

'... I have only just read *Mere Christianity* and *The Problem of Pain* and while I think I got something from reading them I'm blowed if I could tell anyone what I had read! Reading those two books to me was a bit like watching an Open University programme on television. The subject interests me but seems to be on the very edge of my ability to understand. I can follow what's being said but couldn't tell anyone afterwards much about it. I hope you see what I mean!' [BRIDGET, *The Methodist Recorder*]

Uses every opportunity to promote the subject of their adulation?

Another reader of *The Methodist Recorder*, a 'warm Lewis enthusiast,' sent me a copy of his dissertation abstract, outlining his enquiry into the relationship between knowledge of the writings of C. S. Lewis and George MacDonald and the pupils' scores on a questionnaire on moral attitudes, which he had conducted in various secondary schools. He had established a statistical link between the two factors higher than the 1% level of significance - perhaps a more systematised version of the story impact enquiries conducted in the 'eighties by a number of scholars and doctoral students, including myself. However, as this was not 'raw material' it was not appropriate to consult the thesis itself.

These were not always long detailed resumes on each book. Often a mere sentence was sufficient to convey the depth of feeling ...

' ... I read often, as old friends whom one needs to meet: *Till We have Faces,* The

Narnia Series, the Science Fiction Trilogy.' [NOREEN, *Woman and Home*]

'I do indeed remember The Chronicles of Narnia - absolutely brilliant!! I remember reading them over and over again, and have just bought a set for my nephew for his birthday.

I have also read a space story. I believe it was called "The Silent Planet," which I thoroughly enjoyed. He is an excellent storyteller and makes you feel as though you are really there in the world he created.' [VERNA]

'... As he said ... the passion of Aslan ... gets behind our defences in a way that the True Passion (because our concepts are blunted by familiarity) often doesn't.' [BEVIS, Brazil, *Christian Newsworld*]

Coming Home

Sometimes words only were not enough and active involvement of some description was called for - whether it meant the suspension of disbelief or some steps towards identifying with the action.

'Our introduction to his collective works was originally brought about through my sister, who discovered them while working in a children's library in ... New South Wales. *The Lion, the Witch and the Wardrobe* was the first of the Narnian Chronicles we read; and we found the enchanted world which the children entered to be totally absorbing and believable. Gradually we acquired the whole series of books.

Thus it gave us an extra fillip when we visited England for the first time about fifteen years ago, that we were at last in the same country from which the stories had emanated. We especially enjoyed the shock of recognition at seeing the Victorian style lampposts!' [CORINNE, Australian, *The Lady*]

The BBC adaptation reached Australia and on subsequent visits to London they were able to see productions at the Westminster Theatre. She commented, 'As our family has an Anglo-Australian background, we felt that Aslan had finally brought us home again!'

In one case words seemed almost inadequate.

' ... [*The Magician's Nephew*] brought my imagination to life as I lived through the creation; as Genesis 1 was retold in a beautiful and awe-inspiring way. Was this book an influence to "I danced in the morning when the world was begun" or was it vice versa?[14] Words cannot express adequately the thoughts in my mind as I read how Aslan sang and things came into being. I will not say much about this book as sheer beauty cannot be written down ...' [RAYMOND, *Baptist Times*]

He had seen the big images rather than the underlying vagaries of language.

A Way out of Despair

Is it possible that tumbling enthusiasts can perhaps be too intense in their devotion? There was no doubt about one person's enthusiasm, both for the project and for Lewis himself, but in his case it provided something in return ...

'In many ways, the influence of C.S.L.'s writing, fiction and non-fiction alike, is the story of my life, at least after my twentieth year. Though raised in a strongly Evangelical home, I was confronted in December of 1964 with the necessity of making an adult choice as to whether I wished to commit my life to Christ. I chose; but after two weeks of euphoria, I descended during the months of January and February 1965, into what Bunyan called the Slough of Despond, and what I call the "post-conversion Blues syndrome" - what if Christianity isn't true, what if all this is no more than auto-hypnosis? etc. About two months into this desperate time I picked up *Perelandra*. It was, to me, a picture of heaven. I have since learned to speak of the novel in more temperate and discriminating terms. But then, in the rawness of my need amid the melting snows of February, *Perelandra* gave me a picture of that for which I would willingly give away all else, and long before I had mastered my theology and apologetics, that one novel showed me where my heart already lived.

Naturally, I virtually inhaled everything by Lewis I could get hold of over the next couple of years - fiction, apologetics, literary criticism, essays, poetry, letters. Throughout my twenties and beyond, Lewis' writing formed a major part of my theology, my devotional and witnessing life, my writing style, even my choice of professional specialities - I did my Ph.D dissertation in Ren./Ref. [sic] because Lewis was a Renaissance scholar. To this day, at the age of forty-eight, I frequently quote Lewis to myself and, less frequently, to others in a wide variety of circumstances arising out of my professional life in a college English department.

Of all Lewis' fiction, his interplanetary trilogy touched and still touches me most nearly, providing the most satisfying vision I have ever seen of a unified whole - the entire universe shown, in some detail, from a distinctly Christian point of view. I have never lost my fascination with Lewis' ability to include and transform the major features of the old pre-Copernican universe (the "discarded image" as Lewis called it, or, as did Tillyard, the "Elizabethan world picture") in these three novels written for a mid-twentieth century popular readership, and make it good story-telling and compelling reading to boot. It's quite an achievement, and I feel quite strongly that as a group the interplanetary novels - *Out of the Silent Planet, Perelandra* and *That Hideous Strength* - are seriously underrated by Christian academics.

I could go on at length. Suffice it to say for now that I am excited about your project ... ' [RALPH, USA, Direct contact]

MEDIA AWARENESS

Eighteen people indicated that they had either come to Lewis or had their interest in him renewed through media presentation of his books - radio, television, video, cinema and newspaper reviews. In addition, I was also contacted by a representative of BBC Radio North who was planning a series to commemorate the thirtieth anniversary of Lewis' death. He wrote for information, which I supplied and he said he found fascinating; it was a question of whether his proposal was accepted. As I heard no more from him I presume it was not.

Another eight specifically referred to *Shadowlands*, either as the book or in its most popular version as a television or cinema film.

Not surprisingly, Lewis' wartime broadcast talks (later published and eventually collated and expanded as *Mere Christianity*) figured highly in many letters. These were not fiction but factual. They were designed to evoke thought and lead to decision. In many cases they succeeded very well.

A Lost Letter

Though she had enjoyed *Perelandra* and *Out of the Silent Planet,* it was the man himself, in his wartime broadcasts, which, as one listener put it,

'... really fetched me. I was, at the time, a fairly devoted Anglican, endeavouring to make some sense of my religion in all the difficulties of total war. I was a young mother with three small children - husband away in the Navy. C. S. Lewis' talks were like a breath of ozone to me. I don't know if you ever heard one? He has a peculiarly beautiful voice and what he said was so arresting, so unusual, that it really shook me up. I managed to get into Liverpool one day to hear him speak at a mid-day service at the Pier Head Church, fifty years ago now, but I can recollect it as clearly as yesterday. He **really** had charisma and what he said was so full of commonsense that it really "spoke to my condition" - as we Friends say! - and really made a great difference to the way I lived, and thought.

When his broadcast talks were published, I bought them all, and still have them. *Christian Behaviour* was the one I referred to again and again.

I loved (and still do) *The Screwtape Letters* and found *The Great Divorce* entertaining, and the study of the Psalter [*Reflections on the Psalms*] very helpful. *The Problem of Pain* was a bit beyond me - and still is. Later still I enjoyed his autobiography, *Surprised by Joy* and tried to come to terms with *Letters to Malcolm* and the sad one on Bereavement, title I now forget.

I must add one other fact. At one point I was very upset by the current Bishop of Birmingham who was preaching very revolutionary doctrine casting doubts on many established facets of Christianity, and I wrote to C. S. Lewis telling him of my perplexity. He wrote a most helpful letter back (the main feature of it was, **if** the Bishop of Birmingham really believes this, how can he go on being a Church of England bishop? Would you have much respect for, say, a prominent Liberal who talks publicly about his doubts about the Liberal ideas, yet continues to draw his salary as a paid Party member? I was impressed by this. I wonder what he'd say about our dear Bishop of Durham? [who always talks good sense, I think!])[15]

... I felt I must mention this. It was a very kind thing to do, and helped me a lot at the time.' [NANCY, *The Friend*]

Naturally, I responded by asking the writer whether she still had Lewis' letter, to which she replied,

'No, unfortunately, I did not keep C. S. Lewis' letter to me - how I wish I had! Hand-written, too. But at the time (in the late 1940s I think) he was only just another broadcaster, not famous at all. I only mentioned it as it showed a very kind and sympathetic nature. I was young and bewildered at the changes going on around us ...'

For another respondent [KEVIN, *The Universe*], listening to those wartime talks led to buying and on to *The Screwtape Letters*. Shortly afterwards he went to Oxford and two things happened. Firstly, he read the Ransom Trilogy, and then he actually **met** Lewis, not in any specific way but as one of many undergraduates in the religious circles and at the debating societies. He was present at the famous debate between Lewis and Elizabeth Anscombe on the nature of miracles - a memorable evening by all standards as it was there that he also met his future wife.

Pocket Money Book

One of the earliest books to be serialised was *The Lion, the Witch and the Wardrobe*, read, in his persuasive style, by David Davies. This was the means of many children discovering Narnia for themselves.

'My recollection of his books is that I heard *The Lion, the Witch and the Wardrobe* read on the radio by David Davies when I was a child of about seven. It was the first book I bought myself with my pocket money which I had saved. I later read all the other Narnia books but in my opinion none have the magic of *The Lion, the Witch and the Wardrobe.*

Obviously I was unaware that it is allegorical until much later but I have always been aware of its influence, as part of my consciousness.' [KIT, *Woman and Home*]

Those early broadcasts paved the way for other media presentations.

' ... I think it began when I heard *The Lion, the Witch and the Wardrobe* years ago on radio. Then, when it was shown on television all the characters came alive.' [GLENDA, Miscellany, a 'longtime fan']

One respondent wrote enthusiastically highlighting a feature in *The Christian Herald* (5.11.94) on the way in which a television portrayal of *The Lion, the Witch and the Wardrobe* was bringing the Gospel to children in Russia. 'It is thrilling to see the rich heritage of Russian art and culture being channelled into the presentation of Christian truth,' declared the headline. The letter continued,

'We watched the Narnia television series as interested as children ... Mr. Lewis obviously knew we fight more than "flesh and blood."' [GLADYS, *The Christian Herald*]

People seemed to have mixed feelings about the television portrayals, as, I confess, I did on being presented by a Lucy, described by Lewis as 'gay and golden-haired,' who looked like me forty years ago! I wasn't alone.

One young woman in her early twenties had come to Narnia when she was eleven and become an avid reader. When, eventually, she saw the stories re-enacted on television she was disappointed - 'reading the books was much more fulfilling.' [SAMANTHA, *Me*]

Of course, there was a more positive side ...

'... Both my girls were entranced by the BBC TV productions of The Chronicles of Narnia, and I have taken the older one to see the stage productions of *The Lion, The Witch and The Wardrobe* and *Prince Caspian,* which we both hugely enjoyed.' [POLLY, *Christian Family*]

Escape Route

One mother wrote how her children had

'avidly watched the televised version of the Chronicles although we had all formed our own mental picture of what Aslan, etc. would look like.' [VALDA, *Me*]

'It was only when I had my own children that I discovered *The Lion, the Witch and the Wardrobe.* I would be in my thirties then. I just love that book, and thought the television version was superb. Oddly enough, the castle used was apparently Manorbier Castle - and that is a place I already knew well. I do not find the other Lewis children's books so remarkable. Hard to keep up that high standard.' [BEATRICE, *Woman and Home*]

Called to Baptism

There was also a very moving testimony to the way in which television can be used by God to speak to people.

'I have been a committed Christian for the past four years, having been brought up in a traditional Church of England home, I, after my marriage, turned my back on Christianity. However, I dedicated my life again about four years ago ...

Just a few weeks before Christmas I turned on the television and I saw a creature on the screen clawing at the scales on his body as if trying to rid itself of encumbrances. The creature seemed to me in terrible distress. He was in water and gradually became immersed. For an unknown reason **I burst into tears** and at the same time as the creature on the television came out of the water, I **knew** the Lord was telling me to be baptised. I know this television programme was a children's programme either the Narnia Chronicles or another C. S. Lewis book, which had been adapted for television. I knew nothing of baptism by total immersion but I had this confirmed to me within two days when I picked up an *Alive with Jesus* [sic] Bible study and on the first page I turned to, I read, "Believe and be baptised" and on another page I saw a piece referring to C. S. Lewis and *The Lion, the Witch and the [Wardrobe]*! I was baptised ... on February 18th - a wonderful experience. I am delighted to tell people of my experiences, it's a pleasure to share them.' [MAY, *Renewal*]

Two respondents mentioned the plays at Westminster Theatre, but I was also reminded that Screwtape, too, had visited the stage from time to time. A former member of a theatre company wrote of taking her young son to see Sir Donald Wolfit as the solo performer in *The Screwtape Letters.* She commented that she had been a child of the 'Golden Age' of Grahame, Milne and other classics, plus many books now unobtainable - 'but not the Narnia books.' [JULIET, *Harvester*]

One respondent told me about her holiday visit to the cinema.

'When I was nineteen years old, I went with friends to a Christian holiday week at Filey. There we saw the cartoon version of the book. Suddenly, the significance of the story became very clear to me and I was moved to tears. I became a believer myself at about the age of nine and I was glad to discover that a book which I had enjoyed as a child and remembered so clearly could be linked to the faith which I hold so dear.' [DONNA, *Woman and Home*]

Another sent wadges of cuttings - one of which, from *The Times* [3.3.92] contained an obituary of poet Ruth Pitter who 'reduced to despair by her machine-shop activities ... listened to C. S. Lewis on the radio and became converted.' The broadcast appeared 'as manna from heaven to the troubled poet.'[16]

There had followed a lengthy correspondence in which 'Lewis sent her graceful compliments, while she returned sharp criticism of his poetic effusions.'[17] Only later did she actually get to know Lewis, a contemporary. The friendship ended with Lewis' marriage.

This, of course, united two media - the radio and the newspaper. The printed word is an obvious medium for C. S. Lewis. However, not everyone was influenced by Lewis alone.

A Quaker respondent sent me a five-page closely hand-written critique of all Lewis' writings, from which it appears that he 'enjoyed' (if that is the right word) a kind of love-hate relationship with the great man whom he 'discovered' among a batch of newspapers and magazines sent out to the troops serving in Egypt during the war. It was a review of *The Screwtape Letters.* Later that year, in hospital following the battle of

Alamein, he mentioned this to the hospital chaplain and was thereupon loaned a copy to read. Thus the 'relationship' began.

'Shadowlands'

Eight people made specific reference to Brian Sibley's account of Lewis' life with Joy Davidman. As television film, theatre and video it seemed to heighten awareness of Lewis' books, particularly the Chronicles of Narnia.

One respondent sent a copy of the *C. S. Lewis Institute Report* which contained the news that since the arrival of the film "Shadowlands" to America it had 'spawned more than cursory interest in his work.' Orders for books mentioned in the film had tripled in some areas and the 'spring in sales' had taken distributors by surprise. It was noted that since the film left Lewis 'in a sea of pain' it was hoped that book sales of *A Grief Observed* would enable people to 'pick up the insights gained through pain where the movie industry left off.'[18]

'In my final year at college, one of our English dissertations was a completely free choice. During the summer I feverishly read any of Lewis' books, including *Till We Have Faces, The Screwtape Letters* and his *Letters to Children,* plus many critical commentaries, etc. Having seen the play "Shadowlands" and later bought the book, I was also intrigued by his theology. It was this which formed the central focus of my dissertation, which sought to see how the inclusion of Aslan in the Narnian Chronicles had turned this sequence of stories into a twentieth century Christian allegory. Quite how well my argument stood up is questionable; one definitely to my expression, rather than the subject matter, as many critics and, indeed, Lewis himself, had studied this topic, too.' [ADELE, *Me*]

Mainly, of course, it was the human interest ...

'As you have gathered ... I have now read most of Lewis' books, both factual and fictional. My liking of Lewis was increased by a splendid portrayal of him by Joss Ackland in a play called "Shadowlands."

... I could write for hours about these books ... For me Lewis was a great romantic as is the Lord. The whole Bible is a romance between the Saviour and his Bride. In "Shadowlands" Lewis really touched my heart after the death of Joy (his wife) by saying Love was a bridge he had crossed much much too late.' [INGRAM]

Someone else who watched *Shadowlands* 'enjoyed' seeing it on television

'and was so pleased that his late marriage to Joy Davidman gave him so much happiness. I knew just how he felt when she died ... ' [WINIFRED, *Reform*]

Her husband had also died of cancer.

One respondent, who had shared a particularly harrowing experience (cited below, Chapter IV) wrote an unexpected third letter ...

'C. S. Lewis has quite suddenly become important in my life. I purchased the video "Shadowlands" and am now reading same by Brian Sibley. I identify with Lewis and Joy. When she says in the book, "God was more like a cat. He had been stalking me for a very long time, waiting for His moment, He crept nearer so silently that I never knew He was there. Then, all at once, He sprang." He, too, did this with me. Yes ... it was "A severe mercy" ... The Lord, I so clearly see in hindsight, tried the previous two years to attract my attention, so that I could have Giles' continuing emotional and financial help as my husband, but I blew it. He loves me so much that He made events impossible to ignore Him ...

I intend to read the Lewis and Davidman books - to think he was alive during my lifetime and only in Oxford, so near and Tolkien, too. Thank goodness I shall meet them in Heaven. I even feel the stirrings to write, myself, again. I tried in '85 and had some success, nothing published, but reading about Lewis makes me feel inspired.' [HANNAH, *Christian Herald*]

This was echoed by yet another respondent ...

'I have within the last few years gained much pleasure from a C. S. Lewis biography, *Shadowlands* by Brian Sibley. Reading this not only gave me greater insight into the problem of pain and suffering but revived vivid memories of my early teaching days in [the Oxford area].' [JOSEPHINE, FCW Newsletter]

Snippets and Snipes

As indicated, a number of people responded by sending cuttings and quotations. Seven in particular furnished me with a wide-ranging assortment, from obituaries [see Ruth Pitter's above] to information about the C. S. Lewis Centre and copies of the various Lewis journals which, had I chosen this route, would have been minefields of information. Some people simply referred me to them. A few of the cuttings sent lacked source information. Yet others sent cuttings and tracts to back up their viewpoint and where appropriate these are referred to within the main text.

The occasional snippet was amusing, often adding emphasis to the rampant Lewis mania that still existed in the western world. For instance, *The Guardian* of 1.3.94 reported on American Lewis mania, with five hundred C. S. Lewis societies heavily merchandising and a church in California with an 8ft. stained glass window dedicated to 'St. Lewis.' I mention these because the information is contained in a 'send-up' centred on Lewis' fiction. One cutting, a letter in *The Independent,* 22.3.90, even defended Lewis from the accusation of being a 'lousy philosopher'!

However, speaking of windows, my attention was also drawn to a much more tasteful one - the Narnia Window at Holy Trinity Church, Headington Quarry. It is in the form of two panes, depicting on the one, Aslan, Glimfeather, the "Dawn Treader," Puddleglum, the robin and an apple tree, and on the second, Digory on Strawberry, the Castle of Cair Paravel, the Unicorn, Reindeer, Beaver and Reepicheep. The various gifts and armour are spread between the two pictures. Central to both is the gas-lamp. The picture, drawn by Sally Scott, is featured on the cover of this book.

A few were testimonies in themselves, e.g. a letter from *The Independent* written on 24th February 1990, in which a reader had written about returning from the war, 'his faith in tatters' and finding restoration through *The Screwtape Letters* and *Broadcast Talks.* He asserted that it was 'small wonder' that his writing had changed many lives - he certainly 'owed much' to Lewis.

More unusual was the respondent who referred to television celebrity Matthew Henry having chosen a quotation about Narnia in his contribution to a compilation of *Best Bible Bits*!

The serious ones formed a defence against Lewis' many critics, e.g. a cutting from one of the Catholic newspapers (not identified), *circa* 1990. It contained a well-written defence of Lewis against his biographers and other critics by MP David Alton. "Lewis believed in the devil and all his works - and he strongly believed in miracles too," says Alton emphatically. Lewis, he says, had a "resolute determination not to compromise with the truth" and this, he is sure, is why Lewis continues to have such a following.

III
MEETING THE READERS

> *"' ... the Boy is safe. I have blown him to Narnia. But your task will be the harder because of what you have done."*
> *"Please, what task, Sir?" said Jill.*
> *"The task for which I called you and him here out of your own world."*
> *....*
> *"You would not have called to me unless I had been calling to you," said the Lion.*[D]

I asked no initial questions about the people who wrote to me but there were very few who did not share at least one part of their life and nowhere was this more true than in the realms of religion and education.

'HERE I STAND'

I did not make any stipulations on churchmanship, but given that quite a high proportion of people answered my letter via *The Universe, The Catholic Herald* or *The Friend* it was probably not surprising that certain assumptions about my standpoint were made, often in relation to Lewis' own high churchmanship (which tended to worry both Quakers and evangelicals). It seems, therefore, useful to make some record of those to demonstrate Lewis' appeal (well-documented in other literature about him in general terms) to such a variety of denominations.

Mix and Match

There were twenty-nine respondents from Catholic papers, though not all were Catholic. At the same time a number who responded via secular journals also specified their allegiance to this denomination. A typical statement read,

'I should explain that I am a very religious person, a practising Roman Catholic, but on the Left of politics.' [BEATRICE, *Woman and Home*]

As a teacher this respondent found immense value in the Chronicles of Narnia. However, her reason for writing had more to do with the beauty and consolation of *Perelandra*, as already mentioned above, in which she concludes,

' ... this book has influenced me deeply with regard to my religious life - it explains God, the angels and human beings, as well as the position of animals in creation. It is both beautiful and consoling.'

Seventeen people responded from *The Friend*, all of whom were Quakers and automatically assumed that I was. Yet few seemed to have been born into that denomination. One who was, and who seemed frequently to have found himself 'let down' by Lewis, wrote ...

'I read *The Screwtape Letters* first when I was fourteen or fifteen, and re-read it frequently. I was being brought up as a Quaker, and attending a Methodist school. At that time (in the mid-1950s) most Friends, as today, were vague about theology and tended to feel that a profound appreciation of the Spirit was preferable to learned understanding of the Philosophical Letter. Most Friends inclined loosely to a vague unitarianism, and thought that precision questions about the Unknowably Infinite were not very important. But [where I lived] there was still a deep respect for Friends like Edgar Dunstan and Wilfred Tregenza who were known to have orthodox knowledge and opinions. And since Lewis was both orthodox, learned, and yet wittily and straight-forwardly dedicated to making Christianity the central guide to ethical and worshipful **living**, he was very acceptable to most of us. I not only enjoyed *The Screwtape Letters* as highly entertaining, I deeply ingested its unstated thesis that constant self-critical self-examination is a part of Christian life, and that one is assumed to be redirecting one's actions according to the outcome of the self-examination.

There were occasions when Lewis should have been helping me, and he certainly seemed not to. For example, his exposition of the spiritual pride trap of thinking "now I'm being humble" described something very familiar to me, **especially** in its development as an endless chain of reflecting mirrors, as one caught oneself out being smug, and promptly revived the smugness for having caught oneself. Lewis' bluff assumption that in the end "your man's sense of humour" will get him out of it was no help to an earnest adolescent who hadn't yet learned how to combine humour with religiosity.

In a similar way, I got a stone rather than bread when Lewis suggested that it didn't matter if a causal chain of being implied a great chain of Creator-Gods, provided you accepted the first of them. I would now see it as characteristic of him to make a great palaver of following strict logic (as opposed to the woolly intuition of his opponents) until logic stops helping him, whereupon he blandly chucks it out of the window, unaware that his simpler readers now feel he's abandoned them in an untenable position.

Nonetheless, I felt I got a great deal of value out of Lewis, and things like trying not to unduly harass overworked waitresses with "reasonable" demands, and going as far as possible to avoid scandalising other people's ritualist or whatever beliefs, at least when on their territory, have almost certainly become part of my permanent being.' [GLYN, *The Friend*]

Sometimes an element of coincidence seems exaggerated. One reader, declaring that the Chronicles of Narnia had clearly opened up the way of spirituality for her, added as an afterthought,

'Incidentally, at around the same age I was enthralled/transported by the line in "Dear Lord and Father of Mankind" which states "the still small voice of calm ..." Years and years later, after becoming a Quaker, I found it was written by a Quaker.'

This experience led her to conclude,

'We should not underestimate the spirituality of children ... The seeds are sown in the younger years and blossom later when conditions are favourable.' [LORRAINE, *The Friend*]

Also among the respondents were several members of enclosed orders - some Catholics, others Anglican. In one instance the Mother Superior wrote and offered to get some of her sisters to write about their experiences of reading Lewis, which had led them to 'a deeper understanding of Christianity.' She herself added,

'Certainly C. S. Lewis has been one of the most memorable Christian writers of this century and must have reached many people who otherwise had little contact with Christianity.' [NATALIA, *The Universe*]

A Little on Heaven

One of the testimonies sent was a mix of faith and fact ...

'An Anglican friend of mine first introduced me to C. S. Lewis' Narnia stories when we were working together as library assistants. She told me how they had helped her to a better understanding of her faith, but as a very raw convert to Christianity, I was more shocked than anything else by the portrayal of our Lord as a lion and did not go any further with them.

Years later, as a [nun] I met them again and this time was much more interested. I had already met and enjoyed some of C. S. Lewis' theological writings. What he had to say seemed sensible and balanced and his clarity of style appealed very much. His essay demolishing the theory that our Lord could be considered merely as a good man interested me, for this was an argument I had heard from my father many years before. With Lewis, I concluded now that He was either what He said He was, or a lunatic - and there were no grounds whatever for that conclusion.

At first, with the Narnia series, I found them a little "thin," having been a Tolkien fan for many years and judging them by the standards of *The Lord of the Rings*. Gradually, however, I came to see that they were in a different class and had an appeal all their own. My love of them grew very gradually but is none the less strong for that. *The Last Battle* in particular had much to say. **There is so little written on heaven*** (I hope that does not sound a silly remark) and I found his concept very satisfying, and am always moved by the last few sentences, beginning where the children no longer see Aslan as a lion. (My old prejudices on this point died long ago!)

We also had *Till We Have Faces* in the monastery where we lived ... but though interested in it because of the Cupid and Psyche legend, I cannot recall it having any particular meaning for me. Though I cannot recount any dramatic effect of the Narnia books, over the years, as I have read and re-read them, and listened to them being read in the Refectory, I can certainly say that they have helped my development as a Christian and that without their very special flavour there would definitely be something lacking in my life. Like many people, I owe a great debt to C. S. Lewis for making God and the way to Him vivid and real.' [SOPHIA, *The Universe*]

The Significance of Letters

'He first impacted on me in *A Severe Mercy* by Sheldon Vanauken. As a result of reading about his influence on Vanauken and those sixteen letters Lewis wrote to the author, I became very interested in the man as a human being as well as a brilliant Christian scholar. I immediately began to read everything by and about the man.

Interestingly enough, it is his letters that have been particularly significant in my life, especially those in *Letters to an American Lady*. I have come to look upon Lewis as a spiritual director mainly because he has such a practical approach to "godly" living. One line which has comforted and strengthened me many times is *"[Your feelings] are [not] you but only a thing that happens to you. What matters is your intention and your behaviour."* That comes from a letter "To a Lady, 13th June, 1951" in the book of letters edited by Warren Lewis. I could give you many more examples of that kind of message which help me in my struggle as a Christian.

As far as his fiction is concerned, I naturally must say *Letters to Malcolm* which, I understand, is considered "fiction"; and for the same reason. Lewis seems to have understood from his own experience our frailty as human beings and was able to express in words how one can grow through that frailty to what God desires for us.' [PHYLLIS, *The Literary Review]*

This was, in fact, the first time I had heard *Letters to Malcolm* described as 'fiction.' Imaginative, yes; addressed to some hypothetical being, yes. However, to classify it as fiction, unlike *The Screwtape Letters* or *The Great Divorce,* which are allegories, is to undermine the substance of the book which is the serious business of prayer.

Narnia as Icon

It was also evident that, again, Narnia was predominant - in some unusual ways.

' ... some years ago we had the Narnia series read in the refectory and enjoyed them very much.' [NATALIA, *The Universe*]

(Lewis, friend of several religious orders and lover of banquets, would have approved of that!)

A very thought-provoking angle was put by another member of a religious order.

'The only "icon" I've ever found helpful in prayer hitherto was not meant to be an icon at all really. It was Pauline Baynes' drawing near the beginning of *The Voyage of the "Dawn Treader"* of the picture of the Narnian ship when the children find themselves inside the frame and falling in the water. It is so full of important images and hints (by the way the children are arranged, etc.) that it has become for me an icon and enabled me to begin to appreciate some traditional ones.' [ESTHER, *Bulletin of the New York C. S. Lewis Society*]

MOVING OVER

Respondents came from both inside and outside the institutional church. One thing that forcibly struck me as I began to read the letters was the number who changed denominational allegiance (sometimes more than once) and attributed it in some obscure way to Lewis.

A Wholly Congenial Belief

Is there, for instance, any significance in the number of people who became converts to Catholicism after reading Lewis? Some report a distinct connection.

'*The Screwtape Letters* had a profound effect on my spiritual life, and though C. S. Lewis probably did not intend this, it led to my conversion and entry into the Roman Catholic Church in the early 1960s. My family had disapproved of my reading books such as this as I was a growing up, for they feared that my intense interest in religion would prevent me from finding a husband! After *The Screwtape Letters* I went on to read everything Lewis ever wrote, and several biographies on this great man.' [BERNADETTE, USA, *Woman and Home*]

'Later I became a Roman Catholic, and have been one ever since. Lewis of course was not a Catholic, but I found the belief expressed in his books a wholly congenial one. I became a voracious reader of everything by Lewis that I could find. At this moment I have thirty-four Lewis books in my library.' [ORVILLE, Canada, *The Literary Review*]

In a second letter, describing Lewis' reluctance to become a Christian at all, in a parenthesis he equated his own position with regard to churchmanship.

'I became a Catholic in the same way. The Catholic Church did not - then - attract me; I much preferred the Church of England. That was over forty years ago. I now find it impossible to think of myself as anything but a Catholic.'

Two converts both refer to their experience yet don't attribute any direct cause to Lewis' writing: one had gained stimulation from Lewis' books 'both before and after ... reception into the Church' (an event which had taken place during the year Lewis died). Another described himself as 'a Catholic recently converted from the Anglican Church by the grace of God' (that, he adds, 'in the most precise sense.') He continued,

'I have nothing to hold against the Church I was in, and indeed would like to be seen as grateful for the gifts and guidance which that tradition presented me with. **One of those gifts was the works of C. S. Lewis.***

Lewis had left Oxford and gone to Cambridge by the time I went up, but his memory and influence were still around. I had by that time resigned from the Society of Friends and joined the Catholic Church, so I was more open to his influence. (To simplify a lot of complexity, it was easier to be with people who were sure they were right, and equally sure they were bad, than with people who weren't sure what was meant by being right, and unconvincingly argued that they weren't especially good.)' [GLYN, *The Friend*]

For another the move was from the Baptist Church to the Anglican tradition.

'I first discovered C. S. Lewis in 1964, having recently become a Christian through attending a Baptist Church - I was seventeen at the time. Over the next five years I moved from a narrow evangelicalism to being confirmed in the Anglican Church where I found my spiritual home in its Catholic wing. Reading C. S. Lewis was a large factor in the move. He was an author approved of by my fellow Baptists; the books they read were 'sound,' though I soon discovered there were other Lewis titles which were very suspect. I read those too.' [ISAAC, *The Universe*]

And yet another began within Methodism ...

'I was an agnostic in my youth, with a Methodist background, but the Christianity presented to me in my youth was so vague and thin that it had little effect on me, until at the age of twenty-four I underwent an Evangelical conversion of the Billy Graham type. This did not last, but during this period a Baptist minister gave me two books to read, *Out of the Silent Planet* and *The Screwtape Letters*. I enjoyed them both, and looked around for other books written by Lewis. However, I did not commit myself to any Christian denomination, and the Evangelical fervour subsided. A few years later I came into contact with a young man who was a convert to Roman Catholicism, and read the writings of Arnold Lunn and Ronald Knox, and eventually became an R.C. in 1953. But it was C. S. Lewis who laid the groundwork in convincing me of the truth of Christianity, and I still read his books.' [VERNON, *Catholic Herald/Universe*]

One might equally, of course, query the significance of the number of converts from the Anglican and other Churches to the Quakers, given that Lewis was so definite - and so Anglican - about his theology.

'It was the early broadcast talks that really influenced me, that neatly jolted me back into the Church ... and sustained me for many years. Later on I found the Anglican Church less and less meaningful, and was much influenced by Gerald Priestland ... his "Yours faithfully" broadcasts). These, eventually, led me to discover Friends, for which I am eternally grateful. Like many another, I feel I have come home.' [NANCY, *The Friend*]

Converting Ordinances

One respondent, who had attended a Baptist Church in her youth, drifted away and was then converted through reading *Mere Christianity,* after which she looked round for a church to join.

'For some time I attended what was then a Congregational Church, because it was just over the road, and with three children under four my time out was limited. (It is strange that my youngest daughter, not born then, is now a Congregationalist minister. She is, though, the only one out of five who is a Christian). Then I went to a Quaker Meeting, and have been in the Society of Friends ever since.

So, although his influence, under God, was the spur to the most important step in my life, I did not follow Lewis' churchmanship. I wonder if he would have allowed Quakers to be real Christians? Nevertheless I am always grateful to him, and I wish I had written and told him so.' [LAURA, *Writers' News*]

In the case of the two respondents, Anglicans, who met at the Socratic Club the night Lewis and Elisabeth Anscombe had their memorable debate,

'A few years after leaving Oxford, we found that Lewis' Christian orthodoxy was rare in the Anglican Church and we became Catholics. But we have never lost our respect for him and read and reread his books.' LAVINIA, *The Universe*]

'I don't want to exaggerate Lewis' influence on my becoming a Catholic, it wasn't the greatest one, but it was real nevertheless. I read of Purgatory in *The Great Divorce* - despite Lewis' disclaimer in the preface I think it is the only way to read the book - but there aren't many Anglicans who believe in Purgatory. *The Great Divorce* also has the somewhat unusual effect of making Heaven seem attractive and possible. I read [it] round about 1947. The effect was delayed a few years, but it happened.' [KEVIN, *The*

Universe]

Their churchmanship was more a by-product of Lewis' own, and they kept finding pointers to Catholicism within some of Lewis' opinions. For instance,

'In *That Hideous Strength* he expresses great opposition to contraception. That was hardly a typical Anglican point of view in 1951: and nowadays hardly a single Anglican would object. Many of the Catholic flock are, of course, wayward in this matter, but no religious body other than the Catholic Church opposes it. Some more fundamental groups have also taught against birth control. I find it interesting that pagan feminists are starting to object to artificial birth control.'

The "Real Thing"

What about Lewis' own churchmanship? Was he an ecumenist before his time, or what?

One of the two Catholic ladies cited above brought this to mind by writing, '... I strongly support the Ecumenical Movement' in her first letter and filling me in on details of her various involvements in her second letter. [CORA, *The Universe*]

A respondent who declared that he owed to Lewis his intellectual understanding of Christianity, nevertheless identified

' ... The great weakness of Lewis ... he does not enter into inter-denominational controversy, he expounds the basic traditional Christian doctrines, without suggesting to his readers that they should join any particular church. So any agnostic who is impressed by him and asks himself "What do I do now?" gets no help from Lewis and if such a person attends the nearest church, he will probably find that, whatever the moral character of the members, the ideas expounded by Lewis are not to the fore, or are not even approved of - especially the idea of hell and spiritual evil. It is rather an anti-climax.' [VERNON, *Catholic Herald/Universe*]

He does admit that this lack of direction is one reason for Lewis' wide appeal. However, in his own case, it was not helpful.

Another respondent, having begun by referring to a certain 'reverence' for Lewis, is, nevertheless, also critical of his attitude. Like Lewis, she distrusts 'the privileged few' of the 'inner ring,' yet

'To me he was a very representative figure of the Establishment. He was one of "them." This shows up rather painfully when he recommends the terms to use - or avoid - when taking religious subjects to the man-in-the-street. More grotesquely - to me in particular - come his strictures on Church Music ... ' [JOCELYN, *The Universe]*

Lewis' own high churchmanship irked some people, not least Quakers about whom he seemed to have had mixed feelings.

But another found herself a little at odds with Lewis' 'Anglican ideas' which she took 'with a very large grain of salt' and asked in turn, 'What would Screwtape have to say in a Quaker context?' and 'off we went,' the imaginations of herself and her husband taking wing on all kinds of subjects - a 'fun' exercise with an underlying seriousness, perhaps. She actually found Lewis' Anglicanism 'super-male chauvinist'! Lewis, she concluded, was

'A marvellous writer, but too sure of his theology. As an escaped Anglican, secure in the Society of Friends for the last thirty years, I do not like too great certainty in theology.' [HEIDI, *The Friend*]

This issue also concerned at least one Catholic. Three years after becoming a Catholic he had written to Lewis 'and - in effect - asked him why **he** wasn't a Catholic!' - though he stresses that he put it a little more politely than that.

'I did not really expect a reply, but I got one. Quite short and polite. He thanked me for my letter, and said he well saw the Christian charity in it. He then added that he believed that he had "what seemed to him to be answers" to the points I had raised, but he would not give them to me, as I would have answers to his answers, and he again to mine, which would lead to an interminable and inconclusive correspondence between us. Then he wished me well.

I was quite flattered, it seemed to me that he was treating me as an intellectual equal!' [VERNON, *Catholic Herald/Universe*]

In his first letter to me another respondent, after enthusing about his debt to Lewis, had commented, 'This, in spite of Lewis' "High Anglicanism" which contrasted conspicuously with my own fervent "Free Churchmanship" and which ensured, I think, that I never read him uncritically.' Later he added,

' ... I am a convinced Nonconformist, one who does not fit easily into any churchmanship ... and Lewis' churchmanship was - and is - something foreign to me. Yet I have never reckoned it anyone's prerogative to make up their own theology and be nonconformist in Christian basics. I suspect I found a like mind (dare I say) in Lewis (as in Dorothy Sayers).' [PATRICK, *Reform*]

MEETING THE MASTER

Those who actually met and knew Lewis perhaps have a less fluid attitude towards him. One such respondent said he did not find him dominating but one who infected "a note of inspired common sense" in debates. He believes in "Lewis' abiding influence" - indicated not only by those of us who still write books about him, but by the media interest in his stories.

'Lewis - just how he was'

Some wrote with obvious enthusiasm.

'I don't think that when I knew that I had a place at Oxford to read English, my first thought was "I shall meet C. S. Lewis," but he was certainly an enrichment of my time there, which was sheer joy anyway. I never heard him speak on a specifically Christian topic - in a sense I never needed to - his books were like a friend talking to you from an armchair across the fireside. His lectures, however, in the English Schools were a liberal education in themselves.

On the stroke of eleven, he would come stomping down the centre of the crowded lecture hall, shabby black gown hanging off one shoulder, with his big red face glowing like a country farmer's, lean one elbow on the lectern, and without a word of notes in front of him, speak for exactly 55 minutes, the words rolling out in that rich, gruff voice, still with a trace of Ulster drawl.

He used to enjoy lecturing for a term on a theme, with a title like 'Prolegomena to Renaissance Poetry,' and what he gave us was a picture of an age. Quoting from his prodigious memory authors most of us had only just heard about, he would make a period like the 'Middle Ages' stand up in front of you, with its costumes, manners, love affairs, philosophy, geography, science, smells even, until when you walked back down the steps into the High [Street] it was the big red buses trundling out of the Morris car factory at Cowley that seemed to be the intrusion, and the real archaism.

When, years later, I read *A Severe Mercy*[19] there was a tremendous sense of nostalgia - something in me said "Yes, this is how it was, and that is just how he was - in the Oxford of those days."' [BEVIS, Brazil, *Christian Newsworld*]

'1944 Oxford, I was a student, and attended his sermons each term ... Tremendous they were. Evangelicals at that time did not quite know what to make of him, and I remember getting some odd looks from some in the Christian Union for attending them.

He was just then writing the Narnia tales, and meeting Tolkien and someone else at their "Inklings" group one evening a week. His Cambridge sermon, *The Weight of Glory*, was out in a tiny booklet, and that has made a difference to my faith, etc. ever since, also the freshness of his *Broadcast Talks*, etc.' [RACHEL, *Writers' News*]

'Re-conversion'

' ... I was at Magdalen College from 1935 to 1938, and was briefly Lewis' pupil (for Political Science, not for English ...). I was enormously impressed with him, though at that time I had not read any of his books. I did not then regard myself as a Christian (though in fact I don't think I was at all clear in my mind about what I believed).

While I was serving in the R.A.F. in Italy during the war, a relative sent me a number of books, including two of Lewis' (*Perelandra* and *The Screwtape Letters*). I was fascinated by them. They must have played a part in reconverting me to Christianity; something that happened about that time, though I don't remember exactly when.

... I never became an intimate friend of his, but our paths occasionally crossed. My last meeting with him, a casual encounter in ... Oxford ... ended up in a nearby pub ... ' [ORVILLE, Canada, *Literary Review*]

'I found his C. of E. theology less than profound here and there ... but in other places very profound. ... I liked Lewis and I bought and read several of his paperbacks. I thought the best one was *Miracles* and the best fiction *Perelandra*.' [KIRK, *The Friend*]

Some, however, had mixed feelings about Lewis the man, and one lady wrote and explained why she had **not** been tutored by Lewis as a student ...

'I went to all the great man's lectures and they were very entertaining - even my notes seemed to make quite a good read. He, Charles Williams and John Tolkien were great friends and much admired - but when offered C.S.L. as a tutor I declined! I think I was right. He had a reputation for being hard on females ...' [KAREN, *The Lady*]

A Lingering Presence

There were those for whom his influence, long gone in the flesh, still permeated those hallowed halls - interesting when the University distanced itself from his theology. Yet it follows the path set by the young Lewis when, at sixteen, he lighted on *Phantastes* by George MacDonald and declared that it 'baptised his imagination.' Perhaps it was for this reason that his influence spread to other campuses, too.

'Though I sincerely feel that outside my own father, I am not consciously aware of a single individual to whom I owe a greater debt, it has been about thirty years since I started a journey that lasted some fifteen years with Lewis as my constant companion. Now that is not to say that he is no longer with me, but I like to say that I have outgrown Lewis. Not that I am superior in intelligence or in any other sense to him, it just means that I do not depend to such a degree on what he said, and how he said it as I once did. I do not run to him for answers to every question now. But on second thought, that is probably because I have a pretty good idea how he would answer most questions. And knowing how he hated to be lionised, I think he would approve of my quasi-independence. But I readily acknowledge that if I have a firmer footing in this mad world, he had more than just a little to do with it.' [GRANT, USA, *Christianity and Literature*]

This respondent had actually begun his studies in Oxford, but as an American had found the system insurmountable and the Lewis connection was not sufficiently strong to continue, so he had transferred to another 'provincial' (almost) university, where he had succeeded. He admitted that he owed some debt to Lewis, but at the same time, was making a conscious effort to transcend any feeling of dependence on him.

There were also those who, though not students, nevertheless encountered Lewis in the flesh.

' ... One day I dropped in to a lunchtime service in St. James', Piccadilly where Lewis was giving the address. I had vaguely heard of him before but I was very impressed with his clarity of thought and expression and how his very apposite similes shed new light on "difficult" theological matters such as The Trinity and the very purpose of life. After the service I went to Hatchards Bookshop and bought a copy of *The Screwtape Letters* which had been recently published. I read straight through it that evening and since then I have read avidly everything he wrote and most of what others have written about him. He has been a massive source of spiritual strength for me for nearly fifty years and I still read and re-read his many works. As one grows older books like *The Problem of Pain* are a source of help and comfort worth a lot more than most medical advice!' [NIGEL, *Reform*]

A Letter from Lewis

A number of respondents made reference to letters received from Lewis which had been mislaid or thrown away, their potential future value unconsidered. One, however, was unique in having held on to his treasure ...

'When I was at university before the war C. S. Lewis came to give a lecture on English Literature. I'd not heard of him before the lecture and have forgotten what it was about. However, ... one day, waiting to go abroad with my unit, I went into a bookshop and noticed a book by him called *The Problem of Pain* and bought it. In the barracks, three tiers up, with the air full of smoke, I began to read it and was surprised at the subject matter which was not English literature but something very relative to life in the war years. When we went abroad, I took the book with me and when we were cut down to battle-order and had to hand in our big packs, I copied out some passages and kept them in my paybook to read, as I was very impressed by them. During the war I read everything of C. S. Lewis I could get hold of. A friend, who had been a missionary in China till the Communists took over, sent me *Broadcast Talks, Beyond Personality* and *Christian Behaviour*. I came across some other books (*Out of the Silent Planet* and *Perelandra*, if I remember aright) in the mobile libraries that visited the troops. **They were all refreshing waters to a very thirsty soul.*** When I got back home after six years in the army, battered in body and demoralised in soul, my sister had got *That Hideous Strength* waiting for me to read. Not long after that I asked Christ to sort out the mess I was in, taking hold of Matthew 1:21. Life took an upward turn from that point.

I wrote to C.S.L. thanking him for the help his writings had been to me and I still have his reply which began,

> *Yours is at once the most beautiful and the most rational letter of this kind that I have received. I am almost alarmed by it - by the contrast between the sort of man I actually am and the sort of message I have in your case been used to transmit. However, I remember from the story of Balaam that even a donkey can be used for such purposes ...'*

[FRANKLIN, *Christian Family*]

"NARNIA" AND THE TEACHERS

Around twenty respondents indicated that they had first encountered Lewis (in all but a few cases through the Narnia books) at school, either by being directly encouraged to take them from a school library or being handed a specific book, or, most often, by having a teacher read them in class. In some cases these readings had a lasting effect.

'I attended a small country school as a child and the emphasis was very much on reading for pleasure. The teachers read to us every afternoon and, more often than not, the books were by C. S. Lewis. Each one of the books that I read or listened to held me spellbound and carried me away to a world of fantasy and make-believe but the one book that really influenced me and still is top of my list (even now that I'm a grown woman with children of my own!) was *The Lion, the Witch and the Wardrobe.* I first heard the story sat in a dark, dusty classroom listening with awe and wonder to the teacher who read it to us. From then on I lived in the beautiful world of fantasy and could hardly wait to get back home from school and read again the fantastic story.

Later on in my life, when I was training to be a primary teacher, I did a project on the book for one of my humanities assignments and, once again, I relived the wonderful journeys and adventures.

My experience is not an earth-moving one but one that will always be special to me because it cemented my love for literature and has encouraged me to continue to fall back into the world of fantasy each time I open the pages of a book.' [VANESSA, *Me*]

However, one example has already been given above (CHARLOTTE) which expresses some very real concerns about the way in which books of this nature are **used** in school classrooms and the damage that can be done to both books and readers. So, too, an opposite opinion has already been documented of which it is useful to be reminded…

'... when I asked them about this, they were either confused, or uninterested. They saw The Chronicles of Narnia purely as a world of magic and fantasy.' [PEARL, *Me*]

The respondent's research was a preliminary to an in-depth study on children's reading habits. In it she made a detailed comparison with the Biblical texts and incidents, including the miracles, from the Bible - some original, e.g. *The Last Battle* and Noah's Ark. There was also comparison with other well-known texts, such as Tolkien's *The Silmarillion* and Coleridge's *The Ancient Mariner.* She highlighted the different time dimensions, and also detailed the reason behind Lewis' 'attack on "civilisation".' She firmly refuted any suggestion that the Chronicles are allegorical.

This line of thinking would seem to be supported by another respondent's notes on the definition of 'a good teacher' who

'produces, in the taught, effect of **revelation** rather than **learning**. Don't always understand, but feel that one recognises/identifies the "ideas"/"truths" - imagery/symbolism may be previously unknown, somehow it "makes sense" - feeling of meeting with an old friend. These stories provoke, "Of course, yes, I know" response.' [NOREEN, *Woman and Home*]

The Extent of Education

But what of the teachers? We are told that

'Children reject **religion**, mere fact of using this word is a turn off, but all children seem to find deep satisfaction in Narnia books - **feeding** on the story.' [NOREEN, *Woman and Home*]

In the ever-changing climate in our educational system is the notion of reading the Chronicles of Narnia to a class no longer tenable, least of all **because** of its overt religious content (whether or not the children identify it)? And what about the vexed question of class and social mores several teachers raised?[20]

One teacher had difficulty in accepting the 'sanitised' children in Narnia and reacted unfavourably to their elevation to the ranks of royalty (perhaps the least convincing episode in the books, though it speaks of children's wish-fulfilment). Nevertheless, she

'could see the attraction of these stories for a certain privileged type of child - American in particular - and in so far as the Chronicles are able to introduce young people to Christianity and to Christian standards. I have to admit I greatly prefer them to the new vogue of rather twisted imagination as promoted by Roald Dahl.' [JOCELYN, *The Universe*]

On the other side of the argument was a variety of responses, some amusing, some illuminating - all interesting ...

Husband and wife teachers had both read the Narnia books to their classes of primary children, 'who loved them, sometimes even asking to stay in school for more!' One day a pupil borrowed her husband's copy of *The Lion, the Witch and the Wardrobe ...*

'... when it was not returned after some time he enquired about it, and was told that the boy's father and uncle were reading it! It came back eventually quite tattered, but we thought that Lewis would have approved.' [IVY, *The Lady*]

At that time (mid-1992) she added, 'Only one child ever asked me if the books had any deeper meaning, but of course others may have wondered.' Four years later, referring again to her pupils, she said, 'They, too loved them, and several asked if there was a deeper meaning to them.' Clearly there was **some** response from the children, but the extent of it must remain in doubt.

Narnia for All

'[I] was reading *The Lion, the Witch and the Wardrobe* to a class of country children. There were some ten-year-olds and a few boys of thirteen-fourteen from nearby farms - rather tough lads - among them.

As they listened to the story there was absolute silence and I heard a visitor passing through the room with the Headmaster say, "How does she get them so quiet?"

"Oh, just the feminine touch," was the reply.

But it was simply the inspired writing of C. S. Lewis!!!!' [AMY, *Reform*]

'As a schoolteacher in a boys' comprehensive school I found that the Narnia stories were quite acceptable to and obviously much appreciated by boys of eleven to thirteen years of all abilities. Most commonly I used *The Lion, the Witch and the Wardrobe* and *The Silver Chair* as "bonus readings" towards the end of R.E. lessons. Boys would remind me of them if they suspected I had forgotten!' [MYLES]

'Many years ago, when a small girl at grammar school ... my English teacher said, "I have a new book just for you!" And she put in my hands *The Lion, the Witch and the Wardrobe*. So began a love of Lewis that is still growing.' [ELSA, *Woman and Home*]

Moving to an African country one teacher taught a primary class and on alternate years read *The Lion, the Witch and the Wardrobe*, which had been published shortly after their arrival.

And not teachers only, but other pupils ...

' ... I was introduced to C. S. Lewis' writings in the late 1950s by boys at the ... Grammar School ... when I was a pupil at ... [the] Convent Grammar School ... The boys had been taught some theology (which we girls were not) and some of us were interested.' [BEATRICE, *Woman and Home*]

(She, too, became a teacher.)

In some cases the teacher's own life was changed. Having trained as a Baptist minister, one man discovered Narnia ...

'In fact I never entered the Baptist ministry for reasons that had nothing to do with C. S. Lewis. In 1965 during a teaching practice I discovered C. S. Lewis' delightful Narnia books and really enjoyed reading them to junior aged children. I continued to do this for the next twelve years during my time as a classroom teacher. They provided me with enjoyment and insight into Christian truths as well as the children.' [DARRELL, *Reform*]

'Ever since, as a student teacher, I was advised to go and select a children's book to read and comment on, and someone put *The Lion, the Witch and the Wardrobe* into my hand, I was hooked. I have been teaching twenty years and read the books with my class of nine to ten year old girls each year. One year I didn't, to give myself a change, and I really felt that that particular class had missed out.' [SARAH, *Catholic Herald*]

Yet another, admitting that it was 'difficult to over-estimate the influence of Lewis' writings have had on myself, and ... the socially-deprived children whom I teach,' wrote,

'When in my early twenties, I first discovered the "Narnia" books I was "hooked." They seemed to me to contain so much Christian truth that they warmed and enriched my life and as over the years I have shared these books with others, the spiritual understanding has been enriched too. No matter how many times I read a "Narnia" book there is always a fresh insight into some spiritual truth or a comforting re-affirmation of a basic Christian belief.' [CARL, *Church of England Newspaper*]

A Question of Kinship

However, the teacher/pupil relationship can have its dark side, not least if a child claims family connections to the idol of the moment - but when, as their mother explained, **three** children do it ...

'The most difficult thing was each of the children (three) told the same teacher at school, during three different years that they were second cousins of C. S. Lewis, and each time she told them not to lie. I even went to the headmaster about it. She was reading C. S. Lewis books to the children and of course they wanted their claim to fame, and each time they came home ridiculed by the teacher. You'd think by the third child she might have believed it. My father was **furious** - but she never believed any of us!' [LEILA, *Woman and Home*]

LITERATURE AND LETTERS

There remain two other small but significant groups of respondents whose working life and C. S. Lewis had every possibility of being inter-related - those involved in academic pursuits and those who were creative artists.

Hidden Agendas?

It was sometimes the case that Lewis' books, however they were regarded by, on the one hand, narrow Christian circles, and on the other, the academic elite, became the mainstay of an undergraduate's emotional and spiritual as well as intellectual life ...

'At that time Lewis gave me two vital things: first a comprehensible and satisfying intellectual basis for my faith, which the Christian circles I knew then did not (*Mere Christianity, The Pilgrim's Regress* and *Miracles* gave me this); second, in *Letters to Malcolm, Letters of C. S. Lewis* and *The Great Divorce* I was introduced to a much wider vision of Christianity which seemed to me to be much deeper and truer.

... Whilst I was on my ordinary course which prides itself in a high academic standard, I found Lewis' books and general approach very helpful, even though I can now see that some of his arguments are not as unanswerable as they once seemed.' [ISAAC, *The Universe*]

Among academics - Americans in particular - there is an overwhelming enthusiasm for Lewis and all his works, and this was one reason for taking the liberty of approaching individuals as well as contacting the Lewis Journals. Yet, while the initial pilot study during the Mercer University Symposium had been encouraging, this proved to be the leanest quarter of all.

Even the most hopeful of all academic responses, was, at the same time, the most discouraging. The writer was confident that I had been inundated with testimonies - yet to my knowledge, I received none unless they had omitted to refer to the lecture she had announced my project in. Were they waiting to see some groundwork in print first?

Yet here was someone full of enthusiasm, passing my name on to students and professors alike.

'What a wonderful project it is ... I feel so blessed to have the opportunity to teach Lewis - and doubly so to live at the time his life and writing so richly sowed God's love and wisdom on earth.' [ABIGAIL, USA, *Christianity and Literature*]

She made me feel that I was missing something.

Three others promised to put my question to their students and this caused probably the biggest delay in completion, yet I heard nothing from any of them. One put me in touch with a colleague but again, the correspondence was fruitless.

One misunderstood the question and sent a lot of information about magazines and collections, assuming that I was scouring journals for already published letters or looking for people who 'had information.' He was one of a handful who took this line.

Most assumed the existence of a questionnaire as opposed to one question and this clearly caused difficulties not experienced by the many 'lay people' I had heard from. Usually, when I redefined my question, I heard no more. When I did I was picked up on a technicality. That particular letter went on ...

'Lewis' writings affected the development of my personal formation, the development of basic views and perspectives. I call those foundational perspectives. And it is helpful to go back to the several basic texts that help to ground those foundational perspectives.' [WARREN, Canada, *Christianity and Literature*]

Comments in other initial responses ran ...

'... we will be reading *Till We Have Faces* among other books which deal with self-awareness and God-awareness. If I reach any conclusions about the effect of this novel on my students, I will be in touch with you again.' [LYNETTE, USA, *Christianity and Literature*]

'Your letter ... interests me. Perhaps with more thought, particularly after the busy months of our spring semester ... are over, I will have something to contribute.

Lewis' works in general have certainly influenced me, but they are so interwoven that it may be impossible for me to say how his fiction has affected me. *Perelandra* is my favourite, probably because Milton is my academic speciality.

In the autumn of this year I hope to begin a study group at my university to discuss one of Lewis' books each month. Then I can introduce your interest to them.' [XAVIER, USA, *Christianity and Literature*]

One professor wrote to express interest in assisting me, trusting that the information he had to share would be 'worth the wait' experienced through his hospitalisation - but no information was forthcoming.

There were the few, mentioned above, who sent details of their books or their own projects. Other than that, this was the pattern ...

'I am willing to make myself available for such data as you may be seeking. I am very fond especially of *That Hideous Strength* and *Till We Have Faces,* as well, of course, as *The Great Divorce*. I shall be teaching a one-month course in January ... and am looking forward to conveying my enthusiasm to thirty students ...

Perhaps you have a questionnaire, or some guide questions to which I would be happy to respond. And perhaps your format will permit some involvement of my class when the time comes.

I am eager to learn how you are structuring your project and how people respond to C. S. Lewis' fiction. I have found him bracing, stimulating, edifying in **all** of his works, fiction included. I welcome your further correspondence.' [MAX, USA, *Christianity and Literature*]

I wrote, but again there was no reply. Somehow this persistent silence nagged me. Was it that they were all simply too busy? Or that, having realised that personal publicity would be nil, saw nothing in it for themselves or their colleges? Was it the lack of a questionnaire which suggested that this was the way they were programmed to operate? Or was it that my approach did not fit their usual patterns and they simply couldn't cope with it, or didn't agree with/approve of it? It was hard to resist the possibility that it might even be because they could do better and were probably already beavering away doing just that.

In fairness to the Americans, one keen British academic went straight off the subject when he realised that I was **not** asking for 'a paper'!

Beginning with Socrates

One thing the writers and artists who responded had in common was a pre-occupation or concern with Big Issues and Ultimate Questions. One, a science fiction freelance editor, wrote about Lewis' view of science and religion.

'I share Lewis' view that science - or what currently passes as such - has itself become a kind of religion, a binding-together, to use the etymological root of the word, wherein the linkage has become more important to the participants than the actual nitty-gritty of the subject. Though I would not dream of calling myself a really serious student of science, I know just enough about it to know that much of what passes for science today is a travesty of the subject. Witness this week's revelations that all that has been taken as proven in astronomy for decades has been thrown out of the window by the new findings about the density of matter in the universe ... Perhaps I might make the point that Lewis himself was really a magnificent example of one with a really scientific attitude, being always willing to start from the Socratic point of view that he was ignorant, and had to **start** from there. Most scientists are in truth only technicians, building on someone else's viewpoint and taking matters from there. That is all right in itself, but it is the attitude of the technologist, not of the scientist.' [HAROLD, *Writers' News*]

Another (BEATRICE) whose interests ranged round history, social sciences, current affairs, archaeology and religion, loved Lewis' way of explaining creation, with particular reference to *Perelandra.*

Nightmare in Wartime

Perhaps there is a certain significance in the fact that so many of the testimonies of indebtedness to Lewis emanate from the war years when many questions were being asked, people lived under immense pressure and the possibility of death was a daily occurrence. Many, women in particular, were expected to continue living as though nothing had changed and the constant upheaval from city to country was a mere bagatelle ...

'Until I was twenty-three, God - to me - was a very distant "condemning" figure - pointing at all my faults. Because of "background problems" - my late teens-into-twenties were mainly a bleak, frightening (sometimes nightmarish) time. When I was transferred from my London office ... in 1940, I was physically, mentally and spiritually more or less a wreck (though I tried to cover it up). Then, in 1941, whilst alone in an attic bedroom, in my "billetors'" house, I had an amazing - unforgettable experience, of God coming to me, telling me He could do for me what I could not do for myself - get rid of fears, jealousies and complexes, etc. I had a wonderful sense of "belonging" I'd never known before, and an utterly real sense of love: the feeling of His reality and presence was a far more real thing than anything I'd thought possible. I began to go to Church and then some weekly Christian meetings. After the first "wonderment" of my experience, I found it became a "hard slog" to try and work out all the things I was learning and hearing about - in my everyday life.

Could I say - here - that I do have a pretty vivid imagination - that goes with "creativity." I am an artist - and also write poems, plays, pageants, etc. - some serious, some comic ... All this "blossomed" after I became a Christian (though I had always loved drawing) - but, mainly, after discovering a whole new "dimension" to Christianity - and to God: I had found myself beginning to "kick" against certain "stereotyped phrases" - continually, it seemed, used by Christians - and against a feeling that there was a kind of "confinement" of thought outside of which I must not venture. (I do not know how else to describe this?)

Then - I heard about C. S. Lewis! - and *The Screwtape Letters.* I bought a copy and devoured it in almost one sitting and re-read it. I bought *The Pilgrim's Regress* and several others and the effect was rather like the releasing of a floodgate inside me. Here was a man who obviously belonged to and loved the Lord and who had a tremendous intellect - yet who could take me on a "magic carpet" into his wonderful world of fantasy and myth and a new understanding of God - nothing "stereotyped" or "prim" here - but a God who would encourage and use imagination and even fantasy. He (C. S. Lewis) also gave a new dimension to Christian truths one could relate to.

At that particular time in my early struggle to work out in practice the experience I'd had - I almost "clung onto" these books as a lifeline. This may sound "over-dramatic" - but it was true. C. S. Lewis, I feel, helped me to know, in a real sense, the meaning of "and you shall know the truth - and the truth shall make you free" - I shall never cease to be indebted to this very special man of God.' [SYLVIA, *Christian Woman*]

Yet another artist had read *The Screwtape Letters*, found it 'distasteful,' and questioned Lewis' ability to 'uplift' people. She was, she said, fortunate

'that I don't have to try and write about it ... Art gives us experiences just beyond the range of our senses, ideas that cannot quite be grasped. glimpses of an undiscovered country, fleeting indeed yet powerful enough to make the familiar world seem drab, so that a **sense *of* disappointment** is endemic in life.' [YOLANDE, *Reform*]

It was a very powerful letter - the ability to write such letters as well as to grapple with the kind of huge topic Lewis would have revelled in also united them. Just for a brief interlude, reading them elevated this study beyond the boundaries of the common-place - but they nevertheless left me with the realisation that Lewis, who had the capacity to fire enthusiasm and lead people to faith could also spawn negative thinking and scientific questioning.

The exception came with the lady, then residing outside the country, who had found that reading *That Hideous Strength* had fired her own desire to write and was planning a visit to do some research so that she could write an essay - for what and why she did not say. She maintained that Lewis had influenced her but did not say why. She was anxious for booklets so I sent a comprehensive letter detailing where information could be found. When I came to contact her again my letter was returned, so whether that essay was ever written I never knew.

Perhaps, for the present reader, these few thoughtful responses will serve to cushion the real attacks with which Part IV has to do. They challenged Lewis from the standpoint of what he could or could not offer to their own art rather than openly condemning all that he was and stood for. Not everyone proved to be so polite.

IV
AGAINST THE TIDE

C. S. Lewis – 'Evil Incarnate'?

"'Once and for all," said the prisoner, "I adjure you to set me free. By all fears and all loves, by the bright skies of Overland, by the great Lion, by Aslan himself, I charge you - "

"Oh!" cried the three travellers as though they had been hurt. "It's the sign," said Puddleglum. "It was the ***words*** *of the sign," said Scrubb more cautiously. "Oh, what* ***are*** *we to do?" said Jill.*

It was a dreadful question. What had been the use of promising one another that they would not on any account set the Knight free, if they were now to do so the first time he happened to call upon a name they really cared about?'[E]

Criticism of Lewis tended to fall into four categories -

1. **Major criticism**: Attacks on Lewis' Christianity, morals, means and the content of his message.
2. **Theological criticism**: Present-day attacks on the viability of his theology, how much he did or didn't get right, and the niggly points connected with the major complaints.
3. **Social Criticism**: The incompatibility between Lewis' society and the present-day gender and race conscious community. Lewis' perceived chauvinism.
4. **Minor criticism** - Often former addicts who have matured and put him into perspective, separating 'wheat' from 'chaff' according to their thinking, and generally airing their grouses.

In some cases these four areas overlap; usually I have tried to distinguish them, though where this occurs within one response it is not always possible. Sometimes the respondents themselves spontaneously supply argument/counter argument - and frequently one person's experience supplies the answer to another's question or criticism.

MAJOR CRITICISM

The concluding paragraph of a supportive letter read,

'I am saddened by the current trend which links C. S. Lewis with demons and dragons and things satanic and wondered if you were pursuing this line of approach. Your views interest me greatly ... ' [BRENDON, *Christian Herald*]

Back in the early 'nineties I would never have envisaged beginning the main sections of this book by highlighting criticism - criticism levelled against Lewis for his portrayal of so much that was reminiscent of Greek mythology, occult involvement, charges of blasphemy, dissatisfaction with his attitudes, shock at the effects the revelations of Lewis' private life had on people's perception of this popular theologian-turned-storyteller to whom countless people testified to owing their faith and whom many virtually venerated and some would have canonised had it been in their power to do so. However, I would not be true to the nature of this enquiry if I did not present them, for there are always at least two sides to any argument and my role is to offer the evidence from both and to take sides with neither.

Dungeons, Dragons and C. S. Lewis

One of the many cuttings I received pointed up Lewis' antipathy to all things modern, including (surprisingly) radio, 'which he rarely listened to' (and yet made such a profound impression on) - and then proceeded to set out a detailed case for Lewis having been influenced by pagan myths, 'lies breathed through silver' as he called them, enthusing his imagination for God.[21]

A covering letter to a further batch of papers began,

'These enclosures were supplied to me by the Chick Publications Stockists ... in answer to an enquiry.' [MURIEL, *Harvester*]

One enclosure was a paper, 'C. S. Lewis Books - Definitely not Christian' by Sidney W. Hunter, which addressed the thesis that the characters in Lewis' Narnia books 'represent demons and deities from pagan mythology.' It had arisen out of accusations by Jack Chick on his discovery that Lewis' books were being sold in occult bookstores - and he believed it was 'no accident.' The paper examined each of the books and produced a detailed and reasonable argument.

Also enclosed were two cuttings, one from *Battle Cry* dated April 1984, issuing a warning to parents: 'Could these [the Chronicles] lead to this ['Dungeons and Dragons']?' The item, written at a time when the excesses of 'Dungeons and Dragons' were causing alarm, concluded, 'By all means, read to your children. But read them stories of men and women and boys and girls who solve the problems through obedience to God, not through magic and fantasy.' The fact that Lewis himself recognised the inherent dangers and warned against them, though misunderstood, is not taken into account.

A second piece was from the *European Christian Bookseller Review* of December 1989, containing an article on 'White Magic' by Rosemary Dinnage. It was the account of an experience of white magic by Dr. T. H. Luhrmann, during which 'She attended dream interpretations sessions, read the books popular with magical groups (by Tolkien, Le Guin, C. S. Lewis), learned to divine the tarot, did a study course on the cabala' - one small paragraph, duly highlighted. It gave the impression of someone in search of every grain of evidence, at all costs - but that is the mark of a researcher who then sifts and discards because she cannot take all on board.

Interestingly, though I could not recall having seen that article, the following year I was involved, by invitation, in defending Lewis in a feature in the same publication.

Lewis - the Blasphemer

One of two major criticisms to which my attention was drawn involved a charge of blasphemy. This formed the substance of the first negative response.

'In response to the appeal ... I felt I would write and give you my witness as to the significance C. S. Lewis' books have had in my life, though I don't think this is the type of reply you would wish to have.

As a very young teenager in the 'fifties I read the science fiction trilogy. Later in life, when I became a Christian I realised that the language and content of these were anti-Christian. During the 'sixties I was told about the Narnia books and over the years gave many away as gifts. About three years ago I read one of them for the first time (age forty-six). I was reading *The Magician's Nephew* to my children when to my absolute amazement, horror and disgust I found myself on the verge of uttering the Lord God's Name in vain! I managed not to speak it in vain but read it is vain! I read on and found it so used again. I burned the book and decided to investigate the others. I found that Aslan was meant to be a figure of Jesus. I found also that Mr. Lewis then very often had his "heroes" say such things as "By Aslan" etc., in effect advocating the use of the Name of Jesus to be taken in vain. Surely if it is all right for these "Heroes" to take Aslan's name in vain, and Aslan is God, then can't we take God's Name in vain? I shudder to think of all those young people I gave those books to and now run a campaign to have them withdrawn from shop shelves.' [WALTER, *One*]

A Biblical tract, against which Lewis' theology had been systematically challenged, was included.

Five months after I replied - I confess, just a little defensively - a second letter arrived, accompanied by a cutting from *Focus* dated October 1990 entitled 'Lewis Demythologised' which picked up some of the worst points raised in A. N. Wilson's biography and also slammed Lewis for being a 'a theistic evolutionist who rejected Bible doctrine, used profanity (this was highlighted) and believed in purgatory and other Catholic doctrines.' The accompanying letter read,

'I am pleased that you had been glad to hear from me and surprised that you had no letters critical of Lewis. I would presume this to be because Christians do not read his material. I think it would tend to be read by those who are Christian in name only rather than those who are committed to living as Christ has asked us to. After all, what Christians would let their children read blasphemous material and stories which teach that it is perfectly OK, and the done thing, to take the Lord's Name in vain? I think you missed the point I tried to make, I have no objection at all regards the teaching of Christianity and Christian standards through allegory. Many great writers have done so - Lewis Carroll, John White, etc. My objection was solely that Lewis actually takes the Name of the Lord in vain even in his Narnia books and teaches others that it is all right to do so. You say you are "very sensitive" regarding the Lord's Name being taken in vain, why then does it not offend your sensitivity when you read it in Lewis' books? By the way, the teaching of the end justifying the means, as in *Lord of the Rings* for example, is anti-Christian. Bilbo and Co. murdered and killed their way to their objective. Just not Christian.'

Much later another respondent did raise this and numerous other issues ...

'... I read and **loathed** *The Lion, the Witch and the Wardrobe*. The opening was charming. The conclusion seemed and seems to me an essentially frivolous-minded blasphemy. While I don't now believe in the literal resurrection of Jesus, or his death as a sacrificial atonement for sin, my respect for the beliefs of those who do would say that you **cannot** trivialise this into a magic lion dying to save a fairy kingdom from winter, and present the lion as a divine figure for worship. I also deeply dislike children's books which create a child's guilt-making Judas (or otherwise inherently evil) figure from one of the children ...

I have never attempted to read any of the other Narnia books. I'm sure I should hate them.' [GLYN, *The Friend*]

The Inversion of Society

The second major accusation was one of bigotry - a bigotry clearly subsumed in racial prejudice. In this case the respondent found a very close affinity with the Calormenes in *The Last Battle*. He sent no letter as such, but two essays, one entitled 'Bigotry and the "Last Battle",' the other, 'Warriors and Wild Animals.' It was certain that he saw in the treatment of the Calormene a mirror to his own life which left him angry and embittered, convinced that the whole of society was against him. Writing of the events surrounding the likelihood of a Calormene invasion of Narnia, he outlines the murder by King Tirian of two Calormenes, about which the young king subsequently feels guilty ...

'... He and his close friend - Jewel, the unicorn - are remorseful killers. Calormenes would presumably have no such noble Narnian guilt. Tirian surrenders himself to the "dark men ... in a thick crowd, smelling of garlic and onions, their white eyes flashing dreadfully in their brown faces." This is a horribly bigoted picture of the ugly Third World hordes overwhelming Aryan courage. Throughout *The Last Battle* the Calormenes unfortunately symbolise the ... meddlers who at last seize the smug "holy land" of Narnia. The Narnian "crusaders" have lost their moral sureness ... Shift, the vain ape, represents those clerics, particularly the Pope, who tamper with religion to exploit the innocent ... Religion has become a deadly tool for cynical, manipulative unbelievers - such as Shift the ape, Ginger the cat, and the smirking Calormene commander, Rishda Tarkaan.

The viciously arrogant Darwinians feel that man is merely the descendant of apes. Shift, the ape claiming to be a man, promises scientific progress that never occurs;

Shift heralds the apocalypse. For C. S. Lewis, pretentious science is really sorcery and lies. Cursed science is the enemy of religion. ...

... To be Calormene is to be not really human ... In obnoxious Narnia, the racist lies grow ever worse ... Being absorbed into a dark-skinned Calormene nation is the equivalent of death.'

He then turns to the occult objection, but from a different perspective.

'Inside the stable, the occult has emerged. It was in a stable that Christ was born. In a stable, all Narnia perishes. The selfish sceptics who have tried to manipulate faith are now overwhelmed by religion ... [The battle] is an apocalyptic crisis with white Narnian light against brown Calormene darkness. The animals are divided in allegiance between Tirian and Rishda. The less pleasant sort of animals join the callous Calormenes. For Eustace, these "dark-faced" Calormenes are even worse than dragons and sea-serpents.

... The dwarfs are for themselves, not for Narnia or Calormen. "Poor darkies!" scream the racist dwarfs. The Calormenes turn on the treacherous dwarfs, seize them, and throw them into the eerie, menacing stable ... The terrible implication is that the Calormenes are more deplorable than the turncoats of small size seeking a republic for the dwarfs in Narnia.

... This is a Christian allegory without pacifism ...

One miserably concludes that very few Calormenes are assimilated into Aslan's country - a white Christian paradise where swarthy pagans are generally unwelcome. A token Calormene is in the lion's land, though - Emeth ... one more example of the collaborator with white rule against his own people ... The race-hatred is the flaw that enfeebles this story ...'

The story is described as 'this fascist apocalypse.' Narnia is

'... "the inner England" ... with the dark-skinned pagans having been extensively eliminated. *The Last Battle* may have been a gory response to the waves of non-white immigration that struck England in the stolid 1950s. ... Narnia is the journey to oblivion. Narnia is bigotry and carnage. The jarring weirdness of *The Last Battle* makes this a satanic textbook with no honest merit.'

In the second essay, he refers to *The Lion, the Witch and the Wardrobe* ...

'This clumsy, pretentious book seems almost an anti-imperialist fable. That the villainess is so white would appease anti-racist liberals! The witch, with her Gestapo-like Secret Police of wolves, is a Nazi occupier of Narnia. She has imposed a sort of Third Reich that is a perpetual winter - the season of death ... In the wardrobe fascist tyranny has invaded the fairy-tale ...'

To this respondent,

'C. S. Lewis is a negative destroying fate [who] misrepresents Christianity as a violent crusade ... has no constructive criticism of the non-white races ... is the madly burning Cross of the disgusting Klu Klux Klan.' [DIRK, *Dial 174*]

His response is not mere criticism; it is grounded in knowledge of the text, it is well-written, and it is sincere, from the heart.

What lies behind situations that give rise to so much apparent inward anger - panic even? One suggestion was put forward.

'The fear yet admiration of Islam, so constant in European literature ever since the Crusades, is reflected in the Calormenes, Narnia's traditional enemies.' [TANYA, Miscellany]

Another respondent highlighted the kind of situation that can give rise to this kind of radical thinking ...

'We were teaching the children about Christianity at the front line, about the part Satan wants to play in our lives and how we are to deal with it. Many of the children knew woefully little about this subject - they were great with the Bible, with Jesus and with the apostles, but had little knowledge of bad. Most had read *The Lion, the Witch and the Wardrobe* (to fall back on the Narnia stories). The parallel between Aslan and Jesus had been explained, but the White Witch's spiritual parallel was a mystery. She was just a character in a book.' [DAWN, *Christian Woman*]

She had discovered that setting out the full agenda had much to offer.

THEOLOGICAL CRITICISM

'I recently saw a TV discussion programme concerning the merits of C. S. Lewis' religious writing - which conveyed the idea that his "theology" was unsound. **Well! - God certainly used his writing to reach me - and I am so happy to acknowledge this.'*** [NORA, *Church of England Newspaper*]

The main theological criticisms are included in the major criticisms above - those of blasphemy and pagan involvement, and even ardent fans who have admired Lewis at a personal level have permitted themselves to cast doubts ...

'My wife and I read the Narnia books aloud to our children, and looked forward eagerly to each new one being published. I still regularly re-read them for pleasure, although after several readings the religious imagery sometimes seems a little controversial.' [KEVIN, *The Universe*]

' ... though it does remind me that I always have to read over the part where Aslan rises again, **because there was not even the slightest hint of this happening all the way through the earlier chapters of *The Lion, The Witch and The Wardrobe.*'*** [FINLAY, *Success*]

'... And, of course, today I'd say that Lewis' whole idea of Christian humility was radically misplaced, and lay in the traditional direction of Uriah Heepishness, rather than the Psalmist's awe and reverence in the presence of the evident beyond-us grandeur of Creation, never mind the Creator, which makes all one's finite achievements totally insignificant! ... ' [GLYN, *The Friend*]

'I do not like the trick that some theologians have of calling certain things "great mysteries" as if they were not meant to be solved. The clues are there.' [KIRK, *The Friend*]

Much of the theological criticism emanates in part from A. N. Wilson's controversial biography, published at the outset of this enquiry, and discussed below.

SOCIAL CRITICISM

A few respondents highlighted what, for some at least, were barriers to present-day acceptance of Lewis' novels and stories. Even one or two addicts had difficulty in coming to terms with certain issues. Broadly speaking, they fell into two groups - class divisions and gender or other distinctions.

A Problem of Class

An area in which Lewis is criticised is his attitude to other people's lifestyles. As Victor Watson put it in an article sent by one respondent, 'Lewis does not edit out his own prejudices and hatred.'[22] That leads to open attitudes on vegetarians, non-smokers, teetotallers and secondary modern, co-education and 'experimental' schools - and criticism of Lewis for not appealing to children from these schools.

Reference has already been made to the respondent who found Lewis

' ... a very representative figure of the Establishment - one of "them." This shows up rather painfully when he recommends the terms to use - or avoid - when taking religious subjects to the man-in-the-street.' [JOCELYN, *The Universe*]

She felt that Lewis' children were too middle-class to be of relevance to today's children.

A Limited View

'Women don't come off very well in it [*That Hideous Strength*] (do they **ever** in Lewis?).' [KAREN, *The Lady*]

The feature by Victor Watson referred to above highlighted Lewis' attitude, not to women only, but to girls. Having berated Lewis for his attitude to co-education, the spotlight falls on a scene from *The Voyage of the "Dawn Treader"* in which the occupants of a girls' school are described as *'mostly dumpy, prim little girls with fat legs'* - the kind of child chosen to portray Lucy in the television version of *The Lion, the Witch and the Wardrobe?*

And the Chronicles of Narnia and *That Hideous Strength,* though major sources of complaint, were not the only books that provoked reaction. *The Four Loves* is not fiction but it introduced an area which did bother quite a number of people. One respondent reacted to it when she 'started to detect a male chauvinism which [she] did not like too much.' [MOIRA, *Christian Woman*]

This was the nub of an axe which another, otherwise enthusiastic reader, had to grind.

'Most of Lewis' writings still inspire me, except *The Four Loves.* His attitude to women seems unforgivable to me. He downgrades them in every chapter, in some way, and above all, his relegation of parental love to "mere family affection" I find hard to bear. Presumably this is the result of his close relationship with Warnie, loss of his mother, and unsatisfactory father. He **almost** gets it right, in the image of the love between the Son and the Father, but I question that Eros can ever really rival the deep reality, the transforming effect, of becoming a parent and sharing in the creation of a new life. Nothing is more grave, more moving, nothing motivates humans more deeply towards God. Parenthood is the human image of the Divine Love and this is why we venerate our Lady. Lewis missed all that.' [WANDA, Bermuda, *The Universe*]

Someone else wrote at great length what she described as her 'personal run-down' on Lewis' fiction, but however widely she wrote one thread wound its way through everything - her mixed feelings on his attitude towards women.

'Amongst Anglican theology students of the mid 1950s the buzz author was Charles Williams, whose imagery entranced one and all. A younger generation of general readers, including my own daughter, went bananas over Tolkien. These two were, as is now well known, the close friends of C. S. Lewis - part of the group calling themselves "The Inklings."

Williams is now little thought of. Tolkien is a modern classic. C. S. Lewis is still read with immense enjoyment, most of his fiction in print, but he has been viciously attacked for his limited view of **women**. At the moment this lack is the Crime of the Century ...

I think my first taste of Lewis' fiction was *Out of the Silent Planet* - in which there are no human women at all - apart from the anxious mother of a retarded youth who makes a fleeting appearance at the very start. In any event, although female, I was so carried along by the exciting story and its wonderful imaginative sweep that this lack of a Female Perspective bothered me not at all. I did not even notice it.

I already knew, and loved, *The Screwtape Letters*, enjoyed the closely argued theology of *The Great Divorce, The Problem of Pain* ("A little courage is worth libraries full of philosophy" - so true) and *Mere Christianity*. Already they were being pushed aside by new thoughts on the role of the Church, but still sold steadily. Perennials on the Parish bookstall.

At much the same time I read *Till We Have Faces* and was bowled over by this brilliant re-working, and possible explanation, of a strange and difficult myth. I had studied Classics for a time and was convinced that the apparently random and amoral Greek myths held profound truths - somewhere. I was also, then as now, a detective fan so rational explanations of complicated puzzles pleased me wherever they might be set.

By the time I read *Perelandra (Voyage to Venus)* and *That Hideous Strength* some years had elapsed and I found the obvious theology rather obtrusive and action-delaying. Also the **woman** question reared a small head. The young woman in *That Hideous Strength* did not bear much relation to myself nor anyone I knew. Somehow I felt uneasy about her.

Then came motherhood and "Narnia." With three lots of bedtime stories spread over a number of years - right up to the first grandchild, I was drawn ever more deeply and happily into this wonderfully realised "fantasy world." I saw at once its "Christian" bias, but surely it did not matter. In fact I thought then, and think even more now, that no fairy story can be effective without a strong, though preferably not obvious, moral basis. In fact I would go so far as to say this is true of **all** worthwhile fiction and the lack of it weakens and vitiates many of today's technically excellent writers.

One can see the influences. In *The Lion, the Witch and the Wardrobe* there are surely echoes of *The Wind in the Willows*, especially when, aided by the badgers, the children flee from the wicked witch into the snow-deep woods. In later books there are resonances of Nesbit. The grown-ups have disappeared, or are sinister, like the wicked uncle in *The Magician's Nephew* or incompetent as at the awful "progressive" school from which Eustace is whirled. Arthurian Legend is prominent both in the imagery and the Knightly Ideal ...

These days it is obvious to a more sophisticated public that the Lewis who wrote these books, mostly before his rather odd marriage, did indeed lack much in-depth knowledge of **women**. Yet his presentation of female roles was very much of his time. In the 1950s women, of their own free will, were fleeing back to the restricted but comfortable role of Mother and Homemaker. Frilly aprons ruled OK? Hitler's diktat of "Children, Kitchen and Church" was eagerly embraced by those who had lent a large hand in defeating him. It is foolish, and shows a lack of historical perspective, to castigate Lewis for going with the psychological tide of his times.

In any case he described a great variety of admirable women - be they human like Lucy the gently brave heroine of "Narnia," animal, like Mrs. Beaver, or mythic, like the Dryads. His villainesses are full-blooded and resourceful. Psyche's elder sister (*Till We Have Faces*) totally believable. Only "Eve" in *Voyage to Venus* is poorly drawn to the detriment of the whole. Very few authors are without weaknesses and he had fewer than most. In any case I would forgive him far worse faults because of the fabulous yet believable New Worlds he created. The totally satisfying Life-forms he imagined. His straightforward, rational defence of his Faith. His humanity, the humanity of a crusty Victorian born bachelor perhaps, but genial, positive and life-enhancing.

To sum up. For pretty well forty years I have read and enjoyed Lewis' fiction. He ranks with Rose Macaulay, Helen Waddell, Raymond Chandler and a tiny handful of others who give uncomplicated enjoyment with an added dimension. He is "holiday" reading because his plots are so clever, his imagination so rich, his vocabulary so wide. Yet when the book is laid aside with a contented sigh something remains. His fiction is light but not trivial. Theologian and professor, he displays his learning only to enhance his tale or add to our delight. In life he was unselfish and unpretentious. So are his books. Though he **wasn't** very strong on **women**.' [TANYA, Miscellany]

Similarly, another respondent was happy to continue recommending Lewis' fiction, but was less happy with the non-fiction,

'as I have to confess that I now find his style and language rather dated (and sometimes sexist) and sometimes rather patronising in tone for a modern reader.' [ERICA, *Reform*]

Women and the Church

The subject of women's ordination into the Church of England, then still very much in the air, was also raised, one respondent wondering how she and Lewis would fare in debating this issue ...

'There is an issue I should mention - that of Lewis' attitude to women, for which he is criticised. I can imagine that I, myself, would have a long and weary argument with him on this one (during which I should probably lose on points, since he is much cleverer than me!) as I am convinced that the Church has treated women shamefully, St. Paul has been mistranslated and misunderstood, and I cannot wait for the ordination of women, not only to the priesthood but to the Episcopate! Of course, some of Lewis' view, which was common in his day, of the ultimate authority being male, is shown in the Narnia books, with the High King being Peter, etc., **but**, and it is a big "but," he deals with the girls in a very positive way. I never felt, nor feel now, that the girls in the story had less character or influence than the boys. In fact, Lucy has probably the best worked out character of the four children, and some very important roles to play. No one could call the White Witch a wimp, though it is unfortunate that the "wrong" powers should be female-led, the right should be male led. However, that Lewis was a product of our male-written, male-translated, male-led, male interpreted human understanding of Christianity is not surprising. He does at least appreciate that girls like adventure as much as boys, that girls have opinions and influences on a story as much as if not more than boys, and as such his children's fiction is a great improvement on that earlier this century when adventure stories were for boys, and school and soppy, domestic stories were for girls. I don't find the books too male chauvinistic, and would happily give them to a girl to read, knowing her kind will be involved in the adventure, not left behind or relegated to doing the cooking! Lastly, but not least, Lucy is often the one who perceives the "spiritual" first - i.e. Aslan, and Aslan's guidance, and even the High King, Peter, has to eat humble pie and learn from her at times.' [CHARLOTTE, *Church of England Newspaper*]

Women and Men

This perhaps leads naturally to the relationship of women to men in more particular terms ...

' ... I am not really what is called a feminist but sometimes wonder (I wonder, by the way, if your correspondents were men or women, which is another point) whether in fact, women almost like or have been forced by fate to become easily **disciples** of men.' [YOLANDE, *Reform*]

Then there is the question of marriage ...

'I have some conversation in my head with Mr. Lewis on his view of Christian marriage. It is not my experience that the man "usually is, much more just the outsider." If he were the world would surely be a very different place. My experience is of women with a greater sense of love and responsibility towards the great family of human beings and other aspects of Creation. Having said that - and I'm re-reading *The Abolition of Man* again at present, it having fallen into my hands as I was packing - I still enjoy such a sense of him and feel so cheered. That's the word - **cheered**. I have, and continue to have, a blessed life. Meeting his mind/spirit has been one of the blessings.' [UNITY, *The Friend*]

Just occasionally he is given a respite. Discussing *Till We Have Faces* one reader commented,

'... *Till We Have Faces* is quite a complex book, but supple and exquisitely written. I can't say I entirely understand the ending (there's the faintest hint of Christ's presence) but it's a marvellous book, and the only one in which Lewis writes about women convincingly.' [IMOGEN, *Church of England Newspaper]*

She had not felt this about Lewis' attitude to women in *The Four Loves*, not realising that the two books stemmed from the same 'Joy Davidman' era.

One lady even felt she just might have misjudged him.

'C. S. Lewis ... was sometimes rather dogmatic, and also, I thought, rather a misogynist (though according to current thinking I was mistaken there).' [FREDA, *Woman and Home*]

On the other hand, there was at least one who would not even allow her concern about Lewis' attitude to women in *That Hideous Strength* to detract from her enjoyment of this 'smashing story!' [TESSA, *Christian Herald*]

MINOR CRITICISM

Minor criticism was levelled in a number of areas - the books, Lewis' theology and Lewis himself. Some respondents tussled with themselves wanting to or feeling bound to accept all of Lewis when they knew that they really couldn't. Sometimes the passage of time changed their outlook.

Flaws and Fallibility

'I used to love all his books, particularly the Screwtape ones, but now I find them dated.' [GLYNIS, *Success*]

Others tended to balance the argument more carefully. Yes, the books may still be helpful,

'even though **I can now see** that some of his arguments are not as unanswerable as **they once seemed**.' [ISAAC, *The Universe*]

Perhaps infallibility, like beauty, is still in the eyes of the beholder.

Reflecting on the way in which *Mere Christianity* was used in his conversion, one respondent nevertheless takes an objective attitude towards him today. His introduction to Lewis was not helpful.

'In the summer of 1968, I was then aged sixteen, my father thrust a book into my hand: *The Screwtape Letters,* saying, "See what you make of this." At the time I read it as fiction and enjoyed it; perhaps now I consider it the second worst book C. S. Lewis wrote, the worst (in my view) being *That Hideous Strength.*

Perhaps now I see C. S. Lewis as a very great intellectual, a milestone in the challenge to the then contemporary attitude of it being impossible to simultaneously hang onto one's faith and one's intellect. However, perhaps some of his theology is a bit shaky in places: also some of his fictional work is flawed where he yields to the temptation to grind his own personal axes, this being to me what fatally mars *That Hideous Strength,* and through putting the opposite viewpoint into the mouth of Screwtape ... His comparative objectivity and breadth of view in "Narnia" and *Till We Have Faces* make them so compelling.' [TERENCE, *Christian Newsworld*]

Other books in the trilogy also provoked adverse comment.

'I began the Ransom trilogy ... and recall spirit-like creatures called eldils ... However, these books did not inspire me in the same way at all and I did not finish even the first volume. I think the descriptions of Mars or wherever it was were too claustrophobic and there did not seem to be enough momentum to the context and plot (perhaps I was mistaken).' [VINCENT, *Woman and Home*]

And on *Perelandra* ...

'My only criticism would be that Lewis lapses into pedantry sometimes when writing about everyday life. A bit stuffy, perhaps!' [BEATRICE, *Woman and Home*]

'I've read *Out of the Silent Planet* and *Perelandra* - I liked both, as they contain some very, very beautiful ideas, but the character of Ransom is, quite frankly, irritating: he's sexless and cerebral. Lewis' children's fantasies are much more successful.' [IMOGEN, *Church of England Newspaper*]

'If this be Treason'

One of the Quaker respondents submitted a five-page closely hand-written critique of all Lewis' writings, from which it appeared that he 'enjoyed' a kind of love-hate relationship with Lewis. He began with a copy of *The Screwtape Letters,* which he found thought-provoking and during the next few years went on to *The Problem of Pain, The Abolition of Man* and, when it was published, *Miracles.* Then came the fiction.

'In 1949, having settled down in England with what looked then like lasting domesticity and employment, I read his first work, *The Pilgrim's Regress,* and found it silly-clever: in a foreword to a second or third edition he admitted that it struck him in retrospect as very callow. Then came the space/science fiction trilogy! *Out of the Silent Planet* ... was really moving and on the whole convincing, though both his villains were Aunt-Sallyish stereotypes. In *Perelandra* ... I found a great falling-off; everything after the crazily melodramatic end of "Weston" was sheer padding and chi-chi. As for *That Hideous Strength,* I read the original full text in 1950 and came back thirty years later to a slightly abridged one to see whether it left as repulsive a taste as before; it did. This is to me a long orgy of gratuitous gothick nastiness which the moralistic thread in no way redeems. It may be a *roman à clef* vilifying several real characters; the only one which I recognised was the contemptible caricature of H. G. Wells as "Jules." In a later article Dr. Lewis denied this identification, on which I doubt whether an intelligent child of twelve would have been convinced or believed him ... I tried in my own mind to identify "Weston" of the two earlier novels; this was not easy, and my nearest to at all a confident conjecture was J. B. S. Haldane: if so it was an abjectly caddish as well as clumsy portrait and I should like to be proved wrong.

... A year earlier I'd taken a dive back into Lewis with his *Mere Christianity* ... and had found it overall more helpful than otherwise.'

However, when someone objected to Lewis' attitude to pacifism he began to dissect this book more closely, concluding that since

'Lewis, having volunteered for and undergone the horrors of Flanders in 1917 when conscription was not applied to any part of Ireland, had earned the right **not** to be a pacifist ... but I could **not** stand his carping at "fashionable semi-pacifists" meaning those who accepted the war against Hitler as a lesser evil but still frankly and sadly felt that all war still **was** an evil.'

There were some saving factors: Lewis' 'cogent points' on the Sacraments and

'... his careful analysis of the strength and weakness of dualism. Nevertheless, the flavour of donnish superiority cropped out again and again: it seemed worst at a very early stage of the book in his attack on the motives of believers in "creative evolution" [which] does not deserve to be hit below the belt in Lewis' characteristic way.

Reflections on the Psalms, read in 1961, gave me the best impression of him yet. Very soon after his death ... I read *The Four Loves*, and reverted to something near outright dislike: it was a great, valid, promising theme, based on accurate distinctions, but spoiled at almost every turn by over-subtlety and cheap, crude satire. By then also I knew something of his influence on Canon J. B. Phillips ... and on lesser popular apologists like the forgotten B. G. Sandhurst: I began to see the "in-group" atmosphere of which he often sneers in the abstract but blatantly practised in the concrete among his back-scratching fellow Inklings ... and the guru-status which he enjoyed (the word is deliberate) outside that charmed circle among admirers from a lower level. He did not overtly share Canon Phillips' tub-thumping hatred of "Communism" as if there were no other real tyranny on earth, but he could convey it more subtly and intermittently. In the field of fantastic romance I for one find Professor Tolkien more wholesome, but here and there as in the character of "Gollum" he may have absorbed a little of Lewis' darker vision. About ten years ago, when the Lewis cult was gathering momentum almost every month, I found a volume of material previously uncollected or even unpublished with fragmentary stories reminiscent of the ugliest passages in *That Hideous Strength*: their vision was very dark indeed.

I made something of *Surprised by Joy* ... rather more of *Letters to Malcolm*, and quite a lot of the better essays in that very unequal assortment *Fernseed and Elephants*, especially "Membership," "Religion and Rocketry" and the title piece. Again, in other collections of occasional articles, reviews and broadcasts there were lots of good sensible passages marred only by their manner. His own intermittent professions of humility convince as much as those of Mr. Heep.

Anything about his marriage I avoid, and some references to it by one biographer were distasteful. He went through the legal form of marriage to give Mrs. David[man] a secure footing in Britain, which in itself was a decent action, but since it **was** legal he ought to have made it a normal, sanely-consummated union straight away instead of shilly-shallying for the condescending leave of Jack Priest like another Evelyn Waugh. His ambivalence about marriage has echoes of one of my *bêtes noires,* Patmore.'

Following this digression, the discussion returned to fiction - 'and of course to 99% of readers today that means Narnia.' He then went on to refer to Stephen Neill's 'rather cool' references to this series, in which he spoke also of 'his "petulant" language,' warning of 'the fulsome, almost febrile cult of C.S.L. which was growing up in the USA' Hence his amazement when, in one of his last publications, Neill referred to the Narnian stories as "charming"! Following an apparently pained defence of Neill against **his** critics, he lamely assumes, 'he must have found some real appeal in them, and I make any admirer a gift of his commendation, though he did not enlarge on it.'

'One tale, *The Horse and His Boy*, entertained me innocently by several passages which were a very good send-up of that bolting-hutch of beastliness the *Arabian Nights* ... Moreover, the book ends none too vindictively or savagely with the slapstick punishment of Rabadash. As a disciple of good Mrs. Svendsen and of Q.C.A.W., I like donkeys and am sorry to see them ridiculed ... But the Rabadash episode is good clean fun compared with most Narnian visitations. To offset it, even in that story the scratching of Aravis' back is laid on quite gloatingly.

The Magician's Nephew revives ludicrous Miltonian literalisms about fiat-creation, where the Divine piper conjures fully-formed warthogs and other fauna out of the bumps in the soil, and equally gruesome fantasies of stars burning their way out of the sky in lines of meteoric fire. The Magician himself is just a pantomime villain and butt. I accept several critics' views that in other stories the characters of Reepicheep and Puddleglum are excellent creations, but there is much in both tales which they don't redeem ...

The schoolmistress at the beginning and end of *The Silver Chair* is the craziest Aunt Sally of the entire crowd. In that story also you find the gratuitously beastly episode of the "Gentle Giants of Harfang," unctuous blarneying cannibals whose introduction owes nothing to the logic or inevitability of the story - they are simply contrived additions of ugliness and horror, like Nikabrik and the old witch in an earlier volume (was it *Prince Caspian*?). But right on toward the end of *The Last Battle* there is a sideswipe so lightly touched in that you can easily miss its cruelty: the dropping of Susan Pevensie. Earlier she has played a dignified, honourable part in the children's regal dream-life - much more dignified than the sickly Lucy with her abject crush on Aslan - and then one is told with sneers from Polly that at the age of eighteen she has become worldly, shallow and frivolous. Lots of girls do at that age, and so do boys: many of them get over it. But Susan is dropped from the celestial omnibus for her mild silly sins: and in Dr. Lewis' categories, make no mistake, being ruled out of Aslan's paradise means nothing less than eternal conscious torment, as Papist and Pentecostal unite in rubbing it in. ...

If I'd never read any of his fiction, or the trumpery *Regress* which is little more, my respect for him, though this side idolatry, would be much greater. He has influenced my life and thought for fifty years, coming over more vividly as a personality than any other Christian apologetic writer except Stephen Neill ... In some passages Lewis condemns or satirizes donnish vanities which elsewhere stick out a mile from his own record: but if he hadn't been a don he might never have been an apologist of any kind, and we should have been the poorer. Furthermore, the Hooper and Farrar gang have built him up so assiduously in the near thirty years since he died that one can't blame the man himself for a lot of the picture.

This must read captiously and censoriously, making my plea that I've almost always **wanted** to admire him - and that not only because it was the done thing - seem hypocritical, which it is not. If I had to single out a nucleus for my fellow-Quakers to digest it might boil down to *Mere Christianity, Reflections on the Psalms, The Abolition of Man* and very optionally *The Screwtape Letters.* Among the fiction, only *Out of the Silent Planet* would stand a chance. But those are all to be valued.' [OSWALD, *The Friend*]

His final sentence reads, 'Now shoot me down: or, more elegantly, if this be treason make the most of it.' I hope I have done neither. It perhaps reflects what many people feel as they wrestle with what may appear conflicting or contradictory values; it is less vindictively argued than some of the other 'negative' responses because it is prepared to admit that there is a good side as well as a bad side to Lewis' writing. Where he may have misread Lewis, in the matter of Susan Pevensie, he is in company with most others who comment on what he calls 'a sideswipe so lightly touched that you can easily miss its cruelty.' It could well be that Lewis was simply being realistic and true to the unexpectedness of the coming of the Kingdom as outlined in Matthew 24:40-41.

'The Shadow of a Shadow'

One respondent had been an Oxford undergraduate at the time when Lewis was tutoring. She reacted against the Christian content of his books, yet appeared to be a dedicated reader.

'While at Oxford I read *Out of the Silent Planet* and thought it quite wonderful. ...

Perelandra was more Biblical, and not as good (I thought, and also: oh dear, the man is a born storyteller and can't get away from religion: The whole thing was slightly annoying).

That Hideous Strength is a really terrifying book, apocalyptic and severe ... To me, the animal vengeance themes of Arthur Machen and Daphne du Maurier were the interesting bit.

I had left college and was in a job when *The Lion, the Witch and the Wardrobe* came out. Oh, I thought, what a marvellous idea worthy of E. Nesbit, but he's done it **again - why** drag the Christian religion into a children's story? For me, it didn't work. I read all the Narnia books as they appeared, but interestingly, when my own children read them they weren't bothered by Aslan (to me, a rather forbidding headmaster with an invisible cane).

I'd read *The Discarded Image* in the course of work. Also *The Pilgrim's Regress* which I liked very much ... The one which I enjoyed the very most was *Surprised by Joy* because it made me feel I wasn't alone in having had feelings that were "the shadow of a shadow" - always sought, always unattainable. By this time I had turned Agnostic and was a lot more tolerant about other people's religion. *They Asked for a Paper* and *The Four Loves* I found excellent and closely argued.

By this time again I found that the other religious books, *The Problem of Pain* (to an agnostic, no problem), *Miracles* and *Letters to Malcolm* and *A Grief Observed* were not for me. The other one that really "got" me was *The Great Divorce,* which I have read and reread. Whatever one's views, this book has such insight into what it is to be human that it knocks me back every time.

I've never understood *Till We Have Faces*.

Dear C.S.L. What a lot I owe him ... ' [KAREN, *The Lady*]

Writing on *That Hideous Strength* in another comprehensive survey, a respondent commented,

'The only trouble is that sometimes the religious ideas are so explicit in the stories that they mar them and thus they begin to read like a tract, which I don't like. ...

... A final point on that book. My mother has never liked it, because of the gory finale. I suppose the idea for this part came out of Lewis' many nightmares. It is unrepentantly full-blooded, and that suits me, but not everyone. And I believe I remember a letter of his in which he says that children's books should not be "de-gored" or the children will be unable to deal with their nightmares ...

Of all the Narnia books, I am least happy with *The Voyage of the "Dawn Treader"* which I found rather bitty, and *The Last Battle* which is too allegorical and also rather disparate in my view. My favourite is probably *The Silver Chair*, a phenomenal story with the best character of all being the Marsh-wiggle ...'

Apart from those I have read *The Pilgrim's Regress*, which I thought very impressive, and *Till We Have Faces* which I was in two minds about, it is rather out of style for Lewis, I suppose, in my view, a book that manages all right, but is not what he is best at. And lastly in the fiction side, there is *Screwtape*, which for me is a sort of half-way house between his theology and his story telling. It always makes me roar with its absurdity and precision of understanding. I was very struck one time by the idea of fear, that we are afraid of many mutually exclusive things and that the first step to overcoming fear is to realise they can't all actually happen to us.' [FINLAY, *Success*]

Ingratitudes

Another lengthy response began very cryptically.

'C. S. Lewis has long figured in my mind as a leading subject in a series of essays I should like to do, entitled *Ingratitudes*: reassessment of writers who have in one way or another influenced me, yet whose influence I no longer value (F. R. Leavis, Robert Graves and Edgar Lustgarten would be accompanying pieces) ...' [GLYN, *The Friend*]

In reference to *The Pilgrim's Regress* he accused Lewis of, among other things, 'enthusiastically perpetrating the evil guilt-making.' He then passed on to *The Great Divorce* which

'meant much less to me. The image of hell as a brick city of chip-shops and newsagents was very striking - when around this time I first visited Crewe it seemed to capture everything Lewis meant. And the idea of Napoleon's great palace and interminable search for others to blame has stayed with me. ...

But the only George MacDonald I'd read was *Cross Purposes*, which I didn't make much of. So I couldn't understand him as a spiritual guide (Today I find MacDonald's lifelong trust in Providence an inspiration: his books much less rewarding ...)

The "creature on the shoulder" in *The Great Divorce* looked, in the end, like just another insistence that masturbation was sin - only now there was an amazing suggestion that True Believers would successfully uproot it. ... That good people should be left with such a deep sense of shame and worthlessness over something so trivial absolutely enrages me - and Lewis is right on the side of Darkness there!

His throwaway sentence that "Christians don't make jokes about sex because they think it is sacred, not because they think it obscene" strikes me as horrible cant. The sacred is something one **does** make and enjoy jokes about ... The obscene - cruelty, child-abuse, extermination camps - is what one can't laugh about. And things that are sacred are things to be sought out and enjoyed to the full - meeting for worship; Holy Communion (if that's your theology); aesthetic grandeur in creation; great works of sacred art. Christians (especially ones like Lewis) are apparently incapable of keeping their heads and retaining a reverential and appreciative attitude to sex while enjoying it as fully as possible ...

A common catch-phrase among students at the time was that it was a pity Milton wasn't as much fun as *A Preface to "Paradise Lost."* Even so, some clear blots couldn't be missed. The suggestion that Adam might have resolved everything properly by "perhaps chastising" Eve did not escape me as an evil recommendation of wife-beating! And I was puzzled by Lewis' enthusiasm for the misty and unhelpful Charles Williams, let alone Williams' alleged brilliant success in moving a roomful of young people to wild enthusiasm for chastity. As I belonged to the avant-garde and Cambridge influenced intellectual groups of the time, I was not deeply impressed with any of the Inklings' work, despite their (Anglo)-Catholicism. I saw (and see) Lewis' claim to share beliefs with T. S. Eliot that utterly outweighed all questions of literary taste as dishonest special pleading. I saw (and see) many of his conservative literary opinions as deliberately perverse and merely argued to shock and impress his readers ...

At this time I read the *Perelandra* trilogy. They were still usually described as "science fiction" in those days. I enjoyed the first without reservation; was charmed by the second; hated the third. Hated its rancid reactionary fear of modernism, coupled with superstitious beliefs in Satan and the completely dishonest notion that a Satanic cult could ever underlie scientific procedure. Nonetheless, at this time Lewis' concept of "scientism" usefully entered my mind, and became a part of my thinking (Though I suppose now I'd say it has no useful application above middle-brow levels of thought).

On Lewis' death, I was deeply shocked by an obituary article in either the *New Statesman* or *The Spectator* which described the rollicking, bawdy lecherous "Jolly Jack" side of his life - shocked, not by the fact that it existed, but by his completely pretending it away in his devotional writings, which were taken seriously by my mother and other ... Quakers and Methodists who, I felt, had a right to expect that writers who addressed them on religion tried to live lives of complete integrity, as they did ...'

Further, referring to a piece in one of the University reviews, he added, 'the conclusion that Lewis offered much misleading triviality in an enviably readable style seems to me very fair.'

Another respondent, on learning the details of Lewis' private life, had referred to the feeling that 'a small rug' had been pulled from under her. The above response gives the impression that not a rug only but the whole carpet had been swept from under his feet to produce such gut reaction against a writer to whom he was, nevertheless, apparently instinctively drawn!

'Something distasteful'

Mention has already been made of the respondent whose single foray into Lewis' writing had caused her to write ...

'His books to me had never seemed very profound and it surprised me that he had, apparently, many admirers. However, after buying and reading *The Screwtape Letters*, I threw it into the dustbin where it could do no harm. There was something so distasteful about it.' [YOLANDE, *Reform*]

FAILING FAITH AND THE WILSON FILES

Amongst those tending to be critical were a few who began as Lewis addicts and then found themselves doing an about turn. For some it was a feeling of 'growing up' - the most common complaint being that his books were 'dated.'

Unexceptional Wanderings

At times it was just part of the matter-of-factness of life. One respondent, having described his reaction to *That Hideous Strength,* particularly the debate about characters, 'went off' Lewis for a while with the exception of his literary criticism 'which inspired much more respect.' [OSWALD, *The Friend*]

However, he eventually 'reverted' ... till the question of pacifism arose. Later the pendulum swung again with the advent of *Reflections on the Psalms*, which he read in 1961, and so it continued as his reading of Lewis expanded.

Another respondent made a similar comment ...

'I read *Mere Christianity* and [*The Four Loves*] ... the former simply wandered unexceptionally through my orthodox and Catholic mind of the time: the latter left the sentence, "if God is not Love, then Love becomes God" as a more useful observation than most of Lewis' quasi-profound witticisms. I also read *Surprised by Joy*, which interested me, and left me quite sympathetic to Lewis, but made no deep impact.

... In my later years at Oxford I occasionally made trips to Cambridge and sat in on seminars of Leavis'. At one of these, Leavis sneered at Lewis over something on which Lewis was unquestionably right. There had been some general seminar on Jane Austen, at which Lewis had popped up in question time, and remarked that you'd never know from the previous speakers that Jane Austen was supremely **funny**. This seemed to Leavis a classic example of Lewis' insensitive triviality. But I'm afraid Leavis had little or no sense of humour, and none of the still more important sense of **fun**. Lewis is obviously right in seeing that Jane Austen did, though he might not have felt as strongly as others of us that she provides a vital moral touchstone for contemporary life as well.' [GLYN, *The Friend*]

Again, his opinion had fluctuated and he had found himself on the side of 'the enemy.'

A Momentary Halo

There were a few for whom the spark of faith, once kindled, faded, yet the debt to and often fondness for Lewis remained.

One letter was very brief.

'In 1980-ish I read *The Screwtape Letters* and was very affected by it.

I began to see Christianity in quite a different light, and became religious.

I am not now, but it was a phase of great impact which lasted for maybe ten years.' [IRENE, *The Literary Review*]

Intrigued, I opened up the way for the full story, which arrived almost by return.

'In about 1977 I was very confused in my thinking (why are we here?). I was twenty-eight years old, and married, with a two-year-old daughter. My father an atheist, my mother vaguely guilty that she ought to be a Christian.

I really was dead against "religion." I had been brought up as a services child. R.A.F. churches reserve the first three rows of pews for officers, and this was just one hypocrisy I noted.

I started to study the tarot cards. I had a book called *The Tarot Path to Self-Development* which led me to challenge statements, for which I had to refer to a school Bible.

It was at this time when I bought *The Screwtape Letters* by C. S. Lewis after flicking through the pages and finding some flurry of interest in them.

After reading the book, I decided that C. S. Lewis had had similar thoughts to mine, had also been an atheist, but had been warmed by genuine feelings for others, to the extent that he could now recognise the "good" and "bad" in others. I went on with my studies and had a "religious experience" in which I lay on the floor on my back and prayed for an hour or so and afterwards stopped smoking, watching television, biting my nails, and devoted **all** of my time to making my husband's and daughter's lives better. It was the best two weeks I had ever experienced. I wore a halo!! It really felt like that.

Needless to say, I couldn't keep it up.

Now I detest organised religion, seeing that it has nothing to do with genuine feeling. Religion is repetitive dogma to me.

Now I believe we're all a part of everything that matters, that is matter; that we're needed for feed-back by the "overmind," the "all-seeing eye," and that if we weren't needed, we wouldn't be here. This feeling gives me perspective; a right to be here: a feeling I didn't have as an atheist, nor as a prospective Jehovah's Witness, Mormon or Buddhist, which I did consider in the past. Religions are clubs with hierarchy and rules.'

Prize Reading

'As a child I discovered Christianity for myself - no one else in my family went to Church - and became very enthusiastic. My vicar ... lent me a copy of *The Screwtape Letters*, which I very much enjoyed. Some years later, when I won a prize in the 5th form at school, I chose as my prize *Miracles*, which impressed me greatly. Lewis' views on the nature of myth struck me deeply at the time. I am no longer the enthusiastic Christian that I was (in fact, I am no longer a Christian at all), but a few months ago I saw a reprint of *The Screwtape Letters* in the University bookshop, and decided to buy and re-read it. It still strikes me as an extraordinary piece of writing, and carries for me resonances from the distant past, although I now look on the book with the perspective of nearly 50 years more of living.' [NEIL, *Gradlink*]

'Warts and All'

By far the greatest influence in changing attitudes to C. S. Lewis has been A. N. Wilson's biography, published just after I had begun my enquiries. Reason and emotion were varied, but a sense of shock was quite common among readers ...

'I was rather disturbed by what the reviewers said of the contents. They made it sound a very "warts and all" story, with an emphasis on the warts.' [CORA. *The Universe*]

'I was quite disturbed during a programme of 'The Late Show,' which included an interview with Lewis' biographer ...

In the interview the biographer appeared non too impressed by his subject's religious work - upon which I had leaned so much! I felt the biographer admired Lewis' specialist knowledge of mediaeval literature, etc. but discredited his religious work which had "taken in" thousands of suckers around the world ("especially in America").' [MOIRA, *Christian Woman*]

This respondent also pinpointed Lewis' 'remarkably high standard of morality ...' Others found the moral foundation rather rocky.

'... I was appalled to learn from A. N. Wilson's biography that Lewis just wanted to be a don at any cost, and didn't much care which subject he taught. That frivolous lack of commitment to "the common pursuit of true judgment" is undoubtedly what undermined his work, and made him an essentially damaging influence on 20th century literary studies.' [GLYN, *The Friend*]

Some used less strong adjectives ...

'I am an absolute non-academic, a school-leaver at fourteen years. His books were not difficult for me to read, though I sensed great depth and scholarship in them.

... I am now confused by the A. N. Wilson biography and feel some hostility towards Wilson, maybe because he has moved a small rug from under my feet.' [HILDA, *The Universe*]

One man who wrote was an avid reader of everything by and about Lewis, except the Wilson biography which had only just been published, **but** he 'did not like what he said on a radio programme some time ago.' Lewis had admitted his alarm at **'the contrast between the sort of man I admit I am and the sort of message I have in your case**

been used to transmit.' * His verdict?

'The great thing about Christ is that He saves sinners and I am sure C. S. Lewis would have gladly put himself in that class and so he speaks to sinners like me with understanding of our problems.' [FRANKLIN, *Christian Family*]

When he had eventually got his turn in the library queue he commented, 'Most people, I think, are more interested in the treasure it contains! He has given a full description of the earthen vessel.'

'Recently, after the publication of A. N. Wilson's biography, Lewis' religious writings have been scorned. But he did not write for theologians or other "clever" religious people. He wrote for the ordinary honest seeker who wanted to know whether there was anything in this Christian "stuff" and he did it superbly.' [IDA, *Christian Woman*]

Inevitably there were some who shared Wilson's viewpoint. One saw it as a source for good, quoting the Rt. Rev. Richard Holloway who had declared in *The Independent*[23] that 'Lewis' position is strengthened not weakened by A. N. Wilson's brilliant dissection of his personality.'

'And I read A. N. Wilson's biography, which confirmed my final feeling that Lewis was an essentially shallow man.' [GLYN, *The Friend*]

One respondent sent me a copy of a letter she had written two years previously to a literary paper, following its review of Wilson's biography. The first part concerns Wilson's conjectures over the relationship between Lewis and Mrs. Moore. The second point, however, is worth noting here.

'In the Narnia sequence, in which C. S. Lewis was purveying traditional Christian doctrine under the guise of allegory, he was faced with a number of dilemmas. One was how to convey the possibility of eternal damnation without terrifying children with tales of hell-fire. Besides, it was vital to convey the point that damnation is the direct consequence of the sinner's self-will (the gates of Hell are barred from the inside) and only consequently the result of God's wrath (after all, He died to **save** sinners). C. S. Lewis had made the obnoxious Edmund the **type** of the penitent and redeemed sinner; now he had to provide an obdurate and unrepentant one.

I do not myself consider an obsession with clothes, cosmetics and parties a sign of maturity. A demonstrable sense of responsibility for one's self, one's immediate neighbours and one's wider community would be a better gauge of adulthood. Susan has not "committed the unforgivable sin [and] become an adult"; she is indulging in an inordinate affection for the trivial to the exclusion of things eternal; that is, she has wilfully stuck at a transition stage and remained an adolescent. The possibility therefore exists that, with Aslan's help she may still reach salvation at some date after the fatal rail crash. At any rate, one can comfort an anxious child reader with this thought.' [FAY, *Good Stories*]

And from an enthusiast ...

' ... a most excellent book, and a good read. It cuts him down to size so I can enjoy his books without feeling threatened by his super-male chauvinist Anglicanism.' [HEIDI, *The Friend*]

Significantly, those who sent in cuttings had chosen ones in which it was 'highly recommended.'

IN DEFENCE OF C. S. LEWIS

'I believe that a recent biography of Lewis has been written condemning the book *Mere Christianity*. As I haven't read the biography I cannot comment, but as far as I am concerned it was the turning point for me.' [OLIVE]

While a few defended Lewis against Wilson because it was the most topical subject at the time, one significant factor was the number of people who addressed the issues raised by Lewis' critics without for one moment knowing that these issues had been mentioned. Thus they provided a useful counter-balance to set beside the detractions. With one exception they were completely unsolicited and tended to two related but compatible areas - the New Age and the 'Occult'/Pagan question.

Lewis - the New Age Writer!

In one instance the respondent was a writer, who was not happy about the misappropriation of the Narnia stories.

'They have been favourites of mine for many years. I have used some during the course of my teaching, but my chief memory of them is taking them on our family camping holidays, one per year for several years. I would read aloud in the tent, either on rainy days, or at bedtime and the whole family would enjoy them. I would sometimes have to translate some of the more archaic language as I read, to keep the boys' interest. When they got too old to be read to, I read *The Last Battle* to myself for my own enjoyment.

Just recently C. S. Lewis has been receiving a bad press. Have you seen the letters in *The Independent* newspaper this week? One of **my** respondents wrote warning me that he was a New Age writer! I have since read Texe Marrs' book *Ravaged by the New Age* and find there a similar criticism with a quote. On checking the quote, however, I felt it had been misunderstood and taken out of context. I can understand people being worried about his references to woodland deities, and even Bacchus, but I feel that at all times Aslan is seen to be high over all - King of kings and Lord of lords. It is unfortunate that when C. S. Lewis wrote his Narnia series, he did not foresee the rise of the New Age movement and the difficulty some would have with his "fantasy" characters.' [ODETTE, FCW Newsletter]

Another respondent saw it differently.

'One of the things I love most about him is that he embraces both Christianity and the best of Paganism, and there is no conflict; he transforms pagan mythology and gives it new life and a new point to make.' [GEMMA, *Woman and Home*]

The Mother Superior put this into perspective:

' ... this is one of the hazards of life and certainly cannot invalidate in any way what he has written.' [NATALIA, *The Universe*]

The Enemy Exposed

As part of an extremely comprehensive analysis of the Narnia books, one respondent addressed the kind of accusations, cited above, which were being made at the time.

'... There has recently been criticism of the Narnia books as containing elements of the "occult." I do not believe any child would be influenced towards the occult by the mention of hags, witches, werewolves and bad forces in the book. They are always the enemy, are always sinister, dangerous, nasty and against Aslan and the forces for good, which always triumph. Neither are they dwelt upon in such a way to induce interest in practices or occult beliefs - such detail is lacking. Children need good and bad to be described, a spade to be called a spade. Lewis uses mythological and folklore figures and stereotypes to arouse those deep feelings and instincts that can only be satisfied by Christianity, not as an end in themselves. He makes them servant to his aims - and often uses them quite differently from their origins, like Mr. Tumnus the faun - not, I am sure the sort of character a faun was in mythology at all, but a very useful visual for the sort of character Lewis needed.

As a teenager I had my moments being drawn to the occult, but from quite other directions and influences than from the Narnia books. My eventual total rejection of the occult of course came from my acceptance of the "real" Narnia and the "real" Aslan - Christ. I have, during my time at College, and in various voluntary work situations, not least my recent work with prisoners, come across a great deal of occult influence, and I hate, distrust and suspect anything at all occult, having seen the damage it does. I would never endorse anything which I thought would lead anyone to the occult, yet I unhesitatingly endorse the Narnia books. In fact, I would have thought they'd warn against the occult, and the "wrong" sort of magic (i.e. not Aslan's), rather than anything else.' [CHARLOTTE, *Church of England Newspaper*]

'The Occult Question'

Having written an initial letter, which covered his own experiences of Lewis' fiction, one respondent picked up a comment I had made on one of his remarks. He found it intriguing.

'Is this the nonsense, emanating from America, which suggests Lewis was some kind of crypto-pagan occultist? I am not disposed to canonise Lewis, and have even read the A. N. Wilson biography without serious concern, but the items I have seen on Lewis and occultism suggest basic pig-ignorance of the man. His reaction to Yeats, his own admitted vulnerability to occultism (including the temptation of Mark Studdock in the cell at Belbury) shows how he stood in relation to the real occult. And to become worked up about the use of pagan characters and symbols in the fictional writing is to ignore the fact that Lewis regarded the (small) good in such things arising precisely because they were distant echoes of what God is really like.

The comments arise from a literal-mindedness that Lewis himself once inclined towards, until Tolkien argued him round (That's the charitable interpretation!).' [KIERAN, *Renewal*]

He was, it seemed, unaware of the mounting feeling against Lewis for this very reason.

That Hideous Strength was the adult fiction that fired the occult claims, and one respondent saw this as understandable ...

'Yes, I can see why some writers would consider *That Hideous Strength* occult material. It is firstly the fantastic itself, which upsets them, and secondly the use of pagan names. I simply don't agree. I must say, these days I avoid getting into "demon" debates, because it is my impression that a lot of so called occult fear is self-generated, and to deny it is to risk seriously upsetting people. This has certainly been the case with the wave of pulp Christian "New Age" books, and the resulting fear of "green" issues among some Evangelicals, which has been so needlessly catastrophic. The use of ghosts, magicians and so on by writers is surely just a literary device. Of course, there are some writers, whose work involves "mucking about" with dark forces. And I am certainly not implying that the church should altogether reject the concept of devils and the like, I just think that religious people, the fringe elements in particular need to get things in a better perspective. And that is what a book like *That Hideous Strength* does: puts the whole issue of good and evil in its proper perspective, which is quite the opposite to tampering with the occult. One might even suggest that the occult label is often just a way of avoiding the message.' [FINLAY, *Success*]

'Beyond Good and Evil'

One man refuted such accusations by stating that, finding himself 'surrounded by among others "Satanists" and "atheists"' he retreated into his reading of Lewis in order to recover his faith. This statement is paralleled by another ...

'My experiences of "black art" were horrible and very dangerous. "I knew not what I did" etc. It is ten years + since I accepted the Lord Jesus and rejected "the Devil." I still experience a back-lash against the choice I am glad I made.' [PHILIP, *Catholic Herald*]

In his initial letter to me he had enumerated the corpus of Lewis' books in the order in which they had helped him. Almost at the end he added '*The Screwtape Letters* is a favourite of mine (fiction).' Referring to his involvement in 'the black arts' he observed that

'*The Screwtape Letters* show me very clearly that the Devil (and his legion) is/are very much non-fiction.'

Perhaps it really is true that

'... Mr. Lewis obviously knew we fight more than "flesh and blood".' [GLADYS, *The Christian Herald*]

V
IN DEBT TO C. S. LEWIS

From Fantasy to Faith

> *"'I have come," said a deep voice behind them. They turned and saw the Lion himself, so bright and real and strong that everything else began at once to look pale and shadowy compared with him. ... And she wanted to say "I'm sorry" but she could not speak. Then the Lion drew them towards him with his eyes, and bent down and touched their pale faces with his tongue, and said:*
>
> *"Think of that no more. I will not always be scolding. You have done the work for which I sent you into Narnia."'*[F]

By far the greater number of respondents - sixty-four - indicated that they had first encountered C. S. Lewis as children. A handful was actually sixteen or under when they wrote. As noted earlier, a large percentage was introduced to the Chronicles (and some other books) by teachers at school. The ones who found the books for themselves sometimes had more unique and lasting stories to tell while for others it was their introduction to Lewis' many other works. In the case of the children, some of the accounts have been highlighted in other chapters.

These child-oriented responses have been sub-divided into four sections, though they are seldom stereotyped in any way. Because of this there would seem little need for commentary especially as they themselves are a form of commentary on the books Lewis wrote. Each has indeed his or her own story.

JOURNEYS OF SELF-DISCOVERY

Twenty-one in this group found Lewis' books (usually the Chronicles of Narnia) for themselves. A small number received them as gifts. The reading of them provoked many feelings, supplied insights, helped understanding, stimulated reading, became a 'diving-board' to Lewis' other books. The following are not always entire letters for often that first distant discovery led to a much wider reading pattern years later; some are cogent snippets.

Every Child's Dream

'I think that by the time I last read about Narnia, at about the age of fifteen, their biggest impact was an almost religious one. This is quite unusual for me as I am normally not the kind of person who makes a big thing of my Christian upbringing. However, the moments when Aslan returns became for me truly stunning. Although it sounds superficial, the sense that "everything would be all right now" was amazing. It involved a feeling of excitement, anticipation and hope, but also of overwhelming peace.

Nevertheless, this religious facet was not fundamental to my enjoyment of C. S. Lewis. I read the books plenty of times as a child without even considering this aspect. The imagery of Lewis was terrific. I remember first picturing that anomalous lamppost in the wood, surrounded by snow. I desperately wanted to be there! Then there was the Queen with her Turkish Delight and the broken table on which Aslan had been sacrificed. I recall covering my wardrobe doors with paper and trying to recreate that scene in paint. It kept me occupied throughout an entire summer holiday.

Finally, speaking of wardrobes, I think it is probably every child's dream, at least for those brought up on authors like C. S. Lewis and Enid Blyton, to find a secret passage. I certainly tested out the back of my wardrobe a few times (always leaving the door open a crack of course!). Unfortunately, my parents have always favoured houses which are far too modern, and plywood doesn't make for easy rite of passage. And I think I'm probably too old to get to Narnia now.' [ZANETTA, *Me*]

One respondent first read the Narnia stories when she was ten, and somehow knew he was talking about Christ in Aslan.

'I was too young then to understand about allegory but *The Last Battle* remained etched in my memory and I still ponder over the dwarves in the dirty shack who are too blind, angry and frightened to see the wonders around them.' [ROSEMARY, *Catholic Herald*]

Strength Becoming Weakness

'I read *The Lion, the Witch and the Wardrobe* when I was about eleven years old. At that time I had no idea C. S. Lewis was a Christian. I remember particularly the part where Aslan allowed the White Witch to destroy him out of his love for [Edmund]. This had a profound effect on me, and I read it over and over again. It was something to do with the idea of strength becoming weakness out of pure love - and then the joy and relief of finding out that the witch had not really won. I did not at that time relate it to Christianity or to Jesus, I was just deeply moved. As such it did have a great effect on my life, and in some way prepared me for an understanding of the Gospel message which I did not accept until I was twenty-eight years old. Since then I have read all his books at regular intervals and always something new strikes me out of them, but nothing so profound as that first reading.' [HONOR, *The Local Preacher's Magazine*]

Fiction as a Commentary

'I suppose it must have been as a young child, reading *The Lion, the Witch and The Wardrobe* about 1957 that stimulated my interest. My twin sister was also profoundly interested in this novel and we must both have read and re-read this story many times. It has helped me in later years because I did not realise that this man was also a Christian apologist. His further writings such as *Letters to an American Lady* [and] *The Screwtape Letters* have profoundly interested and influenced me.

[These] although fiction I use as a commentary on books of counsel for myself. It reminds me of *The Pilgrim's Progress* and a guide and reference point in my Christian life. When C. S. Lewis speaks about superficially intellectual and brightly sceptical people I treat this **not** as a novel but a man's observation.

The original book I read, *The Lion, the Witch and the Wardrobe*, although fiction, prompted me to read more **non**-fiction books by the same author ... I certainly regard him as a major influence on my Christian life.' [IRVIN, *Christian Newsworld/Church of England Newspaper*]

Re-enacting the Battles

A childhood love of Narnia had worked itself out in a somewhat unusual hobby for one reader.

'When I was a young girl of about eleven to fourteen years I read the Chronicles of Narnia at least four times. It greatly influenced my future reading, and I am now an avid reader of fantasy novels. I am also a member of my local mediaeval society, where we frequently re-enact battles (in shows for the public) which has become a major part of my life. At a recent mediaeval fayre which I took part in I spotted a poster of *The Last Battle* which brought back all the memories of those days and I am at present saving to buy this set of books as I believe they were the major influence to the interests I have now which are my life.' [OONAGH, *Me*]

In Search of Narnia

'I have always loved fairy stories, because of the truths they contain. I grew up in South Africa, and when I joined the library at the age of eight, my father helped me to select books. Although himself not familiar with Lewis, he knew I would like *The Lion, the Witch and the Wardrobe* and little did he realise just how much! I devoured the book. I had been raised in a Christian (Catholic) home, so I immediately realised that Aslan represented Christ. Also, the whole world of Narnia became very real to me and I wished passionately throughout my childhood that I could somehow get there. One by one, I obtained the seven Narnian Chronicles, reading them in the published order, and I was about fourteen when I finally found *The Last Battle.*

... Just as Lewis himself described his original spiritual awakening being connected to a feeling of "northernness," so did I feel. I had never been happy inside the Catholic church, and for years I struggled with the nuns at the convent school I attended when points of doctrine came up.

After leaving school, I spent a few years not quite sure about religion in my life, but again, it was the memory of how I'd felt on reading the Narnian Chronicles which gave me some sort of spiritual hope to cling onto. Nearly ten years ago, I at last found a Christian church which I felt answered my questions: The Church of Jesus Christ of Latter-day Saints, also known as Mormons. That may surprise you, but it teaches the concept of degrees of glory in heaven, and actual bodily resurrection for example. Later, I discovered that Lewis is held in great esteem in my church, and he is often quoted in books and lectures by leading figures in my church.

I felt I had to mention my conversion story in brief because that was in part due to C. S. Lewis. I no longer need to search for Narnia, as I have found it! This does not mean that my love of the Narnian Chronicles has been lessened, as I still read them from time to time; have enjoyed the BBC television productions - though with reservations when they have meddled with the storyline, and when the costumes and characters do not "match" the Pauline Baynes illustrations! - and also enjoy reading other books by C. S. Lewis or about him.' [JANCY, Belgium, *Woman and Home*]

Introduction to Fantasy

'... I was fascinated by the stories and went on to read Tolkien's *Lord of the Rings.*

Having thought about it, reading the Chronicles of Narnia introduced me to a fantasy world, and I have continued looking for readable fantasy novels ever since. Presently favourite authors include Ann McCaffrey and David Eddings.' [HAYLEY, *Woman and Home*]

A 'Haven Away from the Hurt'

'I wish I could say that I had a brilliant childhood, full of fun and adventure, but sadly I can't. I'm not saying that it was all bad, because it wasn't, there were definitely times when I was a happy little soul, but all I can seem to recall of my early years is a lot of heartache and misery.

My father was and still is a journalist and was (now reformed) an alcoholic. Often he would come home, late at night, from work, terribly drunk and abuse my mother.

My sister (who is older than I) and myself would lie awake at night feeling helpless listening to the arguments and the smashing of various ornaments and plates, but it was never discussed with either my sister or myself, it was always brushed over and never spoken of.

My schoolwork suffered, my social life (as I got older and into my teens) suffered, I never had boyfriends as I was too afraid to bring them home and I was too afraid to turn to anyone and I guess it was about this time where Mr. C. S. Lewis entered my life.

On one of the better days my father and I went shopping ... he took me to a large bookstore (my dad is an avid book reader). I went off to the children's section (I must have been about eleven years old at the time) and there was a large very impressive red bound book embossed with gold leaf; it was of course The Chronicles of Narnia. I wanted it so badly and my father, who I have to say that when off the "booze" is a gentle loving man, bought it for me.

In times of despair, which were many, I would read the adventures and become totally lost in the world of Narnia. I was there, it was so real I could feel, touch, see, smell all that was described, it was my haven away from the hurt, I would sit on [my] bed and read until I fell asleep and then I would dream of being in Narnia.

Narnia was exciting, magical and a place that, to me, was real and fantastic.

Of course there were other books, I think I must have read everything Enid Blyton ever wrote, but somehow C. S. Lewis' tales of Narnia were special, they made me feel special like I belonged somewhere.

I am now twenty-five years old but I have not outgrown Narnia. It's still a very special place and just occasionally, quite by accident, I escape there in my dreams.

When I have children I will encourage them to read the Chronicles of Narnia and I hope that they too will be as captivated as I was, only I will do my very best to make sure that they are reading it under a lot happier circumstances.' [RHODA, *Me*]

An extra dimension

'I began as a child reading the Narnia books followed by *Out of the Silent Planet* and the rest of the space trilogy. Even then one could not help but be aware of an extra spiritual dimension. Some years later, browsing in a book shop I came across *Mere Christianity* by C. S. Lewis. Because I remembered his name with delight from childhood I bought the book. It was compulsive reading and I was unable to put it down. He made Christianity sound like the most exciting adventure that ever was, and not just "the same old thing" which makes so many religious books a no-go area for most of us.

From this I went on to read *The Screwtape Letters* followed by anything and everything I could lay my hands on, and found myself completely captivated by Lewis' outlook and philosophy.

Everything I read made me wish that I had known him personally. Living near Oxford ... I joined the C. S. Lewis Society in Oxford which met each month at "The Kilns" - home of the author. At these meetings we would read and discuss some of our favourite books - fiction and non-fiction.

Over the past ten years his work has given me enormous spiritual strength, and if I could choose to meet one person it would be C. S. Lewis.

Because he was so influenced in his spiritual life by George MacDonald (of whom I had never heard), I began to read Lewis' own anthology of MacDonald's work, and this is rich bedtime reading!' [NERYS, *Woman and Home*]

Reflections on Aslan

'As a child of about nine or ten years, I was profoundly affected by the presence of Aslan in *The Lion, the Witch and the Wardrobe* series of books. The wisdom, mystery and hidden truths encompassed in "The Lion" gave me a sense of greater realities than I had realised in my life up to that point. I somehow felt the great importance of the sorting of animals/people in *The Last Battle* but even though I attended a Church Primary School it was a few years later that I realised the Biblical connections.' [LORRAINE, *The Friend*]

'My Childhood Friend'

Less usual in this group were references to *Surprised by Joy*.

'I must have been nine or ten I think ... and can still relive the thrill of discovery that I was not the only person in the world to have "peak experiences."

It was the beginning of the road to discovery that it is "OK" to trust one's own religious experiences, a road that led me through many of Lewis' religious books (though not his fiction till I was an adult) and twenty years later into the Religious Society of Friends. And though I've learned a hundred names for the experience I still in my heart call it being "surprised by joy" so vivid is my memory of the discovery of my childhood friend C. S. Lewis.' [PETRA, *The Friend*]

'An Unimaginable Place'

'C. S. Lewis' works of fiction have certainly had a pervading influence in my life. I first read *The Lion, the Witch and the Wardrobe* when I was eight, and thereafter all the Narnian books as they appeared in the local library. Through them I unconsciously absorbed many basic Christian concepts, which were later to help shape my life, and so lead eventually to my commitment to God's service as a [nun] ...

I read much as a child, but the Narnia books and above all the figure of Aslan remained real to me in a way that the characters in other books did not. It was always more to me than "just a story" - I must have been basically aware of the Christian imagery in the tales of Narnia, as I was brought up in the Church of England, but I did not attempt to rationalise the stories in specifically Christian terms. I simply accepted them and enjoyed them as they were written.

Although God was at that time very real to me, the figure of Jesus was not. I think I can truthfully say that that of Aslan was more vivid in my imagination than that of Christ in the Bible stories I read. Perhaps this was because I felt the world of Narnia could be so close to our own, just through a wardrobe door, and Aslan tended to turn up unexpectedly in all sorts of places, often when he was most needed. On the other hand the Jesus of the Gospels in His earthly life seemed far removed from our own time, and although I knew He was now in heaven, this to my childish mind was an unimaginable place remote from our everyday world. ...

So it is that I have lived and grown with C. S. Lewis' books. To this day the sound of running water in a springtime thaw makes me think of Narnia - and a prayer we say daily referring to Christ as "the Lion of the tribe of Judah" inevitably conjures up the picture of Aslan.' [TAMARA, *The Universe*]

Looking for holes in the road

'I read them when I was eleven or twelve, and was fascinated by their imagery of good and evil, with the goodness of Aslan shining through the whole sequence.

I very much wanted to visit Narnia at the time, and was on the lookout for other ways into Narnia - e.g. holes in the road!

I found the stories really exciting adventures too, and hated each book finishing. They still remain among my very favourite books.

I read them in 1961 or 1962, so the references to clothes, meals etc. were contemporary to my understanding at the time (although not my class!) and this might have added to my enjoyment. I think that for children now some of the references have to be explained - so perhaps making the books more like "double" history - the children's 1950s childhood, and the history of Narnia!

The books were a big influence on my reading as a child, becoming the standard by which I judged other books.' [EDITH, *Woman and Home*]

'The Narnia books, I am pleased to say, were published just in time for my late childhood. My appetite for them was whetted by the serialisation of some of them on 'Children's Hour' (BBC Home Service). I ended up buying all the books and reading them for myself.' [ADAM, *Family Life*]

Under the sideboard

'For quite a few years I would have the same recurring dream that underneath my Nan's sideboard was a little door that only I could get through and only I knew about it. I used to dream that if I crawled on my belly under the sideboard I could push the door open and go into a snowbound, completely different world. I never managed to get any further than a few feet before waking up, much to my disappointment, and tried to go back to sleep to see where else I could go, but to no avail.

... I still sit and stare at that sideboard wondering if I were ever small enough again would I be able to find the door. Also when it snows I like to find a place with no footprints and imagine that I'm the first person ever to have seen that place - I love to make the first footprints and imagine being all alone in a strange world.' [SAMANTHA, *Me*]

A Bit of "Blind Faith"

'I was introduced to the Narnia stories as a child of around eight or nine years. I recall reading *The Lion, the Witch and the Wardrobe* during a summer holiday ... around that period. Eventually and in that year, I managed to read all the books. I remember reading *The Magician's Nephew* and feeling cheated because this book was the historical predecessor to *The Lion, the Witch and the Wardrobe*, as though the Narnia series book order had been mischronicled. However, I now realise that the sense of discovering a prior history to a known period (Narnia and the White Witch) is an exciting and invigorating exercise. I also recall *The Last Battle* and the movement of many previous characters to Narnia following the train crash. I was not happy that the character Susan was not allowed to return, but at that age I was completely oblivious to the arguably Christian overtones of the work!

I suppose that I, born in 1958, am just old enough to have grown up in a less computer-oriented video-consuming age and could therefore appreciate the magic of a novel in ways that children now would find more difficult. This is somewhat paradoxical given that I am now a neuroscience researcher who uses complex computer programs to analyse brain function.

I believe that the Narnia series opened my young mind to the possibility that there might be other worlds containing magic and magical characters. I always wished that something would happen to me, some transcendent experience perhaps, were I to enter a cupboard in the house and walk through the racks of hanging coats, or find a trinket in the street and wonder whether a wish while touching that object would bring some new experience. I was indeed fascinated by many other similar kinds of books such as the E. Nesbit series ... There were also two other books that I recall very clearly, one was called *Half Magic* and the other was called *The Ship That Flew.* This latter book had a profound influence on me but I have since never been able to track it down as the author's name was never one of my priorities as a primary schoolboy.[24]

Well, as the years go by one begins to realise that magical events are alas rather uncommon, and my science upbringing through school and ... Universities installed a rather more sceptical view of the world. However, I feel that my childhood experiences, particularly of Narnia, were in part responsible for my later interest in philosophy and religion. I spent many years studying eastern religions and western philosophy because I had become fascinated by the problems of consciousness and determinism in western science. I feel bound to say that I was not compelled to take up any particular one of these religions as a consequence, my sense of scepticism, part inherited from science, part in my high regard for the philosopher David Hume, prevented me from being sucked into any religion or dogma that requests blind faith in the absence of tangible evidence. In effect, I was, and still am, lacking some Narnia-like experience to change my mind. This is a predicament faced by most people, I suppose. However, I remain certain (without evidence) that our understanding of our own conscious experience is still in its infancy and there are still great and earth-shattering discoveries to be made (not necessarily theistic ones). Perhaps this little bit of "blind faith" has its roots in the primitive child's mind, or perhaps we need an Einstein to overturn our Newtonian view of Neuroscience ... Nevertheless, I am convinced that my interest particularly in **alleged** mystical states has its roots in my childhood preoccupation with magic and transcendental other worlds. This is a theme I am exploring in an article I have been preparing for a long time on the relations between mysticism, psychology and brain function ...

I feel that the strongest legacy of the Narnia work remains the magic of the books themselves. I read C. S. Lewis' autobiography ... and know the house in Bristol in Ravenswood Road where he once stayed. I remember his account of a meeting with J. R. Tolkien ... who rubbished Lewis' use of animals in allegorical form only to write *Lord of the Rings* at a later date ... I have to say that the most potent book for me was *The Magician's Nephew*, particularly, and perhaps strangely, because of the description of the crumbling world of Charn with its cold red sun. I think I assumed that the Empress of Charn was the white witch of *The Lion, the Witch and the Wardrobe*, but I am not sure now whether this connection was explicit ... I was also deeply impressed that an Apple from Narnia (or was it the world of pools) grew into a tree after being thrown by the witch ... and Digory (the professor in *The Lion, the Witch and the Wardrobe)* had the tree turned into a wardrobe after it was struck by lightning. Now that I am reminiscing I also recall the scene in *The Lion, the Witch and the Wardrobe* when all the stone animals are converted back to life by Aslan's breath and another lion running around pretending to be Aslan after being brought back to life, or the drug addiction allegory of Edmund's Turkish Delight!' [VINCENT, *Woman and Home*]

A Sense of Logic

'I started with *The Lion, the Witch and the Wardrobe* at the age of nine (I am now twenty-five) and his work and ideas have been a very strong influence on mine (I am a tapestry designer ...) When I read that first book I fell in love with the enchanted world he created, especially the fauns, dryads and Aslan. I was and still am fascinated by the idea of trees and rivers having living spirits and that nature has a magical dimension. But there is so much in his work that I hardly know what to write about; I think most of all he gave me certain beliefs about life, about right and wrong - that is to say, ideas that corresponded with my own, but lacked any solid shape or form of expression before I read his books.

The firm basis of logic combined with imagination in his books made me feel it was possible to defend the more gentle attitude to life without being airy-fairy; he used logic as a weapon with which to attack those things he loathed, and I think he was successful in the attempt to argue with the selfishness and materialism of modern life.

I remember reading once that reading C. S. Lewis was like opening a window in a stuffy room. This seems very apt to me; when it would have been only too easy for him to lapse into a more elitist style, he made his work accessible to all who could respond to it, and although he used many metaphors, his method of expression was very clear.' [GEMMA, *Woman and Home*]

No More Magic?

'When I was sixteen I wrote a long poem lamenting the loss of childhood (as one does at sixteen). There is a line "Narnia has gone back to the printed pages." Part of the frustration embodied in that poem is from some realisation I had when I was eleven or twelve, which I expressed to myself at the time as "There will never be any magic in the world."

What I had in mind was this image of doors opening suddenly on to other worlds, the sky opening to let me walk through, hearing a magic horn that would call me into another world; where trees could speak to me, where there were talking mice and lions and horses.

... while Narnia was only one of the fantasies I devoured ... it was certainly one of the strongest. I read and re-read all seven books, once we had them all. I remember a Puffin-sponsored competition about the Narnia series, when I was ten or eleven; I picked up a form in a bookshop, went to sit on a bench outside to wait for my father and sister, and before they came out (in about ten minutes) I had answered all seven questions - correctly, as far as I recall.

When I came to read the sources from which Lewis borrowed, much later, I recognised much of the symbolism (Reepicheep casting his sword into the sea of lilies; the stone table and the stone knife; the worlds being only hollows in the greater world) he had used. (Greek and Norse mythology excepted; I'd been reading that since before I read the Narnia books) But what was in the Narnia books belonged to Narnia; only his use of Father Christmas now seems unnaturally borrowed.

I now know that Lewis wrote the death and resurrection of Aslan in deliberate imitation of the death and resurrection of Christ; yet I remember too well how I felt when I first read and re-read it, aged six or eight or ten, to be able to associate it, except intellectually, with the crucifixion. Lucy and Susan, watching it happen, cold and miserable and afraid, and afterwards sitting on the Stone Table beside Aslan's dead body, knowing that the worst thing in the world had happened. And then when Aslan is alive again, and the vivid description of the ride on his back through open countryside in the early morning - beautiful.

The same with the rest; the image of Aslan singing Narnia up out of nothingness into the first morning, and of Aslan roaring the end of the world into the last night; the lamb who turned out to be Aslan in disguise; the mysterious lion who kept following Shasta and Bree and Aravis and Hwin through Calormen and Archenland; I have read commentaries, yards of them, and I know what the Christian allegories are, but the roots of them go down beyond intellectual understanding into me.

The rest of C. S. Lewis' fiction, the science fiction trilogy, *The Screwtape Letters*, I read when I was older - fourteen, fifteen sixteen - and enjoyed it, but the only other work of his that had a similar effect on me was *A Grief Observed*, which I read and re-read addictively when I was sixteen; it was such a strong impression of complete loss and grief that I found it nearly unbearable. So I wrote a novel in which the hero, based consciously on the Cuchulainn type, loses her lover at the beginning of the last book.

I didn't actually like *The Screwtape Letters* very much; I still don't. They gave me the cold shudders the first time I read them, maybe when I was fifteen.

Of the science-fiction trilogy, I like best the middle book, *Perelandra* ... because the description of Venus/Perelandra seemed to me when I first read it (fourteen? fifteen?) the most beautiful description of an alien world I have ever read. It is still completely magical to me now.' [ANNETTE, *The Friend*]

The notion of 'the door' is picked up by another respondent.

'Like many others I was at school myself when I first read *The Silver Chair*. The idea of a door from school to another world is one which I found most compelling. A lasting impression has been given me by the description of the "blaze of sunshine" which "poured through the doorway as the light of a June day pours into a garage when you open the door."' [PRESTON, *Gradlink*]

And as an aside on *The Screwtape Letters* ...

'... I read *The Screwtape Letters* and was impressed and amused. I was an Anglo-Catholic at the time and it all fitted: the book is still a delight - but it's a sugared pill ...' [KAREN, *The Lady*]

NARNIA IN THE CLASSROOM

The effectiveness of the Chronicles of Narnia as vehicles for education has already been outlined in Part III. Respondents reported a range of spin-offs from this activity - introduced at an age (and in an age) when the sense of wonder in a child was paramount, and it was interesting that among Lewis' detractors, there was not one to slam this form of 'filling the time-table' or 'rote learning' or even accuse teachers of 'indoctrination.' Rather, even among those who lost interest later, it was regarded as a positive and productive activity. One respondent reported two experiences of it ...

'Once a friend ...'

'When I was in the top infants and aged six or seven, *The Lion, the Witch and the Wardrobe* was read to us by our class teacher. I think the book was quite fashionable at the time (if that is the right word to use) and the following year, when I had moved into the junior school, we read the book again. This time each pupil had their own copy and we took it in turns with the teacher to read aloud.

My favourite part of the book was then, and still is, when the children reach the beavers' house and have lunch. Then they have to hurriedly pack up sacks and Mrs. Beaver wonders if she can take the sewing machine!

I remember that I liked the book but found it rather strange and there were parts I did not really understand. However, I must have seemed very enthusiastic about it because mum and dad bought me a paperback copy for Christmas or a birthday. I'm not sure which; but I still have it.' [DONNA, *Woman and Home*]

For others it was a case of captivating wonderment, getting 'hooked' and going on with Lewis to other worlds in other times and places ...

'I attended a small country school as a child and the emphasis was very much on reading for pleasure. The teachers read to us every afternoon and, more often than not, the books were by C. S. Lewis. Each one of the books that I read or listened to held me spellbound and carried me away to a world of fantasy and make-believe but the one book that really influenced me and still is top of my list (even now that I'm a grown woman with children of my own!) was *The Lion, the Witch and the Wardrobe*. I first heard the story sat in a dark, dusty classroom listening with awe and wonder to the teacher who read it to us. From then on I lived in the beautiful world of fantasy and could hardly wait to get back home from school and read again the fantastic story.

Later on in my life, when I was training to be a primary teacher, I did a project on the book for one of my humanities assignments and, once again, I relived the wonderful journeys and adventures.

My experience is not an earth-moving one but one that will always be special to me because it cemented my love for literature and has encouraged me to continue to fall back into the world of fantasy each time I open the pages of a book.' [VANESSA, *Me*]

'I have been dramatically influenced by the writings of Lewis. And in fact he has been something which has played a large part in my life over the past two years.

I first became acquainted to his work as a child when *The Lion, the Witch and the Wardrobe* was read to me by a school teacher. From there I went on to read the other books in the Chronicles, as did my best friend at the time. I recall that the stories were held in high esteem by my young mind and I spent rather a lot of time trying to find similar books of the calibre. (I only remember finding one book which matched it called *The Ship that Flew* by Hilda Lewis.)' [MOIRA, *Christian Woman*]

'When we were second-year juniors, our teacher ... read us the wonderful story of *The Lion, the Witch and the Wardrobe*. From then on I was hooked and, over the years, have come to regard this as one of my all-time favourite novels. My cousin very kindly off-loaded his complete Chronicles of Narnia onto me when he had tired of them. Although they were originally a boxed set, my mother sadly threw the box away during a house removal - nevertheless, I still have all the books.' [ADELE, *Me*]

'I have to admit that I've always had a soft spot for the Chronicles of Narnia books. *The Lion, the Witch and the Wardrobe* was the first book I can remember being read out aloud at school - and I thoroughly enjoyed it. As I thought all books must be as good - it made me into an avid reader from a young age. I was told by my English teacher at secondary school that I did so well in the English exams because I read so much. She always remembered me with my nose in a book during school breaks!

I can't believe that not everybody has read the books as they are classics. They also gave me an interest into anything of the "fantasy" nature and I still enjoy reading about myths, legends and love art with anything mythical in it.' [WALLIS, *Me*]

'I was first introduced to *The Lion, The Witch and The Wardrobe* at the age of ten at school, where it was read to us, a chapter a day, after lunch. I thought it was magical, and realised with a great sense of relief that the invention of a personal, imaginary "better world" was not my personal aberration! I read and re-read the entire Narnia Chronicles many times during my schooldays. The stories were simple, but so well written, so satisfying in their outcome, that every time I enjoyed them as if reading them for the first time.' [POLLY, *Christian Family*]

Making Connections

The question inevitably arises as to whether the children did feel indoctrinated in any way. For the most part it appeared not - or else it was explained at some other time.

'I cannot remember when I first read the Narnia books, but I had read them all, and read them all to pieces ... by the time I was ten. I never noticed the Christian mythos until I actually read about it in some commentary on the Narnia books, when I was sixteen or older.' [ANNETTE: *The Friend*]

'Although I came from a Christian family, any comparison between *The Lion, the Witch and the Wardrobe* and Christianity was completely lost on me although I do remember my mum trying to explain to me that Aslan was "like Jesus."' [DONNA, *Woman and Home*]

One respondent's love of Lewis had begun when her English teacher gave her a copy of *The Lion, the Witch and the Wardrobe.*

'The Narnia Chronicles were very new then, and very unusual. I have since used them as text books when teaching, used them as reading books to awaken interest in children with reading difficulties, and used them to explain Christianity with my own children.' [ELSA, *Woman and Home*]

Another respondent even defended her teacher from any suspicion of indoctrination but had to acknowledge that the result bore witness to the influence of the books.

'I can now tell, looking back, that that teacher was probably a Christian. However, it is most important that there was never any mention by her, or anyone in those days [1963] that I can remember, of any allegorical content to the books, nor any connection with Christianity. I was so untaught that I did not myself recognise the sacrifice of Aslan as being a parallel with Christ's sacrifice.' [CHARLOTTE, *Church of England Newspaper*]

Quite a number spoke of going on to other books from the school stimulus of Narnia, but sometimes the schools themselves introduced these more difficult books, the space trilogy included.

TEENAGERS RESPOND

Several teenagers responded, having had their attention drawn to my letter. Of these the youngest was thirteen.

'Calm at the end of the day'

'I am thirteen years old and was introduced to his "Chronicles of Narnia" books at the age of eight, when a Christian friend of my parents suggested that I read them. The first book really enthralled me because of the great amount of detailed description of people and events, which gave me a clearer mental image than any other books I had read in the past.

I have since read all seven books in this series at least twice (some three times) and have also acquired all the books in cassette form. These I listen to every night when I go to bed and have listened to each story over thirty times.

The fascination never dies and I enjoy them because of the good moral ending to each story and the clever continuation from one book to the next.

I find the effect of reading and listening to these stories very calming at the end of each day.

I go to church and recognise the connection between events in Narnia with those in the Bible.' [VINCE, *Renewal*]

The letter bore a footnote: 'dictated to and typed by my mother!'

Two sixteen-year-olds also expressed their feelings for Lewis. In a very mature letter one of these looked at

The 'Proper Evidence'

'I'm sixteen and have been a Christian for just over a year. One of the first Christian books I read was *Mere Christianity* which I found in ... Library. When I was first converted, I was immediately assailed by all sorts of doubts at the amazing claims of my newly found faith. *Mere Christianity* gave me proper evidence, which enabled me to accept these feelings of doubt as just feelings. Although I don't agree with C. S. Lewis' theory on time, he did actually point out it was a theory and showed me it wasn't so important what theory you adopt for something we don't know the answers to, as long as you realise it's only a theory and keep your mind open. On the other hand, his clarification of the redemption was really helpful. I liked his method of illuminating his statements with practical examples, so you can see they are correct and how they work.

She went on to illustrate this with Lewis' demolition of the meaning of certain 'ought' statements - that what he is doing happens to be inconvenient to you and where the blame might be apportioned. She then concluded,

Mere Christianity helped me to defend my faith - both to myself and others. Other books by C. S. Lewis have proved helpful also, but none as much as that, though I enjoyed (**and became better acquainted with myself after reading***) *The Screwtape Letters.* The final Narnia book and *The Great Divorce* gave me some idea of a Heaven, where we will delight in serving.' [YVONNE, *Renewal*]

From the Heart

The other sent me a copy of an Open Study she had done on the Chronicles of Narnia, her 'favourite books.' In fact, with the exception of the collection, *Letters to Children* and Brian Sibley's *The Land of Narnia,* they were the only books by or about Lewis that she had read at the time.

'The Chronicles of Narnia are my favourite books in the whole world and I love to read them over and over again. They have strengthened my faith in God and greatly affected my life in a positive way.'

She recommended that for my purposes I read chapters one, four and five. Chapter four equated the Chronicles with Christianity, drawing also on parts of *Letters to Children* in which Lewis explained some of the incidents in the Chronicles and answered children's questions about them. She looked at the characters Lewis had drawn, and then, using incidents from *The Voyage of the "Dawn Treader,"* equated Lewis' 'exciting adventures' with Christian thought. Chapter five evaluated Lewis' style of writing. It was chapter one, which explains why she chose the Chronicles for the study, that I found most relevant.

'... They are my favourite books and the only ones I truly treasure. When I was first given the Chronicles I was still in Primary School and only read one book out of curiosity. It was only at the age of ten when I really began to read and understand the books. I began to relate to them at this time because I was going through a lack of security in the Catholic faith.

From the conclusions I made of the images in the books, the secrets and the hidden meanings became clearer to me. As they became clearer I also began to see the answers to my problems in my faith. The books helped me to see why I am a Catholic and as a result I took my confirmation ...

For this Open Study on the Narnian Series I called the theme "Christianity." This was because behind the fairy tale adventure type stories the author had engraved his way of communicating the Christian faith which he believed in.' [NATASHA, *Choice*]

FAMILIES INTO NARNIA

A number of parents and grandparents wrote of their experiences of bedtime reading of the Chronicles and their children's reception of them, and of the sometimes surprising influence the books had on them.

A Steadying Influence

'I bought The Chronicles of Narnia for my ten-year-old son when I was about forty years old. He read them over and over and over again. Five or more years later he was shocked to learn that I had myself not read them. It took another five years of his urging and several of my students' urgings for me to start reading them at about age fifty. When I did, I could not put them down and devoured them in about a week! Why did I wait so long? Who knows? The influence of them on me is tremendous but hard to pinpoint. What I believe is that they have moved me in the direction of (toward) the following:

being more open to the mystery of life,
being more questioning of innovations especially but also of tradition,
being more tolerant toward others,
being more patient with others,

being a better listener.' [NORBERT, USA, *Christianity and Literature*]

Another respondent effectively introduced her daughter to the books even before she was born.

'When pregnant with my first child, I returned to the tales of Narnia and read them with renewed intensity, I don't know why. They steadied me with their timeless sense of rightness. When my child was four, I started reading the books to her, a chapter a night. She loved them and now it's time to repeat the process with her younger sister. Both my girls were entranced by the BBC TV productions of The Chronicles of Narnia, and I have taken the older one to see the stage productions of *The Lion, The Witch and The Wardrobe* and *Prince Caspian*, which we both hugely enjoyed.

For me individually, and for us as a family, the Narnia Chronicles are a mainstay of our Christian consciousness; they put across the message of Jesus to my children in an unforgettable, wonderful way that becomes a part of their thinking and doing for ever.' [POLLY, *Christian Family*]

Shared Experiences

It is as bedtime reading that most families share the Chronicles.

'My sons, who are fifteen and thirteen, have been for a long time avid readers of the Narnia books, and before they were able to read my wife and I read them aloud for the children to hear. C. S. Lewis' insight into the reality of the Christian faith comes out very clearly for those with eyes to see, and I am sure I am right in saying that my own and my children's Christian faith have been immeasurably strengthened and informed by these books.' [ARTHUR, *Reform*]

'I think it was in 1950 and subsequent years when my family of three sons were growing up that *The Lion, the Witch and the Wardrobe* and later the many tales of Narnia, became bed-time reading for them. They in turn have passed on these lovely stories to their children who have also the advantage of seeing and hearing them on radio and television. His earlier works, *Out of the Silent Planet, Perelandra* and *That Hideous Strength* were well in advance, both in quality and timing, of the avalanche of "science fiction" books which came in the 'fifties and 'sixties and his skill in getting over the Christian message via an exciting adventure story was truly remarkable.' [NIGEL, *Reform*]

'... We were given a second-hand copy of *The Lion, the Witch and the Wardrobe* when my eldest child was small, and I decided to read it aloud to him. After that we obtained all the Chronicles of Narnia and read them aloud to all our children in turn, in the proper order. Thus I have read the Chronicles four times out loud right the way through in the space of a few years! The books were great favourites with all the children. Our youngest son finished *The Last Battle* by reading in bed till the early hours of the morning, so actually I was unable to complete the cycle! He was just eight years old at the time.' [INGRID, *Woman and Home*]

'Years ago I read the Narnia stories with delight. I'm forty-one now, and so when my children learnt to read the Narnia stories were amongst the 'Classics' I offered them. I have two boys and two girls, who are now twenty-three, twenty-two and twins of seventeen, and they have all shared the delight I felt upon entering the magical world of Narnia.' [VALDA, *Me*]

'I have three of my own children ... and a foster son ... When they were little it was always my job to get them up in the mornings and put them to bed at night. This I always did with prayer and a Bible story. At night I always added a serial reading of the Narnia books and thus read all seven completely through four times to each of the four children.

It was a source of much gratitude to God and a great joy when each child in turn, without pressure, asked to become a Christian. These memories are sweet.' [BRENDON, *Christian Herald*]

Most may hope against hope for such positive results, as one mother put it ...

'I can't say the books have had any significant effect on us but I hope the message contained in them will stand my daughters in good stead through life and perhaps change the thoughts and attitudes of youngsters who do not otherwise get any moral teaching.' [HAZEL, mother of teenage daughters, *The Universe*].

Meanwhile, another mother experienced the cultural drawback in quite a novel way ...

'... my four children loved them all. On her first visit to England at the age of eighteen, my daughter had to squeeze her considerable height into a wardrobe, to see what it felt like. The childhood images in *The Lion, the Witch and the Wardrobe* had stayed with her, you see, and as our California bedrooms had built-in closets, and no wardrobes, she had always felt rather deprived.' [BERNADETTE, *Woman and Home*]

C. S. Lewis undoubtedly had an impact on children and parents alike - so what of the family who were related to him?

'... I suppose when you grow up with something you rather take it for granted.'

RESPONDING TO NARNIA

Much is said about the effects of violence and gratuitous sex in films and television but these days censure seems to be pointed less towards books - except, as we have seen, those considered to be promoting occult practices or perverting Christian principles. Some dismiss any suggestion that children's books could possibly influence anyone either way. That, as at least twenty-seven of my correspondents testified, is simply not true.

From children searching in holes in the road to squeezing into wardrobes (thankfully leaving the door open!) to the nuns imbibing Lewis with their lunch and a mum fighting mediaeval battles, we have already seen the ways in which these stories have influenced those who heard them. Because this section has been about children's experiences in particular it would seem the point to introduce a few of the other accounts since all can be classed as valid responses to reading the Chronicles.

A Secret Country

'You asked did his works affect anyone - well, sort of! My daughter has made a hole in the wall of her built-in wardrobe - this goes through to "Narnia" - a big room above the garage. It's a secret room at the back of her wardrobe - what else could she possibly call it?' [LEILA, *Woman and Home*]

'I recall reading all of the Chronicles of Narnia quite a number of times when I was around eight to twelve years old (I am thirty now) and I believe one or two of his books were read out to us by teachers at Middle School when I was about ten or eleven. The Chronicles of Narnia certainly had an effect on me when I was younger. I lived in a fairly large terraced house then, which had several fitted wardrobes. Sometimes when I was bored or lonely I imagined walking through one of those wardrobes and finding myself in a world full of fauns, satyrs and talking animals, just as Susan, Lucy, etc. did in *The Lion, the Witch and the Wardrobe*. As I have a very vivid imagination I would continue Mr. Lewis' tales with all sorts of other strange adventures partly made up by myself, and in which I had a part. I also recall creeping through an inspection hatch in the wall of an attic bedroom to see where it would lead as a result of reading one of the Chronicles.

I cannot recall the books in a great deal of detail now, as it has been about fifteen years since I read any of them. However, I do often think of one scene which was set in a strange decaying world, at the end of time almost. The hero entered a room where there was a bell with an inscription underneath it saying that he should strike the bell or he would wonder for the rest of his life what would have happened if he had struck it. I think I remember that as I am very inquisitive I would certainly have rung it!

... I also liked very much Lewis' style of writing - some of the imagery was so vivid it was almost like poetry. I also liked the fact that there was usually one unpleasant child - a spoilt greedy, obstinate boy. I just waited for something unpleasant to happen to him! I liked very much the way the books were all about Narnia - I think most children dream of magical places which only they can visit. After reading about Narnia I invented stories about a secret country (called Aquilegia). Unfortunately, I never wrote them down. Though I do remember writing an English essay when I was fourteen about some very strange people with magical powers. So I suppose C. S. Lewis' books influenced me in quite a lot of ways.

I have also read a couple of science fiction novels by C. S. Lewis - one about Mars, one about Venus, but I did not enjoy them very much. Perhaps I was too young - I did read them a long time ago ...' [THEA, *Me*]

'Our own Narnia'

'Although my life has not been "influenced or affected" by the Chronicles of Narnia I well remember enjoying the novels as a boy. My friend and I established our own Narnia, which we named ... a compilation of our joint surnames. We established our camp Cair Paravel and while my friend assumed the title of High King Caspian XI, I devised my own title of Grand King Rilian II. I remember that I had an heir - Crown Prince Erlian.

There were other Narnian associations which I have now forgotten, although I still think of a local pond as Caldron Pool. I do remember that we tried to enter Narnia via some of the established ways but there were no appropriate wardrobes to walk through and no pictures of the "Dawn Treader" to be sucked into. We even tried thinking ourselves into Narnia (like Jill and Eustace behind the gym) but that did not work either!' [PRICE, *Woman and Home*]

One respondent wrote that thanks to Narnia and her four children they now had a cat named Aslan.

And from a cat named Aslan to Narnia at the Nativity. In an enclosed Order of Poor Clares 'somewhere in the world' Narnia figures were used for their crib. 'Most impressive' was the verdict.

And from crib to model islands, constructed by another respondent's young grandson, who eschewed all violent nursery stories in favour of Narnia, which meant 'everything' to him.

Several respondents had based essays or dissertations on Lewis' fiction and one had won a competition at her local library through reading the books. They also found their way into a variety of church services.

Second Childhood

Moving on to adults' reactions, The Chronicles of Narnia led one reader to question her status. She had

'thoroughly enjoyed all the adventures and felt the ending quite "beautiful" ...

They were recommended to me by a friend ... after I had said I had been reading the *Winnie the Pooh* books. Is this second childhood at the age of thirty-two, or have I not left my first yet? My husband said the latter! Incidentally, I now call him "Trufflehunter" and he has nick-named me "Trumpkin."

... I keep on recommending them to friends and will read them again some day.'

She concluded, teasingly perhaps,

'I've seen the wardrobe in an hotel and was quite tempted to step inside. Perhaps next time I will!' [AUDREY, *Woman and Home*]

The written word also spawns more written words, and a number of respondents wrote of Narnia inspiring them or people they knew to write something of their own - not necessarily fantasy, though one respondent did send me a copy of a Screwtape take-off originally serialised in *The Staffordshire Quaker*.[25] One respondent told me that Lewis' views on sexuality in his letters had partly influenced a novel he was in the process of finding a publisher for, another described a chapter in a non-fiction book, while yet another had taken a sentence of Lucy's in *Prince Caspian* that had inspired him to write a play about a government decision to ban Christmas! More seriously, a doctor drew attention to American psychologist Leanne Payne, who had written of how Lewis influenced her in her book, *Real Presence*. He went on to include what could be seen as a controversial statement,

'The effects of some of his thinking is [sic] revealed in accounts of her work in emotional healing ...' [GORDON]

He gave examples from two of her books, *Crisis in Masculinity* and *Broken Image.*

From the written word to other forms of creative art. There have also been a number of musical interpretations, though these were not by respondents themselves. One drew my attention to the 'Narnia Suite' recorded in 1978 by guitarist Steve Hacket,[26] another brought in George Thauben Ball's music for the BBC Radio broadcast of *The Pilgrim's Regress,* while another had got as far as imagining how an oratorio on *Perelandra* might sound - 'Rather Elgar-ish in style,' she said.

JOURNEYS IN FAITH AND THE SPIRITUAL QUEST

Forty-six people indicated that they had received particular help from reading C. S. Lewis' books, fiction and non-fiction, on their faith journey and/or spiritual quest. Sometimes it was what might seem a stepping-stone, a spiritual catalyst, often some imperceptible yet deeply held conviction that these were the words that made the great difference. At others it was a definite experience, some specific moment when time stood still and something was new-born or clicked into place. Such moments may seem rare to some - most of all to those to whom they are given. Some might have considered the prospect impossible until it happened. Historically they may be unique only to the experiencing individual. Often the debt owed was simply because Lewis had put into adequate words what a respondent had found it impossible to express.

A Hug in Heaven

'I grew up in a Pentecostal Church and am very grateful for the teaching I had there. However, when I left school I found myself among the "intellectually sophisticated." I found I could not give a reason for the hope I had in a language they could understand. Very soon, I began to feel my faith trembling at the onslaught of so much modernism. Eventually I fell out of step with the Lord and although I never stopped believing I was no longer interested in the pursuit of holiness. In the Pentecostal Church I attended there was very little encouragement to read Lewis or Schaeffer and thus I didn't even know what apologetics was or who they were.

I then met someone who loaned me *Mere Christianity* and from that time on the confusion and fog cleared. Even now, some ten years later, I read it regularly and give away at least half a dozen copies a year. I have now read nearly everything Lewis wrote - all of it has brought me closer to Jesus.

When I get to Heaven, if we still have power of recognition and memory, I am looking forward to meeting him and giving him a hug for all he has taught me about our Lord.' [DEBRA, *Christian Family*]

In Gratitude to Screwtape

'I have read about the anguish he went through when writing *Screwtape* and can only offer my eternal thanks for this book opened up ideas and realities to me.

Every so often I return to the book to "top-me-up" spiritually. I call it Christianity in action and wish more people could experience its delights. This book has influenced me more than his others - most of which I've read. In fact, I think I'll give them another airing. Your letter was most opportune!

... this man has been my main Christian influence, and has brought me very close to what I feel is the real meaning of life as a Christian in this world.' [ROSEMARY, *Catholic Herald*]

The Courage to Stand

Sometimes the particular insight arose out of the language used.

'How did this "fiction" affect my life? Because it deals with the absolute basics of life - why are we here, how did we get here, how should we behave, what is our relationship with God, how should we view the world-to-come? And yet all this not in a fantastical "New Age" way, not pretending to have contact with other worlds, but quite simply putting basic Christian truths into picture-language and making problems of theology somehow crystal-clear, near and real. One example: why did Christ come into the world to redeem mankind? The reader of *The Lion, the Witch and the Wardrobe* feels and experiences himself the necessity of help (salvation) from never-ending winter and the misery of sin, and rejoices genuinely as the snow begins to melt, as the promised Aslan is on his way, as the witch's power disintegrates. Similarly the reader is aghast at the sacrifice which Aslan takes upon himself, feels the horror of his death, mourns with the children, rejoices again as he comes again to life. The reader is privileged to experience all these emotions, as the story comes to life is at the same time forced to reflect, and on reflection is rewarded since everything makes sense, falls into place, is so relevant to one's own experience.

Some of the (for me) most important "problems" C. S. Lewis touches upon in these books, depicting them so realistically and clearly that they are a great comfort to me are: why does God "allow" evil to exist in the world? (*Perelandra* is a wonderful antidote to this: how a repetition of the Fall was avoided and evil defeated), secondly, the action of Divine Grace. That we are called and given a "kingly" dignity. C. S. Lewis also depicts most vividly how full of life, how interesting, how wonderful to all the senses is life beyond our human life on earth. Of course he cannot tell us exactly how it will feel when we die, what the next world will be like, but the pictures he draws in words make one realise that it certainly will not be negative, static, endlessly dull.

C. S. Lewis has also helped me on occasion to have courage. He depicts many situations where the children have to stand up physically and mentally to evil creatures or terrifying situations. As a reader, I feel the necessity of being brave, not running away, not giving in, but fighting. Evil in his books is so real and tangible that one realises one cannot simply hope it will go away, or busy oneself with other more pleasant things, but one must stand up and fight it.

One extra point which C. S. Lewis brings home to me very clearly is: what a mistake it is to busybody oneself about - what would have happened if ... or will so-and-so be punished/saved for this or that.' [INGRID, *Woman and Home*]

'The Love of my Life'

'I wouldn't say I'd undergone a particular experience in reading Narnia, but rather that pondering on the Narnia books over the years is for me a process closely akin to meditating on the Bible. One delves more deeply as time goes on and there is always something to delight or to inspire, to challenge or to encourage one. I share much of C.S.L's background, having read Classics and having been a life-long member of the Church of England, so I frequently see references and allusions in his works that I might otherwise have missed.' [ESTHER, *Bulletin of the New York C. S. Lewis Society*]

'As a theological student in the 1940s, I was profoundly encouraged by being able to read the thought of an orthodox Christian, who was yet of such an acute mind and fertile imagination as he. I am sure Lewis undergirt my faith, especially through its more formative years, with his *Miracles, Beyond Personality, The Great Divorce* (which I rate very highly) and *The Lion, the Witch and the Wardrobe,* at least.' [PATRICK, *Reform*]

'Beings on another planet'

'I have been a fan of C. S. Lewis far more years than I care to remember. I am also a science fiction addict. It was through the latter that I first came across C. S. Lewis' writings in my late teens when his two books *Out of the Silent Planet* and *Voyage to Venus* came my way via secondhand bookshops. I was at that time searching for confirmation that the Faith I had just accepted was a "reasonable faith" and in some strange way, the thought that "beings on another planet" worshipped the God I knew helped to settle the argument in my mind.

I **knew** that it was fiction and yet ... I have kept both books and eventually many, many years later, also found *That Hideous Strength* which although interesting is not to my mind of such a high, "pure," if that is the word, strain of thought. I still find these books useful for their clarity of thought on various subjects, giving as they do an unusual perspective on what "angels" and "devils" are or might be; plus the chance to think of things like "co-incidence" as being something more than that.

I am certain that these books nourished a young faith and still stimulate me now, thirty years on, in my preaching.' [SEAN, *Epworth Review*]

All Quiet

'When I was working out Christianity for myself (I was a birthright Christian) it was C. S. Lewis who set me on the way, with the utter simplicity of his writing, especially *Mere Christianity, Surprised by Joy* and *The Four Loves*. No contorted thought, no "clever" reasoning, no complex language, just a message so powerful it had to be the pointer to the road to follow. His fiction didn't have the same impact, though I was much taken with the trilogy, and I chuckle when I remember being on tour with a play, and there was no chat in the dressing room as we were all riveted to different volumes of the Narnia books.

But the nub of his importance is his ability to translate his highbrow theology into very simple terms.' [RUBY, *The Friend*]

Clarifying the deeper needs

'... He introduced adult concepts, e.g. Aslan's sacrificial act to save Edmund in *The Lion, the Witch and the Wardrobe*, whilst creating a world in which the young could feel at home. He raised awareness of the everlasting fight between good and evil in an honest simple tale and with visionary power which led on smoothly to an acceptance of Christian faith and of the need to open the way to other children. This faith may have come anyway as I'm a committed Christian but the earlier awareness Lewis instilled of a world without love - what child for instance could not be affected by it being "always winter but never Christmas" - made the path easier. His work helped to clarify the deep need of being able to pass on the faith/love to others in a warm and humane way. We can point the way, when appropriate, to young people seeking answers to difficult questions. My daughter, a schoolteacher, finds her seven-to-eight-year-olds have their imagination stirred in the same way as hers was when young, when she reads *The Lion, the Witch and the Wardrobe* to them - Lewis can seem to induce an awareness of the lost world mankind subconsciously longs for.' [SUSANNAH, *Woman and Home*]

The Heart's Direction

'The lucidity of C. S. Lewis' reasoning and the fresh goodness of his visions has always inspired me. Not only has he altered my sense of ethics, but also my view of the natural world. I cannot look at a high, pale winter's sky - or even purple sprouting broccoli! - without thinking rather wistfully of the beauties of Malacandra. However, the greatest influence that C. S. Lewis has so far had on me, regards my Christian faith.

I became a committed Christian when I was thirteen, but as I entered adulthood I felt a desire to draw away from my faith. I think I became frightened of "getting too intense" and I worried that God would give me a dreadful task to perform if I got too close! In short, I forgot what God was like and hid from Him, lest His demands became too great.

I had read the Narnia Chronicles as a child, but in my mid-twenties I read them again. They were as beautiful as I had remembered them, but the character of Aslan captured my imagination. I couldn't get enough of him, and I would repeatedly read the passages concerning him.

One night I awoke and was overwhelmed by the kind of fear and loneliness that tends to lurk around bedrooms at about three o'clock in the morning. I hope this doesn't sound childish, but at that moment the one thing I wanted was for Aslan to arrive. I longed terribly for somebody warm, golden and bright - awesome but completely trustworthy - to be there.

As I drifted back to sleep besides my snoring husband, I reminded myself that Aslan, however beautiful, was only a shadowy symbol of Christ, and that it was Christ I should really be seeking. From that moment my heart felt as if it had turned round and found its direction. A few weeks later I had a very real and personal experience of being "filled with God." That was over five years ago, and God has been a close reality ever since.

Cynics may find many psychological arguments to explain my case, but as far as I am concerned, Somebody far more real than we can ever imagine, reached me through that series of children's books and changed my life.' [KATRINA, *Woman and Home]*

A Certain Way of Writing

'I am sure I owe my Christian faith in part to discovering his books when I was an undergraduate ... It was not so much what he wrote, but the way in which he wrote it which made me go on reading *The Screwtape Letters*, etc. ... though I never yet have read his other fiction.' [BRYN, *The Local Preacher's Magazine*]

In one instance the academic use of Lewis had personal side effects. Having, years before, used Lewis' books as the basis for a college dissertation, one respondent wrote,

'I still find his Narnia stories incredibly comforting and, although I still find it terribly sad and violent as a unit, the closing pages and especially the last few words of *The Last Battle* are immensely uplifting. While Lewis cannot be said to have given me faith, his writing definitely strengthens it.' [ADELE, *Me*]

Then there were those to whom some 'discovery' in a book provided the faith impetus or experience.

'I was brought up in a Christian home but when at University and first teaching in the late 'sixties/early 'seventies almost completely threw my faith overboard. Having enjoyed Tolkien, Alan Garner and then been frightened a little by Mervyn Peake, I turned to reading John Wyndham and then C. S. Lewis. The *Out of the Silent Planet* trilogy I can remember as particularly helping me to be able to accept another (spiritual) dimension to life apart from the material one and thus being one step along the road to being able to believe. As you'll realise, it's a long time ago now but I remember finding the "angels," worship and picture of "heaven" particularly moving and beautiful.' [VERONICA, *ACT Now*]

'Only the title'

'I have two instances, one of which continues to affect my life, most joyously, although really only the title is involved. Both date back to the early mid seventies when I was a mature student doing my D.E.S. Teacher's Certificate in Religious Education.

A derisory remark by a fellow student about the Narnia Chronicles being ruined by the religious parallels sent me to question my teenage children who had much enjoyed them in Primary School. Their appreciation of the parallels set me thinking and I eventually wrote the main long essay of my course on the subject of Biblical myth in the Narnian Chronicles. I no longer have the essay, which earned me an 'A' grade, so cannot be specific about the title but the influence of the books remains very strong and I still much enjoy reading them.

The book whose title made such a difference to my life is *Surprised by Joy*. The Narnian experience led me to other C. S. Lewis books and this came my way at about the time when I was beginning to endeavour to "practice the presence of God" (to quote Brother Lawrence). After some time I began to be aware of a sudden feeling of warmth and joy at all sorts of odd moments, interrupting but never disturbing what I was doing at the time. I wasn't sure of the origin of the feelings until one day I was looking for a book and my eye caught the C. S. Lewis book and I knew, in a flash, that these sudden, warm, joyous feelings were from God - a sort of "I am here, now, with you" nudge - I was being "surprised by joy"! I am still practising and am still being "surprised by joy" and pray it will always remain so!' [TINA, *The Friend*]

'It is the major experiences of life plus the enlightenment that I discovered in these books that have helped me to see God's hand in the healing process and in true marital relationships inspired by God ... Reading his books, I am certain, gave me an important preparation for Christian experience and a living faith.' [CELIA, FCW Newsletter]

'Stirring the imagination'

'I am glad to acknowledge the debt I owe to C. S. Lewis and his writings. I think it must have been in a copy of *The Listener* that I first read one of his broadcast talks. It must have been near the end of the war and I was in the Services. I had been a Christian since my late teens but my faith had dwindled during my years as a soldier and my general behaviour had slipped, too. That talk printed in *The Listener* gave me a jolt and set me looking for any other publications by C. S. Lewis.

Soon afterwards I came upon his space trilogy beginning with *Out of the Silent Planet*. These books fed my soul as well as stirring my imagination. I later read *The Screwtape Letters, The Problem of Pain, Miracles,* etc. and various books of essays. I was often out of my depth when reading some of these but C. S. Lewis had a marvellous gift of revealing some scintillating truth in unexpected places.

I have read the Narnia books and delighted in them all. I think his book *Till We Have Faces* has had the profoundest effect on me and have even derived help from an American doctoral thesis based on this novel!

I think what helped me most about Lewis was his lucidity. He used his great power to think clearly and his wide-ranging knowledge to show that the Christian faith was totally credible. One did not need a knowledge of metaphysics or philosophy to profit from his writings, especially his fiction.' [LESLIE]

'Taught to be imaginative'

'There are lots of ways we have been influenced by C. S. Lewis ... taught to be imaginative by the space-fiction ... though I never came across nor have since much appreciated Narnia. However it was *Beyond Personality* that really either "broke a log-jam" or "put into overdrive" the development of my faith/understanding/commitment. I came across a copy in the wholly unlikely setting of [a] ... Youth Hostel ... I was cycling alone ... to my brother's ... stopping over a very very hot night at the Youth Hostel. Again I suppose it was the way the short tatty booklet liberated imagination that did the trick. A few weeks later ... I stood up at the conclusion of the final service of an O.C.W. Campaign (which I had helped organise) and gave over my life to this God, whom Lewis had enabled me to make sense of. I was a very sceptical economics student (and still am!) of seventeen and the dedication was also my first call to "the Ministry."' [ARNOLD, *Areopagus]*

Lewis, he later said, had taught him to be imaginative

> 'By his "suspension of "normal" scientific "rules."
> By his dramatic and extensive portrayal of more than the basics re "landscape," etc.
> By the postulation of ethical issues.'

In the end is the Beginning

Sometimes faith was strengthened through the pursuit of philosophical or psychological enquiry.

'In my youth ... I found *The Pilgrim's Regress* and later *The Great Divorce* of much interest and support to my faith. I think the former in particular, with its allegorical treatment of, e.g. Freudian psychology, and the fact that at the end one returns to the beginning, had much to engage my mind, at a time when I was looking for new ways of matching what I had learnt with the obvious misfit between this and life as it actually is.' [ZAK, *Reform*]

For others it was a matter of finding books by or about Lewis that were spiritually or theologically helpful.

'... Of all the spiritual writers, both Catholic and non-Catholic, I have read, Lewis has been of the greatest help to me. I have a collection of eight of his books - in the non-fiction religious genre, plus George Sayers' *Jack: C. S. Lewis and His Times*, and have read many others concerning his life. I am at present reading the daily quotations from *The Business of Heaven*, for the umpteenth time ... I didn't discover Lewis until about six years ago, but for me, as a spiritual guide and an exponent of the Christian faith, he has no equal.' [CORA, *The Universe*]

'When in my early twenties, I first discovered the "Narnia" books I was "hooked." They seemed to me to contain so much Christian truth that they warmed and enriched my life and as over the years I have shared these books with others, the spiritual understanding has been enriched too. No matter how many times I read a "Narnia" book there is always a fresh insight into some spiritual truth or a comforting re-affirmation of a basic Christian belief.' [CARL, *Church of England Newspaper*]

A Sense of Fellowship

'C. S. Lewis has certainly had an effect on my life. I became a practising Christian at the age of eleven, and was enthralled by C. S. Lewis' books right from the start. I have always been a reader, but C. S. Lewis was of special help to me in my teens, while I was still asking questions "left, right and centre" re theology. I went to University ... to study theology, but gave up because of the query re ordination of women.

I have thirty books by C. S. Lewis, and I love them. They have answered so many of my questions re the Christian faith, and have filled me with assurance. For example, I love *The Screwtape Letters, Reflections on the Psalms, Surprised by Joy* and *Miracles*. Also, I have recently enjoyed reading again his collection of George MacDonald's work - a paperback **edited** by C. S. Lewis. I am also impressed with his letters - as recorded in the books edited by W. H. Lewis and [Walter Hooper].

When my children were young, I bought them *The Lion, the Witch and the Wardrobe* and the other children's books by C. S. Lewis, and I was thrilled by them (so were they!).

I have a large collection (several thousand) of theology books, but none are more precious than those by C. S. Lewis.

I'm just off to do a night shift ... [at] a nursing home for sixty-four elderly patients. C. S. Lewis' *The Pilgrim's Regress* and *First and Second Things* are in my bag in the car, in case I get some free time to read! The other staff all watch television, but I find my collection of books (including C. S. Lewis) far more interesting - indeed, fascinating. He strengthens my faith, gives me a sense of universal fellowship, and still fills me with joy and peace in believing.' [JANICE, *Swansea Evening Post*]

Restoring the Miraculous

'I had the misfortune to be young when theologians of a certain mode of thought were busy sweeping away anything in the Gospels that held traces of the miraculous. So, under their handling, the feedings of the multitude became cosy picnics or Messianic feasts; the various healing miracles were given "sensible" interpretations and the Virgin Birth was set aside.

It was C. S. Lewis' theological books and essays that led me out of that barren system of thought into the richer more abundant "faith of our fathers" that he so ably maintained. *The Great Divorce, Miracles, The Problem of Pain, Reflections on the Psalms, Letters to Malcolm, Chiefly on Prayer* and others of his writings have been and continue to be a source of delight and sustenance to me.

The Narnia Chronicles, too, and *That Hideous Strength* and *Perelandra* all bring near that strong other-worldly contact with the life of the Spirit - "The footprints of the Divine are more visible in that rich soil than across rocks and slag heaps.'" [AMY, *Reform*]

Bridging the Gap

Often Lewis seems to have filled a slot church life could not.

'In my early twenties (I am now sixty-eight years) I was given *The Screwtape Letters* by an aunt and from that time have read (I believe) all his theological books.

I was, and still am, a member of the Christian Brethren - although now thankfully worshipping in a live church ... where we are being wonderfully blessed ...

I well remember at that time how depressed I was with my personal and church life. How out of touch the "meetings" were with reality. So much emphasis on typology and drab Gospel meetings. No one to answer all the questions which flooded into [the] mind of a young engineer trying to bridge the gap between endless meetings and ordinary everyday living.

It was into this dilemma that the writings of C. S. Lewis breathed new life.

Every new book - *Broadcast Talks, Christian Behaviour, Beyond Personality* - excited me as I began to see my questions answered and instead of faith being something which was rather shabby and unable to stand up to the world, it was wonderfully relevant - and more importantly - **true**.

At that time I had become very airy-fairy about miracles and - I'm afraid - only too willing to "play them down" as not too respectable for the twentieth century.

What a debt I owe this man for his book, *Miracles: A Preliminary Study*. How this book exposed the trite and unscholarly views I had unwittingly absorbed from other sources.

Similarly his book on Psalms opened new vistas for me. The chapter on Worship answered questions which had "nagged" at me for years.' [PERCY, *Harvester*]

Deeper Magic

Then there is that odd, inexplicable 'God-incident' in which a passage from a book clarifies or illumines a present situation ...

'I think it is vital to give a little background to my reading of [*The Silver Chair*]. I had attended a Bible study at which the leader had asked us what we would say if Jesus were to return that moment and we had the opportunity to speak to Him. After some thought, I said that I would be so overwhelmed with a sense of failure that I could only say "I'm sorry." A few days later I read this ... from "The healing of harms" (pp. 200-2):

"'I have come,' said a deep voice behind them. They turned and saw the Lion himself, so bright and real and strong that everything else began at once to look pale and shadowy compared with him. And in less time than it takes to breathe, Jill forgot about the dead King of Narnia and remembered how she had made Eustace fall over the cliff, and how she had helped to muff nearly all the signs and about the snappings and quarrellings. And she wanted to say I'm sorry but she could not speak ..." (at which I stopped dumbstruck. I then read on).

"Then the Lion drew them towards him with his eyes, and bent down and touched their pale faces with his tongue, and said:

"'Think of that no more. I will not always be scolding. You have done the work for which I sent you into Narnia.'"

Need I say more?' [RAYMOND, *Baptist Times*]

Reaching the Spiritual Emotions

The lines between help along the way and a full spiritual commitment can be very narrow.

'I preached the Cross for years ... but never shed a tear over it till I read *The Lion, The Witch and The Wardrobe.*

Similarly, I preached the Resurrection for years, but was never thrilled by it till I read *The Silver Chair*. ...

My grandfather ... left the Church of England in the 1860s and became a Wesleyan Methodist. He and his family had the privilege of being present at a time of spiritual blessing and power among the mining communities of County Durham in the 1870s and 1880s, and later moved to the coal mining areas of Monmouthshire.

The faith that was born in those times was passed on through the generations, and led to my own exposure to the Gospel ...

In childhood I was taught to pray, and sent to Sunday school, and at the age of about eleven or twelve, I still had a vague belief that God existed. But He played no part in my life or thought. I still "prayed" nightly, because to do so had been ingrained in me from earliest childhood, but my prayers were no more than empty repetition of the same formulas, and I got through them as quickly as I could.

At the age of thirteen or fourteen I began to think more seriously. Soon, I became convinced that there is no God, and - oh dear! - that those who believed in Him were quite below my own level of insight!

In time, a book about life after death fell into my hands, and I became convinced that there is indeed an afterlife; with this persuasion came also a head belief in the existence of God. It went no further than the idea that He existed - He still played no part in my life.

I went to church only when I could not avoid it - that is, when my parents insisted, maybe every six weeks. One evening, I went for this reason, and after the service I was invited to the youth fellowship. I went for the sake of a good discussion, and in the hope of discovering some pretty girls there, but when my ideas were discussed, neither side succeeded in persuading the other ...

At one such evening meeting the question was put to us: "Do you have a sense of sin?" I was perhaps the last to be asked; the others all said yes. I replied that I supposed I sometimes did something I ought not to, but would not go so far as to say I ever sinned.

I continued going to the meetings, enjoying the warm, friendly atmosphere and the lively discussions. Maybe unawares I was also attracted to their Christianity. At any rate I learned more of what Christianity is - and began attending church regularly so as to qualify for the youth meeting afterwards.'

Eventually he learnt the piano and then proceeded to play tunes from the Methodist Hymn Book, one of which was '*What shall I do my God to love/My Saviour, and the world's, to praise?*'[27] It was in reading the second stanza, which included the words 'Whose every sin was counted Thine,' that the truth about sin dawned on him, and he became a Christian - 'humanly, perhaps Charles Wesley's last convert!'

From that point he was taken under the wing of an elderly local preacher who took him to services he was conducting and eventually invited him to take part. However, he wrote,

'... despite the fact that God had opened my heart to believe that Christ died in my place at the Cross, and despite my desire to recapture and relive the holiness, zeal and love of bygone Methodism, my **emotions** remained unmoved by what had happened at the Cross ... till the first time I read C. S. Lewis' *The Lion, the Witch and the Wardrobe*, I think in 1973. There, where Aslan takes the punishment of the guilty Edmund and dies in his place, and later rises again to a victorious life, I saw afresh what really happened at Calvary: I was the guilty rebel against God's Law and standards; God's word requires that "the soul that sinneth, it shall die" and I was to receive the wages of my sin, which is death - eternal death; but the real Aslan, Jesus the Son of God, took the punishment due to me, died my death; and having fully satisfied the demands of God's justice, rose again with an indestructible life. And as I saw it in Lewis' story, for the first time I wept over the magnitude of what Jesus did for me at His death and resurrection: the greatness of what I had been saved from, and the greatness of the sacrifice that had been demanded to save me; the greatness of the Person who had died in my stead; the wonder of the everlasting life that was won by His work at Calvary: I saw it afresh, it broke my heart with gratitude, and I wept.'

But that was far from the end of Lewis' influence. A second book also had a profound effect on his spiritual experience.

'The trouble with reading C. S. Lewis' stories aloud to one's wife or husband is, that some passages are moving enough to get the reader rather too choked up to continue - and the listener, being equally moved, is not able to continue the reading either!

One story that moved me to tears of joy is *The Silver Chair,* and I ought perhaps to explain that I am most of the time a rather staid, unemotional man who acts guided by logic and principles. To my disappointment, some may even see me as remote and a little cold, though I would not wish to be so. But it emphasises the power of Lewis' writing.

When I first turned to *The Silver Chair* ... I had been preaching since I was eighteen, that is, for some eight years. Like so many other people, my grasp of God's truth increased by stages ...'

The third stage involved the realisation that

'the Christian will not spend his eternal life as a disembodied spirit, but that we await a resurrection of the body at the end of history - a resurrection like that of Jesus Himself.'

Following that he read the final chapter of *The Silver Chair*, "The Healing of Harms".'

In this chapter the children witness old King Caspian, whom they had known as a youth on a previous visit, dead, and all stood and wept over him. Eustace is then invited to drive a large thorn into Aslan's foot, from which comes one large red drop of blood which splashes over the body of the King. Immediately the King begins to change, to go back in time until he becomes a youth - alive again. He equated this incident with the achievement of Jesus' blood on the Cross, through which 'Death is swallowed up in victory.' Just as Caspian and Aslan are reunited, so Jesus and those who love Him shall be together for ever. He concluded,

'I wonder how many congregations over the years have heard me read from that chapter when preaching on the resurrection? For **that story** is what brought the choking to my throat, the tears to my eyes, and the excitement to my heart, concerning the coming resurrection of the body. For me, C. S. Lewis changed it from being a fact acknowledged in the mind, to being also a thrill and joy of the heart, never lost in all the years that have followed, and one day to be fulfilled when the Lord Himself descends from heaven with a shout, and with the voice of the archangel, and with the trump of God: and the dead in Christ shall rise.' [LAWRENCE, *Christian Newsworld*]

First the Head ...

'I came across the book [*Mere Christianity*] when I was eighteen and going through a period of agonising about "why was I here" and so on, and at that time, and since, it has been to me the best defence of Christianity I have ever read. It does not begin by talking about God and sin, etc., as most religious books do (which puts non-believers off straight away) but begins right at the beginning with the fact of there being a moral law outside ourselves. For me, his arguments have been so clearly reasoned and defined that they are indisputable and they made Christianity intellectually respectable to intelligent people. I think his chapter on sexual morality, too, is brilliant - I often have to remind myself that Lewis was writing soon after the war when sexual morality seemed **then** to him to be lax, and I wonder what on earth he would have made of how much worse it has all become in the last twenty years!

The chapter, too, on pride - and on forgiveness - for me are also excellent. I lend the book to people who show interest in Christianity but would not be impressed by the "let Jesus into your heart" approach.

What I am really saying is that the book convinced me of the truth of Christianity, so my head was converted; it took many more years for the heart to follow!' [NINA, FCW Newsletter]

'A Window into My Soul'

'I was raised in the fellowship of the Church from infancy and the discipline of worship, prayer and Christian training were as much a part of my life as eating and sleeping. Despite this nurturing I did not come to grasp the full relevance and reality of Christ in my life until, at the age of **seventeen**, I began to read Lewis' Chronicles of Narnia which were recommended to me by some of my peers who at the time were immersed in a kind of Christian renaissance for youth (*circa* 1970). I experienced a great deal of ambivalence with respect to the enthusiasms, etc. of these "friends" but because of my personal circumstances I agreed to give the "Chronicles" a try - feeling very silly about reading children's "fairytales" (typical of my intellectual arrogance!). I should explain that I was in a state of deep inner turmoil at this point in my life which lasted for a period of about four years. In this emotional upheaval I was desperately seeking integration and peace (Shalom!). Most of my difficulties I now understand to have been a latent and acutely disruptive emergence from adolescence. The course of my life since then has largely been the result of the inner conflicts and resolutions experienced in that period. C. S. Lewis was my primary evangel who spoke to my heart with amazing familiarity. The clarity and intimacy of his work, as I experienced it, brought the reality of Christ into the very centre of my life. Suddenly, in an expansive flash of retrospective I saw the presence of God with me in Christ in every detail of my life's story. Always bothered by the distancing "otherness" of the Church, the Bible, and all things sacred, I **suddenly** discovered the sacredness of **all** ground. I knew much about the God of judgment and law (or at least felt I did) at that juncture, but the revelation of a God of saving love was an overwhelming and startling experience for me. Lewis showed me the true landscape of my soul as the common territory of humanity and also the province of God in Christ. I too was surprised by joy (I later read the autobiographical book by that title as well as numerous other writings including two of his "science" fiction works - *Out of the Silent Planet* and *That Hideous Strength*. I have also read his *A Grief Observed*.

For me Lewis was a window into my own soul. He spoke the truth (Truth) which began to "set me free" and which opened, finally, the "door" against which Christ had been knocking. I have not referred to him for a while now although he remains the chief apologist of the faith (next to Paul, of course) for me! (Thank you, Lord, for this man's beacon of wisdom and insight which, for me, has been an incredible reflection of Your light!).' [TED, *Reform*]

FROM FALTERING FAITH TO FULL COMMITMENT

The accounts of the ways in which C. S. Lewis' books had a direct or incidental bearing on a faith commitment are as many and varied as the people who wrote them. As has been seen in the previous section, it has not always been proved easy to set them into categories so for this particular reporting they have been divided under the headings of the various books responsible. A separate section accounts for multi-book influence, but in most cases it is the works of fiction that are deemed significant.

The Chronicles of Narnia

'In 1977, I was at crisis point - suffering from depression and approaching the suicidal. A colleague at work, a Christian, took an interest in me. As she put it, I "ate Christians for breakfast." In my teens I had attended an evangelical church of the "thou shalt not wear make-up" type. According to their injunctions, I had read the Bible daily and prayed (to a vast, empty void). The Bible bored me rigid, but I "obeyed the rules."

I later threw this meaninglessness over. I was virulently anti-Church and anti-Bible. How should my Christian friend help me? I would not name the name of Jesus even (I couldn't say it) and I poured scorn on The Church. She lent me C. S. Lewis' Chronicles of Narnia - all seven of them. I devoured them - at the age of thirty-seven years, in two days flat. I laughed in delight at them, but I mostly cried an ocean of tears through them. How much I wept. What I now know was the Holy Spirit brought them alive to me. *The Magician's Nephew* told me how evil came into the world. *The Lion, the Witch and the Wardrobe*, the first I read - oh, it was the Gospel, pure and simple. Aslan I could relate to. How I wept when he died - and wept great tears of gratitude and amazement when he returned to life. How I recognised the intimacy of his knowledge of the children and the talking animals. What hope was aroused in me - could this be true - happiness and freedom beyond my wildest imaginings? - And so I read, in fact, about Jesus - the parallels were so numerous. In *The Horse and His Boy* I learned about prayer, as Aslan walked by Shasta next to the chasm, going into Archenland. In *The Last Battle* I learned about the defeat of death - I identified particularly with Puzzle the donkey, whose ears went down when he met Aslan, and then his ears went up again. Every time I read the end of *The Last Battle* - "a wild hope arose in them ... the term is over, the holidays have begun ... " how profoundly grateful I am. This is because my depression was caused by the death of my grandfather and of my father and the near death of my mother, when I was four years old. In *The Last Battle* I was reading about what I couldn't face, in a way I could face it - because it gave me hope.

Since 1977, when I decided to "give it a whirl" (i.e. talk to God), I have had to go through a lot of inner healing - and some very hard times, looking at things I wouldn't look at, they were so painful. Whenever I felt particularly hurt, desperate, etc. I re-read the Narnia stories - I have lost count of the number of times I have re-read them. Before I could name the name of Jesus I could discuss "Aslan" with my friend - what he (or He) was like, how he reacted, what he stood for - till I made the transition to Christ Himself.

... The Narnia stories are truly "Good News."' [ZOE, *Renewal*]

The Screwtape Letters

'I first came across his books as a teenager in the late 'fifties, and they certainly played a significant part in my own pilgrimage to faith. My sister (four years my senior) was converted at a university mission and came home with a determination to "save" me too. I was at the stage of rejecting my earlier Sunday School ideas (our parents were not churchgoers themselves but brought us up with good middle-class standards of behaviour). My sister lent me *The Screwtape Letters* to read - and I am certain that it was that book which enabled me to come to terms with the concept of good and evil, and of a life and influence beyond our own world, and thus set me on the path leading to faith. I still remember its impact. I then moved on to *Mere Christianity*, which laid a firm foundation for a rational faith, counterbalancing the emotional fervour of the evangelical (Anglican) church I was drawn into at the same time (though I needed that evangelical faith to bring me to the point of commitment). By the time I was eighteen (and going to university) I had read several other of his books, including the Ransom novels, which I loved and read over and over again. It was *Perelandra/Voyage to Venus* which had the most impact at that time, helping me greatly to come to terms with the doctrine of sin and redemption.

... I am married to a ... minister and thus have access to a lot of theological writings, but none of them have had the impact of C. S. Lewis - we need more books that are written for the ordinary layperson, dealing with theological issues in a down-to-earth, practical way.' [ERICA, *Reform*]

'A scientific, lapsed church member, I argued a lot with my army chaplain whilst in a POW camp. He was very patient and one day lent me *The Screwtape Letters*. That convicted me of guilt and I admitted it to him, whereupon he lent me *Broadcast Talks* and that encouraged me to request re-admission to Communion.

A few months later the chaplain ... suggested that I be ordained. This I did in 1950 and never regretted it. Now I am retired after forty years of fruitful ministry ...' [HUNTER, *Renewal*]

'I was brought up in the narrow confines of a small Cathedral City, where there was a great deal of religion of a rigidly conventional type. It was not until I went to College that Christianity began seriously to challenge me. My final surrender to Christ came after I had been given a copy of *The Screwtape Letters*. I cannot describe the effect this book had on me, it was like a mental bombshell. It made Christianity topical, rational and fun! I owe a great deal to that book and to others of his writings which I read subsequently, particularly his various essays.

I am now in my late fifties but continue to "visit" C. S. Lewis frequently.' [URSULA, *Christian Woman*]

'... I read *The Screwtape Letters* at the age of nineteen years as a convinced atheist. A few weeks later I received a revelation of God's reality and placed my trust in Jesus Christ. *Mere Christianity* had a great impact on my new found faith and over the years [I] received much help from the writings of C. S. Lewis and George MacDonald.' [MELVIN, *Christian Newsworld*]

'One day I was in my minister's study, having a chat with him. The walls were covered with bookshelves and for no apparent reason he suddenly reached up and fetched down a paperback. "I thought you might enjoy reading this," he said, handing me the book. The cover had a picture of a strange looking devil-like creature on it and was called *The Screwtape Letters* by C. S. Lewis. I had never heard of the book or the author, but as someone who enjoyed reading I was always glad to find something new.

C. S. Lewis was the first writer I had come across who seemed really at home with the concept of eternity. For someone brought up with a "social gospel" view of Christianity, this certainly stretched my mind.' [OLIVER, *Renewal*]

'C. S. Lewis was a great influence on my Christian beginnings in my teens and continues to be, ever since.

The first I heard of his incisive and witty style of apologetics was when, as a fifteen-year-old evacuee living with Methodists and attending the local chapel ... I heard the minister quote from *The Screwtape Letters.*

John Wesley used to try out his sermons on his fifteen-year-old servant, I'm sure I've heard. Well, Lewis spoke to this fifteen-year-old. I devoured "Screwtape" joyfully. Then I heard Lewis' broadcasts, now together in *Mere Christianity*, and appreciated them in print.

I think I've read most of his books over subsequent years, though not much of the work that's been published since his death - still on my waiting list.

Every year or so I re-read *The Great Divorce* - the ideas behind the images are deeply profound ...

Perhaps the piece that has moved and influenced me most of all, which I return to, and read to other people, and quote most often is Book 4, chapter 9 in *Mere Christianity*, "Counting the Cost" - quite superb.' [TONI, *The Local Preacher's Magazine*]

The Pilgrim's Regress: Re-defining the Christian

'The background is that by the age of fifteen, I was a nihilist materialist (and inevitably an atheist). I enjoyed arguing the issues, but was not budged. One thing that I particularly resented was the attempt of liberal clerics on school radio R.E. broadcasts to make me a Christian by re-definition - I knew that if my beliefs were Christian, then anything could be called "Christian" and so why bother with the label? I was particularly contemptuous of the argument "God is the focus of our life" : "Everyone has a focus to their life" : "Therefore everyone believes in/has God." (Aristotle would have called that the fallacy of the undistributed middle, I suspect.)

Anyway, I went to university and in my second year, encountered the Pan paperback *Out of the Silent Planet.* I purchased and read it with much enjoyment (science fiction being a taste of mine). The implications of Maleldil, Oyarsa and the Bent One were obvious enough to me [I was astonished that many readers did miss the point when I later read Lewis' *Letters*] but it was a good story. I later acquired and read *Voyage to Venus* and *That Hideous Strength.* Both enjoyable stories, and why not make stories based on assumptions which are known to be false?

It occurred to me (or perhaps one could equally truthfully say that the Holy Spirit led me) to see what else Lewis had written. A check through the library shelves showed ... relatively little - just the odd-sounding *Pilgrim's Regress* (the unannotated version). I ploughed through it, and found it interesting. Lewis seemed to be addressing arguments that I knew and advanced (most of the book relates to the "Northern" frame of mind - which is mine). It was plausible certainly, but ... in September 1989 ... I found a copy of *Pilgrim's Regress* in [another public library] - and this one had notes, which confirmed that I had got his message right.

After graduating ... in June 1970, I went to ... university for an M.Sc. course (one year), [which] university had two books by Lewis, *Miracles* and *The Problem of Pain* ... [they] seemed convincing - really, the argument for there being a God seemed as strong as the argument against (not stronger, but as strong).

I was then invited to a meeting organised by members of ... Christian Union living in my hall of residence. Ever ready for an argument, I went along with the guy in the room next to mine. A grand debate raged, and I held up my end (possibly more than held it up, for I later discovered that I had left an impression as a hardened anti-Christian) so the debate shifted to my neighbour who seemed more sympathetic. One of the Christians asked him of some problem, "Have you tried praying?" (He hadn't, and didn't.)

That was an interesting question. Obviously, if there was a God, it was important to know. Lewis had demolished or weakened my arguments against the existence of God and against the coherence of Christianity, but had not convinced me to the contrary. It seemed reasonable to try an experiment, for if there was a God, He could answer prayer (and if there was no answer, either there was no God, or God didn't care). So I prayed (on a regular basis) that if there was a God, He would let me know about it. Nothing more than that.

The meeting was in November, I suppose, and by early January I became aware that if I did believe in God, and I did, there was a whole lot of other things that He wanted me to do...

Amongst a whole lot of other things, like attending church, Bible studies, etc. I acquired the Narnia books (which I knew about, but had not read properly) and as many Lewis paperbacks as were in print in 1971. They were interesting and helpful reading, but so were many other books, and they had to take second place to the Bible.

Moving to Northern Ireland in October 1971 was interesting (in more ways than one, for the Troubles were building up to their worst level ever, and [the] University had kindly placed me in new accommodation - two hundred yards from the Falls Road, with an army post across the road!). The Christian Union Bible study that I attended struck me as fragile - the others held strong orthodox views, but somehow it struck me as brittle. They were right, but they would be hard-pressed to defend their rightness against arguments I could have deployed (That feeling faded, but of recent years, I am returning to the view that I was correct.).

C. S. Lewis was not approved reading, having been categorised as "Not Sound" ... I wasn't really sound either, being prone to ask questions like "Why?" and respond to the answer. There were many people in the C.U. who would have sought to dissuade my wife from marrying an English non-conformer.

One problem was that ... for an awareness of sin, one must believe in a moral law that has been broken and a God who has been offended. Believing in neither God nor moral law, I could not follow that road. For me, there were issues that had to be settled first - everything else followed on as a logical corollary, and formed not so much a chain as a cassette.

I can't help feeling that Lewis would have been (is?) pleased that *The Pilgrim's Regress* was used to bring me to Christ. He was disappointed in its impact, but I think he would not have begrudged the effort of writing it, as the tool to bring just one lost sheep to the shepherd.' [KIERAN, *Renewal*]

The Great Divorce

'Two books by C. S. Lewis have been very important in my conversion to Christianity. These are *The Great Divorce* and *Mere Christianity*.

I was brought up as a Catholic, but at University decided that all religion was "superstition." Then, in my mid-twenties I got married and started to think about the meaning of life.

A colleague at work, a committed Christian, who later became a pastor in his church, provided the religious discussion and argument that I needed. Then he lent me a copy of *The Great Divorce*. I read it and enjoyed it and handed it back to him saying that it was very clever. "Clever!" he exclaimed in disgust and the next day he brought me a copy of *Mere Christianity* and said, "Read this."

I did and I still have that same copy which I have re-read many times. The book enabled me to see that Christianity could be believed by intelligent people. It did not make me believe but opened my eyes to the possibility and desirability of faith. Over the next few months, helped by the Vicar of our local church, I became a Christian.' [IDA, *Christian Woman*]

'I have read most of Lewis' writings, and found them all profitable. One that I have most enjoyed rereading, and sharing with others (sometimes even in a class setting) is *The Great Divorce*. While the encounters with each of the "ghosts" offer deep insight into our human condition, perhaps due to my own calling as an ordained pastor, I find the conversation with the "Episcopal Ghost" to be the most powerful of all.

It struck me sharply when I first read it, during my college years. And now, as I have been in the ministry some ten years, I find myself thinking back to it periodically. It warns me against my natural inclination to intellectualise the faith. I tend to place too much emphasis on academic pursuits and credentials, and this simple encounter reminds me clearly of what my calling is truly about. In essence, it says to me: "Return to your first love."

I can think of no more important message for any pastor about the place where we will eventually spend eternity than these: "We know nothing of religion here: we think only of Christ."' [ALVIN, *Renewal*]

Multi-fictions: Engaging the Imagination

'I think I can safely say that I am a Christian today because of C. S. Lewis. Not because of the direct effect of any one thing he wrote, but more because of the background, the mental climate, the imaginative landscape, he provided.

I was brought up as a Roman Catholic in the pre-conciliar Church, which gave me plenty of ideas about God but no experience of Him. Christ was a remote figure and religion was not something which engaged the imagination. That was left to books to do, and once I stumbled on the Narnia books at the age of ten I found a whole new literary experience: stories which were enthralling at the level of plot, but which at a much deeper level rang true in a way I couldn't possibly have articulated at the time. In particular the character of Aslan filled me with an intense longing - I wanted more than anything else to encounter him and in some way belong to him, but although I knew that he "was" Christ, the idea that my allegiance could somehow be transferred left me feeling cold and flat. The joy and life and vibrancy I associated with Aslan did not at that stage have any connection with the God or Jesus I heard about at school and in church.

In my teens I read the Ransom trilogy, which again chimed in with my sense of a greater reality, if only I could penetrate the veil between me and it. I wanted to see and understand, to be part of the "company" which stood against evil in *That Hideous Strength*, but there seemed no way to bridge the gap between my actual experience and what I so much wanted to be true.

In the end I came to a real crisis of faith, brought up against the realisation that either there was more to God than I had been shown, or that He did not exist. At this stage I read and re-read C. S. Lewis, both fiction and theology, because while I was reading them I could believe. Once I stopped, I was out in the cold again. Eventually, at the right time, God manifested himself to me in a quite unmistakable fashion, and, as with Jane Studdock, my "world was unmade" - and immediately re-made. The greater reality which I had known of intuitively and which C. S. Lewis had kept alive for me became part of my experience.' [KATHRYN, *Catholic Herald*]

A Knock at the Door

One respondent was diagnosed as having M.E., from which developed a number of other illnesses and allergies, compounded by the mixed and often less than sympathetic attitudes of some in the medical profession. Her desperation for solutions to the unanswered questions all this raised and a search for a personal faith to hold on to led her to Christian reading ...

'I could write a complete volume if I put all of the last six years in print, suffice to say, that with my life turned upside down inside out, and within a sea of physical and mental pain, at the point of considering suicide, I had a knock on my door. It was two J.W.s They in a way rescued me. However, as the Bible study started and pressure to become one of the flock increased, and family anti-J.W.s stormed, I prayed, I read, I became confused, but deep inside I could not become a J.W.

I was given C. S. Lewis' *Letters*. In that I recognised a mind which was alert, searching, was tormented and although reading was exhausting, I became intrigued by the writer. Our daughters often spoke of *The Lion, the Witch and the Wardrobe*, also Narnia. I had taken little notice; I then saw on the bookshop shelf C. S. Lewis' *Mere Christianity*; I am not clever enough or knowledgeable enough to tear the book to pieces, but for one who has always been aware of God, no doubts about him only of myself, his book was and still is a source of encouragement. That whatever the struggle, God is God, Jesus is our Saviour, and the Holy Spirit is always at work.

I may never read all of his work, but I am grateful for what I did read. I know that God is pure love. I know that Jesus is my Saviour, and I am hoping in all my sinful being to receive the Holy Spirit ...

C. S. Lewis speaks a common language and I have pointed many people to his books, hopeful that they will find some useful means of recognising themselves and hopefully our total need of God our Creator, Jesus our Saviour and the Holy Spirit.' [WENDY, *Christian Woman*]

Non-Fiction Books

'After a Christian upbringing and commitment as a young person I lost my faith as a result of challenges made by friends and colleagues when I started work in a scientific establishment.

I searched for several years to regain my faith until eventually as a result of some Christian lady patients who prayed for me and reading *Mere Christianity* a challenge was made which resulted in my turning again to Christ. The methodical way C. S. Lewis took one through all the arguments and counter-arguments and claims finally stating that if one had doubts he recommended reading the Gospel story and asking oneself if as a result Jesus seemed like a madman, a devil or the Son of God. This challenge succeeded where years of searching had failed and I became a recommitted Christian eternally grateful to those patients who so faithfully prayed and to C. S. Lewis whose clarity of mind and statement cleared the way.' [OLIVE]

The Conductor of Life's Engine

One respondent wrote of the way in which a copy of *Christian*

Behaviour had come his way, 'unsolicited,' then 'put into my raincoat pocket for secure keeping.' He then shared his story.

'Since my early teens when my father died it had grown upon me that the philosophy of Communism "From everybody according to his ability to everyone according to his need." [sic] Living that theory filled my life for 20 years but an element of dissatisfaction kept creeping into my life as it did not seem to be working out. "The best made plans of mice and men often go astray."

With this on my mind I found myself on an underground train going in a different direction to which I had planned to so changing over platforms at the first opportunity finding the book in my pocket I was moved to start reading it. At this point it seems right to add that my training was as a practical engineer, so no doubt I looked on life and its operation in engineering terms. C. S. Lewis used this description in his first section but of course he put the possibility that God was the Conductor of Life's Engine that following with the Cardinal Virtues and (The Great sin) pride caused me to see my life in a different way and I accepted his challenge ...' [MARK, *The Friend*]

The Reluctant Convert

'I admit to being a "fan" of Lewis' writings - over thirty years now and I submit one or two instances when something he wrote made a particular appeal to me. I was converted at twenty-eight years of age in 1952 in the most unlikely circumstances, coming from right outside the church.

I had heard of Lewis, but the first book of his which I read was *Surprised by Joy*. And in it, I read at the end of Chapter 14 about a **reluctant** convert. I knew such people existed - I was one - but in those days one didn't admit it publicly, for we were fed on a conception of every convert being 100% desirous of getting into the Kingdom - you didn't, so it was inferred, look around for a chance of escape or have to be dragged into that Kingdom. And so discovering that there was at least one other reluctant convert enabled me to view my own experience in a more acceptable light.

And then in *Mere Christianity* Book 2, Chapters 4 and 3 occur thoughts which are possibly the most widely used C. S. Lewis quotes: "*Either this man was and is the Son of God - or else a madman or something worse ...*" When I first read those words, words which commented on the deity of Jesus, I had never experienced any teaching on the divinity of Christ which expressed the idea so overwhelmingly or so clearly and unarguably. I could never have any doubts after hearing that, "*the man who was merely a man and then said the sort of things Jesus said would not be a great moral teacher.*"

And lastly, *The Weight of Glory* - a sermon, included in *Screwtape Proposes a Toast and Other Pieces*, and one which I would like to have heard in person (I have read somewhere that this was his finest sermon.) Two parts of it come to mind:

Firstly, the paragraph which begins (near the sermon's end), "*And in there, in beyond Nature, we shall eat of the tree of life,"* and continues, *"What would it be to taste at the fountainhead that stream of which even these lower reaches prove so intoxicating?"* In fact the whole paragraph is quite exciting as Lewis portrays what he believes lies before us.

Lastly to the paragraph which follows that to which I refer above and the phrase, *"it is hardly possible for us to think too often or too deeply about that (the glory) of his neighbour ... There are no* ***ordinary*** *people. You have never talked to a mere mortal ..."*

In the fellowship where I am, there is a member who washes the floors at [a supermarket]. Another man spent his working life clearing the weeds at the sides of the roads. Menial tasks - but what will they one day be like? I thank Lewis for bringing to us this reminder of our future glory - I've never heard anyone else put this to us.

And then there was the Big Ghost in *The Great Divorce*. He met Len at the gates of Heaven and wanted to know "what about Jack, whom Len had murdered?'" Finding a murderer in heaven was enough to make the Big Ghost want to go home again ... What I learned about the infinite nature of God's Love and forgiveness!

... Somehow the SF books did not get through to me in the same way, but I did enjoy the Narnia books when I read them (in my forties!). ...

In closing, I would mention that it is my experience that those who have read C. S. Lewis deeply are thin on the ground in this part of the world. In fact, I've never knowingly met any! As rare as the devotees of Mahler!' [QUENTIN, *Harvester/Aware*]

Six years later, in a postscript to a change of address letter, this respondent wrote,

'I now have a fellow addict in ... Church. He has called his son Jack!'

A Borrowed Bible

'About thirty-two years ago I read *Mere Christianity*. I cannot recall why I did so, unless I was attracted by the economy of the title, for I was then thirty-two years old, and had been an agnostic since the age of sixteen, when I left my Baptist Church in which I was one of the bright young members from whom much was expected. In the meantime I had steadfastly refused to enter a church or even to sing carols, as a matter of intellectual honesty.

C. S. Lewis' book converted me. It was not a dramatic event. I realised that I had begun reading, thinking, "Oh, that is what Christians believe" and ended it, to my surprise, thinking "We Christians believe ..." I borrowed a Bible from the Public Library (I didn't want to buy one, for money was tight in those days, and I might not really take up religion.) Then I looked round for a church to join. ...' [LAURA, *Writers' News*]

A Book by Lewis

'At the age of twenty I became a Christian through reading *Beyond Personality* by C. S. Lewis. Before going into the forces at eighteen I was a member of a church and was deeply involved in many aspects of its life. I did not, however, have a personal knowledge of God through Christ.

I became more and more aware of my spiritual need, largely through meeting true Christian believers, but also through certain events in my own life.

During a period of leave, the sense of need became very intense. In a bookshop I purchased a copy of this book and read it during the course of a very long bus journey. I had been brought up in a rather liberal church and had many intellectual difficulties about the Christian faith. My sense of need was driving me towards Christ but my intellectual difficulties were keeping me away from Him. It was Lewis [who] helped me so greatly on these difficulties.

At the end of that day, in my own bedroom, I surrendered to Christ. This means that a book by Lewis was the last and decisive link in a train of events which God used to bring me to Himself.' [PARRY, FCW Newsletter]

'If, Lord ...'

'Early in my marriage (1959) - having a very fulfilling and rewarding teaching career I was nevertheless at a "loose end" during the evenings, as my husband was a professional musician ... I had absolutely no church background but had met Christians during my T.C. [sic] years. I was totally cynical and ignorant of any spirituality.

One evening I visited a friend and pleaded, "Have you got any reading material?" She gave me a pile of books one of which was C. S. Lewis' *Mere Christianity*.

I had no inner knowledge that I was "seeking" as I read it. I finished it in one reading and I remember feeling that I **must** re-read this book! This I did the following evening. I found myself on my knees praying, "Lord Jesus - if this is true - if you are there - if - if - if ??? - if you forgive me my sins I promise I will follow you totally."

I had no emotional reaction - until the following morning. On awakening I **knew** He was with me!!

I did not know **any** religious terminology - nor did I own a Bible - but through *Mere Christianity* - my entire life was changed and transformed. Two years later my husband also became a Christian.

My faith has deepened over the years and I have had the joy of leading others to Christ.' [NORA, *Church of England Newspaper*]

VI
HELP, HOPE AND HEALING

The Therapy of Reading

'"Yes," said the Lion in a very quiet voice ... "He has died. Most people have, you know. Even I have. There are very few who haven't."'[G]

A number of respondents stated that Lewis' books had 'helped' them in some way - though not all were specific.

'Years ago someone gave me C. S. Lewis' *The Screwtape Letters* and this book made a great impression on me, and I've often found it a support.' [FRAN, *Success*]

This made two statements:

The book made a great impression;

She had often found it a support.

Each statement rouses the same question: how? In what way? Without the answer to these questions the statements could mean anything or nothing. All I could do in the face of such a question was to despatch an s.a.e. and hope. Few came back. When they did it was often with the kind of reply, 'It is so long ago now I can't remember - I just **know** it did.'

Sometimes the explanation touched on areas dealt with elsewhere.

'I am not able to summarise how his writings have helped me ... except to say that he has the gift of being able both to stir the imagination and also to put the profoundest truths in everyday language - both of which means were used by Jesus Himself.' [DAMIAN, *Church of England Newspaper*]

'I don't think I can tell you anything very definite, but C. S. Lewis is so lucid and so logical, his writings have helped me with many questions that are in my heart and mind, in my Christian experience. Also *Mere Christianity*, which I have found one of the most helpful, is referred to in the book *Born Again* which is the true and amazing story of Charles Colson (of Watergate fame). I gather it really was the biggest help to him during his conversion and ultimate happiness.' [REBECCA, *Woman and Home*]

Academic Advantages

'Being an academic he was able to communicate theological concepts and truth in a way that was profound yet simple, and at times humorous (particularly *The Screwtape Letters*). His writings I found needed to be read and digested slowly to absorb his insights into Christian truth. Many of his ideas ... have helped me immensely in my own personal life, and have given me interesting revelations of the plan of God and the work of Christ.' [GRETA, *Woman and Home*]

At other times it was merely academic - the 'use' of his books in dissertations, etc.

Lifeline to Sanity

There were, however, exceptions. To one he was 'a lifeline to sanity' during university finals.

'I became a Christian at the beginning of my final year at [university] in October 1970. Someone introduced me to C. S. Lewis the following Easter, and I read all the Narnia Chronicles during my finals - my lifeline to sanity! He has been one of the greatest influences in my life since then ...' [JANINE, *Gradlink*]

For another the lifeline was even more taut.

'I set out aged sixteen or so to write a totally new and original style of poetry. I put immense effort into this "work" for sixteen years. To avoid any plagiarism, I never read any other verse. Towards the end of this effort at total originality, "words-trance-power," I was writing things beyond conscious levels of my own knowledge, etc. - part of the attempt to be Nietzschean self-god, etc. I had no title for this work ... until as it became completed ... that which I called my masterpiece wrote "The Satanic Power" ... and said to me: "No - you are **my** masterpiece." I thank God I promptly threw all I had written into the bin ... and (I was terrified for several years ...) I rejected that which revealed itself as utterly evil. In returning to the Christian Way, several of C. S. Lewis' books greatly helped me ... I confess that the evils I met through drugs, black art, the whole "beyond good and evil" business remain a serious and seemingly relentless menace to my faith and sanity etc. In this context the Christian good fight is a real conflict between Heaven and Hell. Often it is very perilous. Since I now never write verse, I do read the works of others.' [PHILIP, *Catholic Herald*]

A 'Quick Fix'

One respondent described Lewis' work in terms of 'a tranquilliser' or 'quick fix'. She had been introduced to Lewis through a Christian boyfriend from whom she had eventually parted and this had left her very distraught.

'However, and it is a very big however, it was when I split up from Ashley that Lewis' work came into its own. During that time (and we have never got back together) I experienced pain and suffering like I had never known before. Therefore I turned to Lewis' work and saw it in a new light. Here was somebody who knew what it was like to suffer and what was more could see reason in it. To me this was a great comfort. And it still is. I must confess that his books have been something of a tranquilliser to me on occasions.

Chapters towards the end of *Mere Christianity* have held the greatest relevance and were something of a healing balm on my wounds. Lines in *The Problem of Pain* had a similar effect. ...

I have not read any of his work for about six months, but still take regular doses when I need a "fix." I still ache for Ashley and have never got over the break-up although I do not devote my life to his memory but get on with the rest of my life.

... Therefore, let it be said, that I leaned quite heavily on Lewis' work after my break-up with Ashley. And I feared I may become something of a C. S. Lewis historian, which was not something particularly healthy for a woman in my position.' [MOIRA, *Christian Woman*]

Comforting Connections

'Comfort' is a word some used to describe the effectiveness of the books.

'*The Screwtape Letters* had a profound effect on my spiritual life ... The chapter on spiritual dryness where the soul looks at a landscape from which all traces of God have disappeared - and still believes - is one that I have often read and quoted throughout my life. It was comforting to feel connected with someone who felt as I did, but could express the feeling with such clever and poetic language.' [BERNADETTE, USA,

Woman and Home]

'As one grows older books like *The Problem of Pain* are a source of help and comfort worth a lot more than most medical advice!' [NIGEL, *Reform*]

Alternatively, one called it being 'earthed.'

'... I worked as a house surgeon and then became a missionary surgeon ... for sixteen years, I found *Miracles* and the Space Trilogy were very valuable in combating foolish ideas that arise from studying psychology, as well as the ridiculous assumptions that the overweening pride of human beings produce. Upholding the validity of reason in *Miracles* saves one from a lot of nonsense. *Out of the Silent Planet* emphasises that beings from outer space are far more likely to be better, more loving, more "humane" and intelligent in the fullest sense, than us, rather than out to destroy us - the attitude of most "civilised" humans to extra-terrestrial visitors compares well with the attitude of the cannibals in the south sea islands to the first missionaries! The peon of praise of God at the end of *Perelandra (Voyage to Venus)* is above anything similar that I have read and was a source of joy and inspiration in the vicissitudes of work on the mission field.

Later, the Narnia books were in themselves an inspiration and I still turn to them when I feel I am psychologically becoming too earthbound, and failing to live in reality.' [NATHAN, *Reform*]

LEWIS AS THERAPIST

One thing that did come across, whether acknowledged or not, was the therapeutic role the books played, which is not the same as spiritual direction or enlightenment. This relates to a healing process, whether mental or emotional, and may be achieved through the dynamic of the book as a whole, or through identification with the characters in the book.

'It depends where you're standing'

I was sent a very brief note enclosing two double pages from *The Magician's Nephew* which depicted Uncle Andrew's reaction to the appearance of so many animals and his inability to distinguish the words being spoken or their interest in him. Puzzled, I hazarded a guess at the message being conveyed, viz. that "what you see and hear depends a good deal on where you are standing ... also on what sort of person you are," but that did not tell me what the sender herself saw and heard. She replied,

'... Maybe my response to your original letter was somewhat too precipitous and not wholly appropriate!

The passage drew me because it reinforced a perception to which I'd been introduced during my social work training - namely, that much therapy is based upon empathy being available whilst painful projections are withdrawn.

Uncle Andrew's plight appeared to offer a classic example of what can afflict the human condition, in these terms. That young readers should be introduced to these concepts earlier rather than later, was most cheering.

I suppose what I saw and heard was that which validated earlier theory, and which renewed the challenge to myself concerning that of Uncle Andrew in me!

It affected my life by stimulating me to continue in my efforts to integrate conflicting and contradictory experiences - and to use the understanding of these complex issues in the interest of others - hopefully!' [SHELLEY, *The Friend*]

One respondent wrote of what could be called 'a sort of therapy.' Her husband was a lay pastor now hospitalised and clearly very ill. Both had led incredibly busy and self-giving lives with little time for reading, yet, perhaps initially through hearing Lewis' wartime broadcasts, her husband had acquired a great knowledge of his thought, and

'C. S. Lewis loomed great in later years as he remembered learnt passages and was often quoting at most unusual times of day and night amongst conversations far more learned.' [RENE, *Reform*]

Lewis, she maintained, 'made the Man' who, even seriously ill and in a low mental state, could remember Lewis' teaching.

Two specific accounts stand out, the first, though outlined somewhat obscurely, an acknowledged therapy, the second, achieving a similar end, a deliberate identification with the characters.

'The Single Furrow'

'I still acknowledge a large and important debt to one of his books in particular, which undoubtedly supported me when things were very grim indeed, and probably saved my life also. I feel therefore that I should write to you ... if I am to disentangle the strands of something I have up to now accepted without much question ...

Up to the moment of reading your letter I had only been sure in a general way that Lewis had helped me a lot at a particularly bad time. To sort matters out in detail: I read the *Perelandra* trilogy nearly forty years ago and was enormously moved (I can still recall the sensation) by the moment when Ransom, feeling sure he cannot bear any more, has a vision (or was it an audition? Memory, after so long an interval, does not provide the answer ...) which convinces him that it is of the utmost necessity to persevere with the task given him. The general symbolic aspects of this episode appear to have woven themselves pretty firmly into the fabric of my life, as I now begin to appreciate.

At the time I naturally supposed my very strong response to be simply a reader's reaction to a powerfully written scene. More recently however I have wondered just what degree of influence it may have had on my life. Some of that influence is clear, but there is a puzzling extra dimension which could be seen as pointing to some kind of precognitive insight, though as to accept that is of course to set aside our usual concept of time as a linear flow, I am reluctant, until I have thought more about it, to do more at this moment than record the facts.

Certainly, though, there was no way in which, at the time of reading, I could have been aware at any conscious level of the decades of severe illness which lay not far ahead, nor of what personal importance the scene in *Perelandra* would come to have for me during that period. Yet, when I began to be profoundly ill with very extreme and even life-threatening depression (I am not using words exaggeratively - if nothing else I nearly died at one stage of sheer de-energisation) then the recollection of the moment from *Perelandra* would come to mind, always when things were at their despairing worst, and when no way forward appeared to exist. So far, then, as it is possible to speak of events which did not happen, this recollection seems to have prevented me from attempting self-destruction when that appeared the only option.

That last statement is, if unprovable, at least a reasonably likely and therefore acceptable assessment of one aspect of the situation. Beyond that lies a strange area which, were it not for the wish to write to you, and the need in that case to do so fairly soon, I would rather disentangle far further in my thoughts before putting them on paper.

After much hesitation ... I find I can probably best begin by saying that, long before I had any real understanding of what had caused my illness, and was therefore still in the position of putting up with what could not be sorted out, I nevertheless formed the firm conviction that I not only needed to survive at all costs but that my survival had some kind of reference beyond myself. I explained this by the general theory that, if depression arises in the individual from social pressures acting on them, then a full understanding of one's own depression could well result in having information to feed back in to society at large. Yet I imagined the contribution I might make as being in the nature of a single furrow in an already pretty well-ploughed field. I certainly had not the slightest idea then that I would in fact slip through the net and become a survivor in a situation where, as it seems, others do not survive, or not intact in the way I have done ...

I do not recall that I drew at the time any parallel between *Perelandra* and my need to survive for reasons beyond myself, probably because it would not then have been clear, as it now is, that "reasons beyond myself" in fact meant on others' behalf. (I find it very hard to put such words on paper.) Nor could I have known then that the solitude of Lewis' protagonist would have a resemblance to my own aloneness - diagnostically speaking ...

It is also possible to say, in a limited way, that I have been chosen (though emphatically **not** in the terms of Lewis' story), in the sense that the individual is forced willy-nilly into trying to find the right response to the pressures of society upon them.

And there was more; though it is, I may say, to my embarrassment that I recount the following very personal episode. Still, the story has to be told fully, or not at all. You will remember that I spoke of the depression as "life-threatening." In fact I had, at one point in the illness, a near-death experience. If you are familiar with the literature on this phenomenon you will know that, in many cases (as in mine), there is a moment of choosing whether or not to return to life. My choice certainly carried with it in my own mind the implication that I would return in order to complete the task of sorting out what was wrong with my life. ... this episode occurred early on in the period of treatment [and] before I had any conception of the unusual nature of the illness and its consequent possible value to society at large. It also must be said that, when the moment came to make this decision, I had already formulated the idea, some time before, that my investigations into the illness had some larger significance. No doubt that belief influenced my choice.

To clarify all this: what happened to bring [me] to the point of seeing my situation in the way I have described was that, in the course of my intensive and prolonged private therapy I uncovered a very early childhood trauma of a pattern not generally recognised nor, equally, charted in the text-books. Yet it is unquestionable that other, similar cases must have occurred and indeed will still be occurring. The chief reason for the gap in medical knowledge would appear to be this: as the trauma results in great and disabling physical weakness (hence the near-death experience), many traumatees (is there such a word?) may well simply have died in childhood. Again, others who may have survived longer have probably not been correctly diagnosed. Certainly, along with the notable dearth of other cases which might be said to coincide with my own, there are now conditions recognised in which people may suffer from, in some cases, quite extreme physical weakness but without any fully understood cause. I believe these are the only clues at present to where the other sufferers might be.

I also note that the skilled private treatment I eventually found for myself (and this, by sheer good luck, with one of the few practitioners with any understanding of the condition) took, even so, eleven years to reach the true answer. I assume that the Health Service is unlikely to have that kind of time available to do the very deep digging that is required, and that is another reason for the **apparent** rarity of this particular condition.

It does seem quite likely, therefore, that I have passed through an experience which others, for one reason or another, are unable to achieve for themselves. From this my thoughts pass to the fact that there are, at last, some signs that those early childhood traumas are coming generally into the open. The medical profession has indeed got a long way already, and there is much public awareness. But even the professionals have not in general yet reached the area I know so much about, perforce. Although it is not clear what I can do, what is quite sure is that I am in possession of knowledge (and good inside knowledge at that) which might be of benefit to others. My timing is good, too! Earlier it would probably have been impossible to shift medical opinion in an area which was ignored because not known to exist.

I do not really understand what the connections are between my reading of *Perelandra* and these matters I have described here. I can only speculate that any journey towards a goal of an importance which is not purely personal very likely contains something like a standard set of ingredients.

Despite the uncertainty surrounding much of what I have written here, I felt sure, once I had embarked on this account, and especially as I am not clear what you are looking for, that I should put all the facts, at least as I understand them at present, at your disposal, for you to decide on their value for your purposes.

I only wish I could have presented a clearer, better thought-out account, but that at this stage proved not possible. I certainly need to thank you for the opportunity to set these things out at some length. The exercise has been of great benefit to me: I can only hope it will be of some help to you also in your research.' [SIMON, *Literary Review*][28]

Here is a struggle for self-expression and at the same time a very important psychological pointer in the relationship of the book and the reader's mental, emotional and spiritual response to it. It called to mind how psychotherapist Wilhelm Stekel (*circa* 1923) began his investigations by ascertaining what books his patients were reading - such was the perceived influence of reading on the human subconsciousness.

The second account covered half a century and was at once intensely personal, clearly painful, and very lengthy. For all three reasons I have had to edit it, though on the last re-reading, less than originally intended. It is an account of identification with one of Lewis' characters and encounter with another.

'Eustacia Clarinda' - The 'Distinguished Freak'

This is the kind of story that today's heightened consciousness of the rights of the child would not tolerate: a story of repressed childhood, thwarted ambition, suffocated talents, moving into emotionally scarred adulthood in which love was minimalised and a lifestyle and persona enforced that well-nigh killed the real individual struggling to be free. It was sent to me with a note that declared, 'What a fascinating time you must be having!'

In her story, the respondent produces two clear inter-acting character studies - one in which she identifies herself with Eustace Scrubb, the other in which her mother personifies for her the role of Screwtape.

In her initial letter to me she had indicated that,

'*The Screwtape Letters* proved to be the most significant influence ... and this might well be described from one point of view, as "a work of fiction" ...

In 1942, when I first encountered *The Screwtape Letters*, I was an Oxford graduate of 25 years, on the staff of a mixed grammar school ... I was dedicated, heart and soul, to music but the subjects I taught were History and Economics.

The book was so enthusiastically recommended by one of the junior mistresses that I quickly asked to borrow it. At a first reading I was so impressed by the wit and the powerful pleading that I bought a copy for myself and recommended it to others.

Two phrases leapt out of the pages at me - "All that is not music ought to be silence" - "You have always been insolent when you dared - "'

Those two phrases unleashed the pent-up emotions of twenty-five years - her lack of musical education over against her love of music, her mother's unforgiving attitude, the background of parental disagreements, her own unforgiveness of her mother for humiliating her in company over the first serious love affair of her life, and not even allowing her to choose her own clothes ...

'... I had gone into a luxury shop and bought myself some extremely expensive fur-lined boots. All I can say is that round those boots "the noise of battle rolled" - endlessly! I was being reckless, squandering my money like that. Did I suppose I was suddenly in the millionaire class because I'd begun to earn my own living? I had no clothes sense - never had and never would have - and so on. However, I returned to school in triumph with my boots, and very thankful I was to have them. But, of course, despite my independent status, despite my years, despite coupons, despite everything, my mother continued to try to assert her "right" to dress me!

As I read and re-read *The Screwtape Letters* I felt that there was an astonishing amount in it that seemed to speak to me personally. My conscience was not happy about her. It was her insistence, her determination and, in the last resort her money (a legacy) that had taken me to Oxford. Was it fair immediately to walk out on her? It was "smother love" rather than "mother love," but could I doubt that she was devoted to me? Was not the real trouble that I was an only child? ...

All the implied injunctions to humility, patience, long-suffering to generosity of understanding smote me again and again. I resolved that from now on I would try harder. Perhaps if she sensed in me a willingness to see her point of view, it might induce her to come half-way, and treat me as an adult and not as a child. My parents received the news of my change of heart derisively. My father was an agnostic, and could not conceal his disappointment that I'd fallen for this nonsense again. My mother slotted in alarmingly to the "sharp tongued old lady at the breakfast table" as portrayed in Letter III. Particularly apt was the query, "Is she piqued that she should have learned from others, and so late, what she considers she gave her such good opportunity of learning in childhood? Does she feel she is making a great deal of 'fuss' about it?" - C. S. Lewis chose just this moment to come on the air in one of his Broadcast Talks. My parents - miraculously upholding an armistice in their eternal quarrels - vied with one another in deriding him. His weird accent. His condescending manner. The highly questionable grounds on which he had based his conversion to Christianity. The intolerable superiority, speaking *de haut en bas*, to make things easy for those of limited intelligence, and so on and so forth.'

This and the increasing seriousness of asthma attacks made her decide on a move.

'My mother nearly went berserk. She bombarded me with letters urging me to stay where I was. The headmaster was delighted with my efforts: it was crazy of me to move into unknown territory. However, move I did - into the Fens, and for eighteen months came as close to happiness in my lot as the profession might offer. I made heaps of friends. There was a very active Music Circle. I made a success of this appointment as I had of the first. Peace broke out! In the relaxed atmosphere of summer 1945, we had an amazing interlude during which we seemed a united family, and my mother and myself on the affectionate terms that a mother and daughter ought to be.

It all might have happened in the ordinary course of events, but I doubt it. I attended Church as regularly as I could: I bought other C. S. Lewis books, including *The Pilgrim's Regress* and *The Problem of Pain*, and I sought every opportunity to promote understanding, peace and reconciliation.

So far so good up to and including the summer of 1945.'

Her introduction to *The Voyage of the 'Dawn Treader'* took her back to childhood and identification with Eustace Clarence Scrubb.

'"*There was a boy called Eustace Clarence Scrubb, and he almost deserved it. His parents called him Eustace Clarence and his school-masters called him Scrubb. I can't tell you how his friends spoke to him, for he had none ... His parents were very up-to-date and advanced people. They were vegetarians, non-smokers and teetotallers and wore a special kind of underclothes. In their house there was very little furniture and very few clothes on the beds, and the windows were always open"* - The remaining characteristics are certainly not mine, for I loved animals; but I made up for the deficiency by growing up a dedicated feminist, an enthusiastic hymn singer and impassioned egalitarian.

My first mistake was to opt for the wrong sex. So certain had my parents been that I would be a boy that they had not even got a name ready for a girl. Very early in life my mother put that fatal question, "Which do you love better, Mummy or Daddy?" to be rewarded with the diplomatic evasion of an infant Talleyrand - "I love you both the same." It was a lie. I adored my father. Physically and temperamentally we were very close - so much on the same wavelength that speech was often unnecessary: we knew exactly what the other was thinking. You may judge how very much more painful this made my parents' quarrels, many of which arose from disagreements as to the way I ought to be brought up. With my father it was a word to a blow, with instant repentance and reconciliation. Even when the terrible words were spoken, "If only you had not been born I could have got a divorce," I found it easy to understand the appalling stress under which he spoke, to convince myself that he did not mean it, and to return to the affectionate terms which always prevailed between us.

My mother was utterly opposed to corporal punishment. She had come to child-bearing late in life, and was only a year or two from forty when I was born. She was an excellent mother in laying the foundations of first class physical health. She was a devoted nurse in sickness. She was even on the look-out for clever, off the cuff ways of educating me, music lessons commencing at three and a half and algebra at four! Both were decisively and violently rejected! Punishment came in the form of refusal to speak to me or have anything to do with me. On one notable occasion this lasted not for hours but for days. (I was looked after by the servant.) Later she would reproach me for my backsliding, and each new delinquency was tacked on to the end of the previous score, so that one never had the relief of a clean slate and a fresh start.

It was "at my mother's knee" that I was introduced to the Christian religion, exactly as C. S. Lewis would have wished. Not content with exhortation and Bible stories, my mother reinforced her campaign with the family Bunyan. Indeed, the "pilgrims" seem to have wended their way into the standard junior reading of those far-off days. Louisa Alcott introduced them into *Little Women*, Mrs. Nesbit into *The Treasure Seekers*; and my mother seemed to take it for granted that I, too, would become a little pilgrim. But the book I received was the full, hideous Victorian edition which contained not only *Pilgrim's Progress* but also the "Holy War." It was profusely illustrated, and was, indeed, one of the most frightening and repulsive books I have ever owned. It was at a very early age, therefore, that I was indoctrinated against the Roman Catholic Church, the illustration of the evil Pope lying in wait to ensnare the unwary was particularly graphic. But the image of a kind, rescuing, loving Jesus did make the most profound impression. In my childish mind He came over as something of a cross between Robin

Hood and William Tell.

The first challenge to this "inner world" came from my father. He detained me one evening just as I was about to go to bed and told me all about a man who had stood in the middle of the street with a stop watch challenging God to strike him dead for blasphemy, if He really existed (Bradlaugh did this, I believe). To me at seven years of age it was all rather puzzling. I could see that my father was frightfully tense about something, but I was terribly sleepy and really rather baffled as to what he expected of me. Into the room burst my mother, shouting at him something about millstones and being cast into the sea. In a moment, I was grabbed and flung out into the passage whilst my parents raged at one another within. Eventually my mother emerged, joined me in my bed upstairs to sob her heart out, until we both of us fell asleep through sheer exhaustion.

The second challenge came sometime about the same age from a traumatic experience with a swarm of village children, who suddenly jumped out on me when I was on my way, alone, to a children's party. They claimed that, having caught me at last, they were going to hand me over to a policeman to be locked up forever; and having obtained their fill of amusement from my bewilderment and agony of terror, only agreed to let me pass provided I promised I would never divulge what had happened either to my family or anyone else. The details were wrung out of me a long time later. Sent on an urgent message, I took so long over it, because of the detour I made to avoid this black spot, that an explanation was required and yielded amid near-hysteria and floods of tears.

It was about this time, also, that I said goodbye to the quaint Dame's School I had attended since the age of four, and was transferred to the village school. My prudent mother had noted a special scholarship attached to it, just tailor-made for me!'

As with Scrubb, the school made its mark and changed her, and all the 'treats' in the world could never have compensated for the daily fear in which she lived, though they - visits to the theatre and ballet and even the cinema - and an endless supply of books helped a lot.

'It was a heady brew! It was made all the more intoxicating by the fact that not the least restraint was placed on my reading. At a very early age I discovered that to have my nose in a book brought approval, occasionally commendation, and consequently I read anything and everything. ... any whim of mine could be quickly indulged. Within a day or two my father would return from his city office and put the book into my hand. Obviously my mother had wrung a promise from him that he would never again tamper with my religion - a promise he kept. But he spoke with enthusiasm of the Russian Revolution where ordinary common people had seized back the country that the rich and lordly had stolen from them. World War I still cast its black shadow over the area, and on November 11th I witnessed humble people sobbing, sometimes fainting around the war memorial. Pacifism was the only answer my father insisted. I nodded my head sagely: very well, I also was a pacifist!

Years later when I encountered Danny Kay in "The Secret Life of Walter Mitty," I could not but give a smile of recognition. Life became tolerable only through the consolation of day-dreams.'

Yet still that inner world was invaded by her parents' 'jangles' ...

'... On one occasion of supreme black humour they even had a terrible row as to which of them had broken my spirit - each blaming the other, and with the Head of the village school thrown in for good measure! But sometimes my abstraction was suspended by an experience so wonderful that the very peace of God seemed to descend on me. Such was one summer's night when my mother took me into the woods to listen to the nightingales. Then, indeed, "all that was not music was silence." I never forgot it.

At long last "Eleven Plus" examinations arrived (I was just turned ten!). My father called for us in the car and held out his hand for the last paper I had taken. What answers had I given? I replied quite cheerfully until halfway through, when he suddenly interrupted. Throwing the exam paper over to my mother, he exclaimed furiously, "Mucked it up! Mucked it up! Get in! Let's get out of it!" It was a terrifying drive during which we cut corners, exceeded every speed limit and avoided crashes by what can only be described as a miracle. There followed an agonising month awaiting the results. Nothing could ever repair the harm that was done in my realisation that my parents' love was not unconditional, that they had no faith in me, and that if I had failed in this test I had most likely failed for ever. In the result, I had won every scholarship in sight, including the special one so much desired. In my prayers I thanked Jesus almost hysterically that I should be leaving that Hell-on-Earth at last. Nothing else mattered very much.

The new school certainly deserved its reputation as the best in the entire area. It was six miles away, and was so slanted towards university entrance that it did not even offer a Domestic Science course. It would be pleasant to be able to report that my feet touched down on the rock and that my troubles were over. Nothing of the kind! Now I would be matched against the cream of two counties and it was up to me to beat the lot! Not only were terminal exams the new nightmare, but I must excel in games as well. Rejected previously because I was a "toff," I was now kept at arms' length because I was a "scholarship kid." Besides, living six miles away it was difficult, if not impossible, to strike up intimate friendships with families we could not meet in the ordinary way of life. However, when I grew old enough, I was permitted to stay on late for drama rehearsals and country dancing, both of which I liked.

... Whilst we were on holiday a friend of the family asked me "what I most enjoyed at school." It was casually put. I saw no reason for an evasive or diplomatic reply. "Singing and dancing," I told her. I was unlucky. The friend went straight to my mother with it, saying how surprised she was. Surprised? My mother was outraged! But for once I stood my ground. As I saw it, school was an infliction like rain or snow that I had to put up with: examinations were something I was forced somehow to contrive to do well in. It was altogether unreasonable to expect me to "enjoy" this process. Incredulous and blustering, my mother actually heard me say that music was the one consolation for school life. My great sorrow was that I had never had a proper musical education. "You had your chance when you were a little girl!" she protested. "And what about Oxford? Have you given up your ambition to get there?" **My** ambition! I shrugged. "It's too late now," she said. "Yes I suppose it is," I agreed. The subject was dropped. Life continued as before.'

The compulsion to make it to Oxford brought with it the necessity to circumnavigate Latin in order to do so and in this she was helped by her father - but in the event, funded by her mother, a lasting area of contention.

But like Scrubb, she changed - found freedom, friends and fulfilment, if only for a season. Only too soon was it apparent that she was "'not their sort."

'It was terrible to have a vision of myself as they now saw me - from the wrong background, wearing the wrong clothes, clad in lisle stockings, never silk, never having heard of a deodorant, and scorning talc and perfumes. I was alone again, broken-hearted amidst my shame and disappointment.'

Then she discovered the University Operatic Society.

'"Surprised by joy!"? Never! but never!! in my entire life had I lived in such utter ecstasy! My father most generously posted me a cheque to cover the over-heavy subscription and other incidental costs, giving me his blessing and hearty approval. It was a novel experience for me to awake each morning to infinite delights, almost to dance around the streets of Oxford crooning extracts from the operas to myself and shouting to the wide open space, "Oh let this never stop! Let it go on for ever and ever and ever!" It was with difficulty that I fitted in lectures and tutorials: for I had been invited to take part in the college play and was obliged to go to rehearsals for that as well.'

But following graduation there was still Mother, now ill with angina, who

'expected the end of the war to bring everything back as it had been in 1939 and when this was so obviously unattainable, she raged against fate, my father and myself almost as though she had taken leave of her senses. It was a bitter winter. Rain seemed to be falling ceaselessly. Twenty foot waves lashed the shore.

She had already convinced herself that Oxford had been the greatest mistake she had ever made in her life. It had turned me into quite the wrong sort of person. Look at me - sulky and discontented. I didn't know how to cook. The meals were rotten. Well, yes, the fish was delicious, but she couldn't eat fish for every meal.

Eventually her physical state deteriorated so alarmingly that the doctor packed her off to hospital as an emergency case. This gave my father and myself a brief respite from the day and night watches we shared, for we were in a pretty groggy state ourselves.

Hospital treatment restored her mobility. The warmth of spring brought an improvement in the weather.

"Get back to teaching," my father urged. "You have done all you can, and you're only being made perfectly wretched here."

It was only too true. My mother had, I suppose, been warned against these terrible frenzied crises. She now spoke to me more in sorrow than in anger, "It will all come back to you after I'm gone. You'll realise the way you've treated me and your heart will smite you. But it will be too late then."

... My mother died nine months later. Some kind of reconciliation was patched up, and her attitude softened a little before the end. Nevertheless, my father and I were left in a sad state of shock, from which we found it difficult to recover.'

Then her own health gave way, leading to a horrific series of ECT treatments which almost drove her to suicide.

'... Self-destruction was rated a sin, but Jesus would understand. In a way the Crucifixion itself was a kind of vile, prolonged suicide - At this point my hatred of all I had had to suffer at the hands of "them" made me draw back. Why should "they" win? I was only thirty-three: why should my life be flung away?

I prayed as I had never prayed in my life before - simply "Help!"

What was it? A voice? An overwhelming conviction? "Only one more and you will not have to go again!"

I turned back, feeling strangely reassured and comforted.'

Only with the eventual death of her father, in his eighties, when she was fifty-one was she able to begin really to take control of her life and plan for the future, which included being herself for possibly the first time in her life. She had affected a persona which her mother had seen as a bid for emancipation, but to her 'was merely a defence mechanism - an armour-plating - protecting an intense inner loneliness.'

Exactly the picture Lewis had in mind as he left Scrubb in the cave, 'thinking nasty dragon thoughts' until he discovered first-hand how very lonely a dragon can be!

Her story told, she summarised the phases by reference to the world (especially religion), science, and C. S. Lewis in particular.

'There was more than a hint that Lewis regarded pacifism as a soft option as against conformist militarism. As far as I was concerned Jesus had settled the matter once and for all - "They that live by the sword shall die by the sword" - I could never imagine Jesus piloting a bomber or standing to the guns for a naval bombardment. That we were obliged to fight Hitler was a cruel necessity, but it was impossible to feel anything else but horror at this circumstance.

I was amused by Lewis' ingenious defence of "intemperance." I had never heard of intemperate card players or golfers brawling, raping or frittering away their entire week's pay, and leaving their families starving, but I should have been interested to meet one. I judged that Lewis liked his tipple.'

She was, however, critical of 'the triumphs of Wormwood and Screwtape,' seeing them as 'rather trivial' when set 'against the background of bombed cities, genocide and mass starvation and disease.'

She also made one other observation:

'Lewis' boy was only too obviously a freak. It has been my (rather painful) task to demonstrate how such freaks are made. So - as a distinguished freak myself I am not too sure I fall in with his idea of "Liberation through Religion." Nor am I too happy about his warning, later in life, that "We have no Right to Happiness." Possibly "Right" is not the best word, but I would have said that happiness is the rich loam into which the delicate plant of personality sends down its roots. On the physical plane, also, the body has its needs, and when these are endlessly frustrated, there is almost bound to be a crisis in health. There are plenty of animals that cannot live in captivity. How much less so the delicate and sophisticated human organism.'

Yet, in spite of her criticism, she found tremendous affinity with C. S. Lewis himself. They had, she said, much in common ...

'A secret inner life developing very early -

Considerable pressure to shine academically -

A parent (of the same sex) with whom we had serious and occasionally violent emotional problems -

A ready acceptance of University life.

Inhibitions against courtship at the appropriate age -

It is, indeed, curious that we each had a school we detested. Lewis was enfranchised: I was not. We each owed mastery in a vital subject to a coach. Lewis reacted favourably to being barked at by "Kirk." I responded instantly to the gentleness and courtesy with which I was treated by my Economics coach. To both of us Oxford came as something intoxicatingly enjoyable after terrible stress.'

Encompassing the philosophies of Plato and Aristotle, religion and Shakespeare, she then reached her relationship with Jesus ...

'The curious result was that Jesus came to me as a friend, an inspiration and a "safe stronghold," with the strongest possible urge to be a rebel.

He clearly came to Lewis as an invader, ruler and judge, with an equally strong urge to be a conformist.

But in the Army of the Lord the fighters are astonishingly varied - as varied as the make-up of each Christian soul. I always think of Lewis as of Thomas Picton at Waterloo, turning up for the battle in his top-hat, and already in desperate pain from the wound he received at Quatre Bras, but tightly strapped up and on his feet, determined to be faithful to death!

Undoubtedly the Socratic Club was Lewis' finest hour, when he threw his hat into the ring against all-comers, with students fighting to get in to watch. If not converted to Christianity at least these latter had their ideas tumbled around sufficiently violently to make them consider issues more deeply than they otherwise might have done.

Truly a very worthy, a very gallant gentleman!' [JOCELYN, *Catholic Herald*]

In the course of her account she also picked up Lewis' comment on the menace of science as she compared the warnings of *That Hideous Strength* with her real-life horror in the hands of psychiatrists and ECT. She had been too conditioned to submission to realise the potential harm it held for her.

'AT HOME WITH CHARACTERS'

In some notes accompanying her main letter, one respondent observed that it was

'... really possible to know and "feel at home with" [characters] from Narnia; - *Pilgrim's Regress*, mastery of characterising. Clear division between those fallen and seeking whom one can "love," and those [who have] chosen [the] wrong way who become repellent.' [NOREEN, *Woman and Home*]

Eustace Scrubb was a character a number of people cited, not least in the initial pilot survey when the direct question was posed, 'Which character, if any, do you most identify with and why?'

'Eustace. My answer is rather childish, but ... well, Eustace is most like me. Or perhaps it is because he is the one character in whom we see the most development. He is also the most complex (excepting Orual) and therefore the most **real**. Joyful but moody; Christian but reverting to old ways. My conversion parallels Eustace's conversion.' [PL20]

'... one of Lewis' pictures has often come back to me as an expression of the Christian life as being a "death to self" - that of Eustace being stripped by Aslan of his layers of ugly dragon skin. As a Christian I see myself often making efforts to "live a more Christian life," to "shed some layers of selfishness," but in the end I know only God can achieve in my life what I would want Him to - and I know of no better or more effective expression of this outside of the Bible than this picture of Eustace finally giving way to the lion's claws. Indeed, I have shared this passage before now in the context of a day set aside at work for staff to explore their own values and beliefs.' [KINGSLEY, *Gradlink*]

Here, too, some people also cited Screwtape. When I had originally conducted the survey in connection with my doctoral studies just one person had made the claim - in retrospect, almost prophetic. Now there were others, for

'Characters like Screwtape are far more memorable and effective than any sermon or notebook!' [DAWN, *Christian Woman*]

One respondent to the initial survey answered, "Screwtape - always in difficulties (Everyman).' [PL19]

'Real Characters we know'

'His characters, though animals, reflect real characters we all know.' [GLENDA, Miscellany]

In fact, other characters with whom respondents identified (sometimes not uncritically) were spread across human, fantasy and animal beings. On the human level there were Peter, Edmund 'the sinner,' Susan and Lucy Pevensie and the 'children' in general, Shasta, Sarah Smith, Queen Orual, the Artist in *The Great Divorce.* Fantasy characters included Merlin and the Dwarves, while one respondent named Puzzle the donkey in *The Last Battle.*

'The parabolic nature of the books was something that dawned on me at quite an early stage. However, I recall that, with each reading, each story came to mean more and more to me. In particular, *The Lion, The Witch and The Wardrobe* helped me to answer the question: Why did Jesus have to die? I recall identifying with Edmund in the story.

... There is nothing very profound about my childhood identification with Edmund. He was the "sinner-type" (on reflection, perhaps, the only one there is in reality). He was the one "bought" by the atonement. The other three were too unbelievably "goodie-goodie" for me to identify with.' [ADAM, *Family Life*]

'Susan Pevensie, the shallow young woman in a fragment called, I think "The Shabby Lands."'[29] [OSWALD, *The Friend*]

(Not so much a character identification as an assessment.)

'I do not myself consider an obsession with clothes, cosmetics and parties a sign of maturity. A demonstrable sense of responsibility for one's self, one's immediate neighbours and one's wider community would be a better gauge of adulthood. Susan has not "committed the unforgivable sin [and] become an adult;" she is indulging in an inordinate affection for the trivial to the exclusion of things eternal; that is, she has wilfully stuck at a transition stage and remained an adolescent. The possibility therefore exists that, with Aslan's help she may still reach salvation at some date after the fatal rail crash. At any rate, one can comfort an anxious child reader with this thought.' [FAY, *Good Stories*]

Then there was 'Lucy - for her adventurous spirit and imagination.' [PL3]

'Lucy - I identified very strongly with her emotions and actions as described throughout the Chronicles. The things she said, did, felt, and thought would have been very similar to the ways in which I would see myself reacting in similar situations.' [PL15]

'I have always been a very visual reader; when reading a book, I'm inside the story, seeing both the printed page and the images from the page. I still feel regret when I reach the end of a story that I would like to continue. In the books, the children from our world were always drawn into Narnia at the beginning of the story - through a door, or a picture, or by a trumpet-call; and had to leave at the end, through a door or the sky. This is a kind of frame within the book; the children enter the story, and then have to leave it, just as I, reading the book, had to enter and then leave.' [ANNETTE, *The Friend*]

'... I grew very fond of the fictitious Narnia characters who, I felt, portrayed Christian characteristics charmingly and simply to the children's level of understanding.' [BRENDON, *Christian Herald*]

'I've had the privilege of telling some children first *The Lion, the Witch and the Wardrobe* and second *The Horse and His Boy*. The best part of it was that I didn't find it possible to read the stories as written - that would have taken ages. So I had to summarise and prepare. As I did, I found myself delving deeper and deeper into C. S. Lewis' mind and actually knowing the characters.

When I came to *The Horse and His Boy* I realised that I'd had to squash the first story up so much that I may as well re-tell this one in my own words. So I began: "My name is Shasta ... " and I told the whole story in the first person. For those minutes as I read, and for the hours as I prepared, I was living in another world. Sometimes I found myself in tears (only in preparation) as Aslan climbed the lonely hill "and he was so sad. His great head hung so low that it almost touched the ground" - as Susan and Lucy wept "though they hardly knew why" - as the White Witch brought down the stone dagger, as Shasta (I) sat among the lonely tombs and a cat came to comfort him.' [RAYMOND, *Baptist Times*]

'... If there is one character in literature I would like to be like it is "Sarah Smith" the lovely and loving Lady whose retinue is of all the young people she had loved.' [TONI, *The Local Preacher's Magazine*]

'Orual. In many of the other books the good people are simply good and the bad ones unquestionably and repulsively bad. But here is a bad person who wants to be good, thinks she is good. We see her struggles - they're just like our struggles (or at least mine).' [PL26]

'I identified with the Artist [in *The Great Divorce*] whose original intention in painting had been to communicate the Light he had been given - his first love - but over the years had come to do the painting for its own sake. He was told that he would never really **see** the country if he was interested in it only for the sake of painting it.' [PL8]

'Probably Merlin in *That Hideous Strength*. Although wholly **man** with nothing of the spiritual about him, he was in touch with the true nature of the Earth (as opposed to the Nature of the English Romanticists or contemporary American ecologists).' [PL18]

One respondent declared that she 'didn't care for Aslan,' adding,

'I must be one of those dwarves who went on doing their own thing at the end of *The Last Battle*.' [KAREN, *The Lady*]

'... I identified particularly with Puzzle the donkey, whose ears went down when he met Aslan, and then his ears went up again.' [ZOE, *Renewal*]

'The Virtuous Pagan'

One incident towards the end of *The Last Battle* has been subjected to much criticism elsewhere. However, most of my respondents who actually referred to it did so with warm approbation.

'I like what happened to Emeth the Calormene - who served Aslan by another name - that somehow all good is service to Aslan.' [ZOE, *Renewal*]

The crucial word is 'somehow,' for there are many who cannot see it that way - yet curiously in this study they seemed to be few - but a stumbling block of first order it remains, since it can be seen as a watering down of the uniqueness of the Gospel - a uniqueness Lewis was, for the most part, at pains to stress.

It may be that while Lewis himself was probably only at pains to satisfy his child readers by rewarding Emeth, he did not realise what a hornet's nest he was creating in doing so.

'Another incident in the book which made a great impression on me as a child, was that of Emeth, the young Calormene who worshipped Tash in good faith and so was claimed by Aslan as his son. This was probably because my own father was Jewish, and although still a child, I had already encountered nominal Christians who were prejudiced against him on that account and considered him beyond the pale.' [TAMARA, *The Universe*]

'In many ways the eschatology of *The Last Battle* seems to me one of the profoundest things he wrote. Three pictures remain vividly with me: the dwarves huddled in the stable, so determined to be fooled by nobody and nothing that they cannot see the beauty of Aslan's kingdom and the richness of the banquet, to which the stable is just a doorway: secondly, the young Calormene warrior who had gone through the doorway in search of his god Tash, and to whom Aslan says ... that when he was seeking the best that he knew in Tash, it was truly Aslan that he was seeking; what a wonderful way for a Christian to be able to approach people of other religions; and the third, the moment when Peter, the High King, pulls shut the door on a dead and frozen Narnia, and they all turn away to go "higher up and further in" [sic] to Aslan's kingdom, and find that **here** is the true Narnia, of which the earthly Narnia had been a mere copy and reflection - what a way of looking at Heaven!' [BEVIS, Brazil, *Christian Newsworld*]

IN FACE OF DEATH

One of the most helpful and therapeutic areas touched upon has been that of death - approaching death, encountering or experiencing death, and speculation about what lies beyond. The most poignant account received was from a mother whose dying son had found help from his reading of *The Last Battle,* and who

'... shortly before he died at the age of ten and a half in 1975, loved C. S. Lewis' *The Last Battle* just because it was all about dying and going "On" ... *The Last Battle* really helped ... as he had already experienced the reality of God Himself in a spiritual experience he had had.' [UNA, *The Universe*]

'When my youngest little son wept when he realised he was one day going to die, then Narnia came into the family ... How many children and adults have those stories comforted.' [TESSA, *Catholic Herald*]

In Face of Love

'The most profoundly affective was *The Last Battle*. Like most teenagers, I went through the stage of being **terrified** of dying/the second coming/the unknown future. At twenty I was beginning to realise that these are all things to look forward to, not to fear, but this was head-knowledge, not heart-knowledge. So I embarked on reading *The Last Battle* with some trepidation. I can honestly say that Lewis' inspired thoughts on our spiritual future were the tool that Jesus used to clear out all the teenage rubbish. After reading the book and seeing the happiness and love that Lewis depicted I was forced to go on my knees before the Lord and confess my apprehensions, and accept in faith His promise for my future. Now I can truthfully say that I'm looking forward to dying, and to the fulfilment of the second coming. At last I can read Revelation!' [DAWN, *Christian Woman*]

Others found help through the Chronicles as a whole, either in being enabled to face death or in the hope of it.

'As far as I can recall ... they [The Chronicles of Narnia] became a means to convey to my sons ... an idea of my values and what I was about; an escape from a dark and disordered present and an anchor into a different reality from the one with which we, each in our separate way, were grappling. At the end of this period some decisions were made with immense difficulty. My first son committed suicide at seventeen and I left my marriage.

I still do not pretend to understand the significance of [my son's] life to him but I know what it was for me; the great catalyst that allowed me to make contact with the occluded parts of my difficult childhood and make some reparations; to view the world afresh with eyes of wonder and openness.

The journey which I took with and through my children led me further and further from my husband's view of the world and changed me, from his stance, quite threateningly, so that he did everything in his power to thwart my growth. With hindsight I have much sympathy, given his background, for his responses. He could do no other, but nor could I. We now have quite a warm relationship - a limited one.' [UNITY, *The Friend*]

'Every time I read the end of *The Last Battle* - "a wild hope arose in them ... the term is over, the holidays have begun ..." how profoundly grateful I am. This is because my depression was caused by the death of my grandfather and of my father and the near death of my mother, when I was four years old. In *The Last Battle* I was reading about what I couldn't face, in a way I could face it - because it gave me hope.' [ZOE, *Renewal*]

One respondent [GERALDINE, *Reform*] included 'The hope of life after death' in her resume of the various signposts she had found in the Chronicles.

Coping with Grief

Not surprisingly, perhaps, testimonials to *A Grief Observed* were prominent. Of the thirty people who specifically addressed the subject of death, from whatever angle, nine cited this book as a prime source of help and understanding.

Lewis published *A Grief Observed* anonymously following the death of his wife, though some of his friends saw through the pen-name. In many cases, if not most, reading that one book led to others.

'[In] 1985 our son ... died suddenly and unexpectedly just before his first birthday. What followed was a waking nightmare of physical, mental and spiritual trauma. About six weeks later I went to see our GP who in conversation recommended I read *A Grief Observed*. As I started reading the first page I cannot describe the release I felt. I was not going mad, here was someone describing exactly my physical symptoms and mental state!!! What a relief. As I carried on reading I found that C. S. Lewis was describing his experience of God at this time which was identical to us, "the gate of heaven slammed shut and bolted," the feeling of being bereft of Him was our experience exactly. I can honestly say that book was like a companion, when no one else understood here was someone who did. At that time we were members at a "Restoration Church" who teach that God is almost duty bound to give us what we want. I found that C. S. Lewis brought balance to this viewpoint and in his other works makes one realise one's obligation to our Father and not the other way around! We also found *The Screwtape Letters* to be very important in bringing one down to earth! I think every Christian should read it regularly as a lesson in humility!

A few weeks after discovering C. S. Lewis I heard about the Narnia series and bedtime was such a joy for me and our four remaining children as we delved into the treasures of these books. My husband was working abroad at the time and he took the book of short readings of C. S. Lewis' works which he also found helped him a great deal in his walk with God.

I can honestly say that C. S. Lewis' books were the greatest influence on me at the worst time of my life along with my Bible and a book by Edith Schaeffer, *Affliction*.' [FELICITY, *Christian Herald*]

The influence of *A Grief Observed* has spread far beyond that first relationship and that has been the beauty of the correspondence which has come from friends, spouses, partners, children, siblings, as well as from bereaved parents, teachers and other carers. Frequently that influence was due to earlier encounters in similar situations with the Chronicles of Narnia.

'I discovered C. S. Lewis through reading *The Lion, the Witch and the Wardrobe* to my younger brother and sister. This was after the death of our mum ... when they were approximately three and five.' [FENELLA, *Writers' News*]

In a second letter she elaborated on this ...

'At that time of my life, following the death of my mother, I found the story reassuring, and felt the Lion was very reflective of Jesus. I felt a great sense of love for humanity from the Lion. I certainly needed to feel some love, and though I would have interpreted it then as spiritual love, years later, when I met my husband, I realised I was looking for emotional love, physical love, sexual satisfaction, though of course, the two are not mutually exclusive, and neither negates the other.'

In her first letter she had mentioned her encounter with *A Grief*

Observed ...

'Then in 1984, I was widowed at the age of thirty-five and "rediscovered" Lewis and found *A Grief Observed* very therapeutic because he pulled no punches. Around about two to three years later BBC Television put on "Shadowlands" and I thought that too was wonderful.'

In her second letter, she explored her reading of *A Grief Observed* more deeply ...

'What I found spiritually helpful ... was Lewis' honesty about his feelings, and his courage in questioning his faith. I do not attend church, and my study of philosophy made me realise that Christianity does not have the monopoly on truth. I believe all we can honestly say is that we simply don't know, and keep our minds open for a sense of adventure.

In fact, my psychotherapist pointed out to me that the image of the Madonna and Child can be very damaging, the contented, blessed mother, the baby that never cries, when for most of us, the actual experience is quite different. It is a very powerful image, and no wonder many of us feel depressed during the Christmas period.'

The Hidden Face of God

'It was the only one to help me of the many I read at the time when I lost my husband. It helped to explain why God seems to hide His face from us in our hour of greatest need. In fact, I would say my religion was of little comfort to me once the funeral was over. But this is how life is, apparently.' [RITA, *Catholic Herald*]

A while later this respondent wrote again.

'I have re-read [*A Grief Observed*] - it still has an enormous impact. His anguish comes through which one could identify with so well at the time. It is not clinical, nor platitudinous or sentimental but rather down to earth and completely frank. For instance the paragraph beginning, "Meanwhile, where is God?" on p.7. A door slammed in your face - yes - this is exactly how it was with Lewis, I also was not in danger of losing belief. We find it again in unexpected places, in trivialities seemingly. I remember being alone in a garden and glancing up to see a neighbour coming across the grass with a cup of tea. I think we are intended to plumb the depth of grief in order to be whole persons. The balm **does** come from all sorts of sources. Lewis does not mention this but I do find it fascinating the way he argues himself back into belief. A bit of *The Screwtape Letters* here in reverse. I find it helpful that he concludes there is a God because even those couples who "feast on love" (p.9) realise there is something more to life than their perfect bliss in each other's company.

There are few books that deal with this facet of bereavement - this questioning of the presence of God. I read one by Michael Hollings quoting poetry of E. B. Browning; this was a solace, too.

To sum up, the real nub of Lewis' appeal is the fact that one identifies with his anguish and travels right through it with him, questioning the Godhead.'

A Miracle of Healing

'My late husband died in May 1970, and, as I think, is common to many people so bereaved, I felt as though I had literally been cut in half or at least had had a limb sliced off. Shortly afterwards friends invited me to go and stay with them for the rest of the summer ... in Ireland, by way of recuperation and to do something towards restoring my spirits.

Another friend, whom I had known for years, was to meet me at Dublin airport and see me on my way ...

I made my way to [the] airport half alive, moving like a zombie, and throughout the flight I read Lewis' *A Grief Observed.* The effect was nothing short of uncanny - and I am not given to mystical experiences; but by the end of the hour's journey I felt so completely healed that I was almost ashamed, thinking that my friend would find me so calm and "normal" as to seem callous or indifferent. It was something like a miracle.' [CAROL, *Catholic Herald*]

'A most beloved older sister-in-law, dying a long, slow, tortured death from MS, regarded Lewis as her favourite theologian, and died stoically, and accepted everything. *The Discarded Image* I used continually through college as background. No matter what area he touched, his models are consistent, tough, believable, true. His poetry I love. 'The Bridge is Breaking' - I think that's the one about Joy - wonderful. His spiritual writings are a tremendous inspiration, because his faith is so strong. But there is the image that has maintained my faith through thick and thin - *The Silver Chair* - the enchantress is seducing them into believing that there is no sun - but Eustace declares that he would rather spend his life looking for the sun, even if he never finds it, than accept her subterranean (hellish) world.'[30] [WANDA, Bermuda, *The Universe*]

'Never Say Goodbye'

A non-Christian had been engaged to a Christian, who died very suddenly.

'I had that Easter visited for the first time the church he attended ... He was so happy that I enjoyed the experience. My whole world fell apart at his death. I was not a Christian but that Good Friday in church, a message was given from the Lord to someone there via the minister ... On Easter Sunday morning [the minister] told me the message was for me. It was 1 Peter 4:12-16. How true this was. The Sunday after Giles' death, I found myself at [the church] and that evening, I came forward to acknowledge dear Jesus in my life.

An American minister I met recommended me to read *A Severe Mercy* by Sheldon Vanauken, which is where I came to know C. S. Lewis. He features in this book very strongly ... The last words he says to the author before his death are, "Christians never say goodbye." These words comforted me tremendously in my grief as I came to learn through God's Word what death really means. It has been and still is a very painful time for me, also struggling to be the way the Lord wants me to be, but I promise you, I wouldn't want to be the person I was before Giles' death. I have reserved the plot next to [his] grave, so that we will rise together and stand before our Lord and this comforts me greatly. On my gravestone for Giles and for everyone who sees it will be the words, "Christians never say goodbye."' [HANNAH, *Christian Herald*]

At about the first anniversary of his death she wrote a second, very depressing, letter, which, nevertheless, concluded with a postscript ...

'... had Giles lived, I would not have given myself so much to the Lord - I've read so much about Jesus this past year - so Giles had to die for me to progress the way the Lord wanted me to - so, yes ... [his] death was "a severe mercy" ...'

Eight months later, out of the blue, a third letter arrived, already cited above but relevant in this context, too.

'C. S. Lewis has quite suddenly become important in my life. I purchased the video *Shadowlands* and am now reading same by Brian Sibley. I identify with Lewis and Joy. When she says in the book, "God was more like a cat. He had been stalking me for a very long time, waiting for His moment, He crept nearer so silently that I never knew He was there. Then, all at once, He sprang." He, too, did this with me. Yes ... it was "A severe mercy" ... The Lord, I so clearly see in hindsight, tried the previous two years to attract my attention, so that I could have Giles's continuing emotional and financial help as my husband, but I blew it. He loves me so much that He made events impossible to ignore Him ...'

'Speaking to My Condition'

One respondent had been interested to note the comments of A. N. Wilson with regard to the help *A Grief Observed* had given to countless people, and wrote ...

'It was suggested to me by a CRUSE counsellor two months ago, about nine months after my partner died, also from cancer in her early middle age, that I might find the book helpful. I had commented several times to him that I was frightened, yet I didn't know what of. Furthermore, I felt that I was continually waiting for something - or someone - yet I didn't know what or whom. Reading *A Grief Observed* was quite astonishing because Lewis seemed to have experienced and to have been able to record so clearly what I (and presumably all those thousands of others!) was experiencing too. While it has not had life-changing significance for me, it has had enormous value in enabling me to deal with my grief better than I might otherwise have done. I value it very much as a book which "speaks to my condition."' [MORGAN, *The Friend*]

This was followed by a series of passages married up with the respondent's own feelings ...

"No one ever told me that grief felt like fear." I was amazed by this opening sentence. Here was someone voicing so exactly what I had been feeling. It felt like a sort of homecoming. [p.35]
"There is one place where her absence comes locally home to me ..." and following to the end of the paragraph. Sexual longing occurs but can be difficult to acknowledge. It's helpful to have it recognised so simply and openly. [p.12]
"Grief feels ... like waiting, just hanging about waiting for something to happen. It gives life a permanently provisional feeling." After almost a year, however busy I am, I am still waiting for something to happen. I am relieved that Lewis too felt this permanent "provisionality" - it helps to make sense of a feeling which those outside the bereavement, however supportive they are, seem to find hard to understand. [pp.29-30]
"I think I am beginning to understand why grief feels like suspense" and following to end of paragraph. Again, Lewis puts into words so succinctly and directly the frustration of having no target to aim at, either alone or together. [p.41]
"Tonight all the hells of young grief have opened again." Lewis understands very well the odd unexpected pinprick of memory (through whichever sense it comes) which awakens a misery as sharp as it was in the first few weeks. [p.49][31]

To sum up, it is less Lewis' strivings to make sense of H's (Joy's?) death, but rather his descriptions of the various stages of grief which I find have especial significance for me. I have the impression that he would have found it impossible to voice his feelings face-to-face with anyone else. Somehow, his journey through grief is the more vivid and understandable through being just that much distanced on the printed page.

He enables the bereaved to say "Yes, I know exactly how you feel" - a comment which bereavement supporters are warned not to use to the bereaved!'

'... Much more recently, I have found much comfort in the **early** passages of *A Grief Observed*, after the death two years ago of my beloved partner in life - he was drowned on an adventure tour holiday. My own understanding of Christianity has much evolved ... and the inability to match experience with faith - as taught in doctrine - has led me much further into "living with doubt" and away from some of my earlier evangelical certainties (except those of my own experience of God). As an openly gay Christian I see, too, the need for a continual reappraisal and *aggiornamento* of the old automatic rules.' [ZAK, *Reform*]

One teacher had found

'*The Last Battle* of particular help to myself and others with whom I have shared it at times of bereavement - particularly the last paragraph ...' [CARL, *Church of England Newspaper*]

As well as facing the death of others, there were those endeavouring to cope with their own eventual death.

'Last year ... I reached an emotional and psychological crisis. I became obsessed with the inevitability of death and the fact of death seemed to render the entirety of life futile and absurd. In short, I came face to face with the implications of my own atheism. There were several things that brought this on: the death of a friend, the father of my closest friend whom I had known since my late teens, the births of my own two children and my growing awareness of the passage of time, even reaching forty years of age - all contributed to my state of mind. My childhood fear of the dark returned, but this time from a logical cause - its likeness to the darkness of death. I suffered panic attacks and acute depression.

In this state of mind I came upon *Surprised by Joy* ...

In a few short pages the fallaciousness of my atheistic and materialistic assumptions - assumptions I had ceased to be aware I was making so deeply ingrained had they become - became obvious. I was now a theist and at the same time already half-way out of the pit of despair into which I had plunged.' [BYRON, *Catholic Herald*]

An essay 'Have we no right to happiness' was the most telling for one respondent because it seemed to speak directly to her own situation, but when she read *The Problem of Pain* she wrote that it

'terrified me, and I have yet to face the kind of ordeal he so stoically bore in his own, and his wife's death. It is not a book for cowards, and I am a coward.' [WANDA, Bermuda, *The Universe*]

One respondent referred to the positing of a theology of death.

'More recently I came across *The Great Divorce* which moved me deeply and helped me along with my struggle to cope with a theology of death - a brilliant book ...' [ERICA, *Reform*]

A LASTING HOPE OF HEAVEN

'**There is so little written on heaven*** ... and I found his concept very satisfying ...' [SOPHIA, *The Universe*]

Both *The Great Divorce* and *The Last Battle* posit an attractive and plausible picture of heaven - what it looks and feels like, who will get so far, how they will appear, who will go 'farther up and farther in.' More astute minds will detect a hint of an 'intermediate state' which may or may not be meant to be equated with the Roman Catholic belief in purgatory, the very name of which does not suggest an attractive place.

'I read of Purgatory in *The Great Divorce* - despite Lewis' disclaimer in the preface I think it is the only way to read the book - but there aren't many Anglicans who believe in Purgatory. *The Great Divorce* also has the somewhat unusual effect of making Heaven seem attractive and possible. I read [it] round about 1947. The effect was delayed a few years, but it happened.' [KEVIN, *The Universe*]

For readers of C. S. Lewis, however, heaven is made more real and more attainable and - since there has to be a counter-balance - hell more credible and to be avoided at all costs. Evil is real.

'... It was C. S. Lewis who first woke me up to the **reality** of spiritual battle. Of course I believed in Satan, but I didn't do anything about it. What was there to do? I realise now that, at the very least, we must be aware of Satan and of the spiritual battle going on around us - and for us - in order to be sure that we are listening to the right voices. As Lewis demonstrates extremely well, Satan's is often the voice of logic, who can advocate selfishness and make it sound righteous.' [DAWN, *Christian Woman*]

'Likewise it was so stimulating to read a book which handled the theme of heaven and hell in such an original way as Lewis does in *The Great Divorce*. I cannot remember that my B.D. studies gave me any guidance on this theme, and my imagination, in particular, was barren and empty in this direction. The "solidity" of heaven and the utter vacuity of hell - and the "nothingness" of the personalities of those who refused God finally, I found most helpful.' [PATRICK, *Reform*]

An Image of Heaven

What kind of image of death and heaven do the books create? It seems that one is needed.

'As for Heaven I feel a need, as probably many people do, to have a picture in my mind of what it might be like. C. S. Lewis' vision contains so many of the right elements. Obviously I don't envisage it like Narnia, as that is only a story, but the happiness, beauty, comradeship, lack of suffering, agelessness, ability to be superhuman, meetings with dead relatives and friends and the continuing presence of God all seem essential parts of my vision.

"I have come home at last ... This is the land I have been looking for all my life, though I never knew it till now."

"The term is over, the holidays have begun." This is what heaven should be like. The *"Farther up and farther in"* point to the growth and development to be found there (as in *Jonathan Livingstone Seagull*), the fact that it is *"only the beginning of the real story."*

I suppose there is nothing to be found here that is not in the traditional teaching of the Church, but Lewis' ability as a storyteller gives it body and makes it seem real ...' [OLWEN, *The Universe*]

'I was most impressed with his image of Heaven becoming so real that men locked into the physical realm could not impress so much as a blade of grass. It clearly pointed out how the physical world we perceive as hard and fast is really less than a shadow compared to God's Truth.' [PL10]

'I grew up in a non-Christian home, and my favourite books, which I continually re-read, were the seven Narnia books. I remember a deep longing to go to Aslan's country, which was described in *The Last Battle*.

I became a Christian when I was twenty-four and about two years later I was walking home from work when the thought suddenly struck me that some day I would be going to "Aslan's country" when I went to be with our Lord in Heaven.

Since becoming a Christian I have read most of Lewis' books, and am continually amazed at the depth of his thinking; I have just finished *The Problem of Pain* which contains, to my mind, the best description of Heaven and hell I have ever found.' [JACQUELINE, *Christian Family*]

'... It is wonderful in this day and age to be able to "pretend" and escape from all the seriousness of modern-day realities. There is certainly an underlying message in the Chronicles, which may reflect Mr. Lewis' personal thoughts on Life and Thereafter, particularly revealed towards the close of *The Last Battle*. The Chronicles' effect upon me is that the religious overtones have certainly set me thinking about what Heaven may be like and what Life After "Death" could be for those who conduct themselves properly in **this** world. (Perhaps Mr. Lewis is in Narnia himself now!)' [HARTLEY, *Me*]

'*The Last Battle* ... had the most profound effect on me. I had been raised with a vague idea that life after death meant we floated around as disembodied spirits, but these "resurrected" beings were flesh and bone. Heaven seemed to be divided into degrees (or layers), with the most sublime existence found inside the walled garden where the most faithful Narnians and other denizens of Lewis' imaginary world received their eternal reward.' [*JANCY*, Belgium, *Woman and Home*]

As mentioned earlier, this respondent finally found her spiritual home with the Mormons who teach the concept of degrees of glory in heaven as well as actual bodily resurrection. She concluded that she no longer needed to search for Narnia for she had found it!

A Yearning for Heaven

But how accessible is it?

One young woman had written to her mother about her daily reading sessions with her nine-year-old son and the letter was passed on to me.

'... The relevance to our everyday walk with the Lord, our "journey," is amazingly accurate. Jill in *The Silver Chair* forgot to remind herself of Aslan's rules every day and consequently got off course. Shasta in *The Horse and His Boy* is so authentic in not being aware of Aslan's presence and in feeling sorry for himself that he has so many tasks while others rest (like Luke 17:7-10 again!). And as we sat down last night, having just finished *The Horse and His Boy*, I thought [he] had read them all, and I was so happy that there was another to read: *The Magician's Nephew*. I really look forward to it every day. And I realised partly why is because I (we as Christians) have that yearning to step over into Heaven and be with Jesus, but we can't. But the kids with access to Narnia could. And they could be in the Lord's presence.' [KIM, USA, personal contact]

'It makes me feel that perhaps indeed we all go to Heaven, but we need to see with our eyes and heart that we have arrived there. And then we must go for ever forward because more and more will be opened up to us.' [ROSEMARY, *Catholic Herald*]

A Concept of Eternity

How is heaven, as a place, equated with the concept of eternity? Lewis has already been seen as a writer 'really at home with the concept of eternity. [OLIVER, *Renewal*]

Reading *The Silver Chair* enabled one respondent to realise that

'... the Christian will not spend his eternal life as a disembodied spirit, but that we await a resurrection of the body at the end of history - a resurrection like that of Jesus Himself.'

He concluded,

'It was good to get my belief straight, in line with Scripture, about the resurrection to come, but it wasn't something I got excited about: it was a fact tucked away in my mind; a piece of Biblical information; but not a cause of joy, anticipation or excitement.' [LAWRENCE, *Christian Newsworld*]

And what about Judgment?

'The thing that has influenced my thinking most, though, is the last judgment and the idea of heaven in *The Last Battle*.

When I now try to think whether I am prepared to face God on my last day, I think of it as a personal encounter - whether I can look God in the face and be satisfied with myself - as with Aslan and the Narnia creatures.' [OLWEN, *The Universe*]

'In my preaching ministry to adult congregations I have frequently used passages of the Narnia stories to throw light or illustrate some principles, e.g. *The Silver Chair* dialogue between Aslan and Jill - "Remember, remember, remember the signs - and pay not attention to appearances," etc. and the judgment scene in *The Last Battle* where the animals approach Aslan - some with love, others with fear and hate.' [MYLES]

One respondent commented on the account of Lewis' 'appearance' to

J. B. Phillips as documented in his book *Ring of Truth*, which had also been scathingly referred to in several of the cuttings sent to me.

'... soon after Jack Lewis died he appeared to see him sitting in a chair looking well - an experience he couldn't explain but seemed to find comforting. Yet I don't think he had met C. S. Probably like me he had absorbed a lot of the wonderful words of wisdom he had written.' [WINIFRED, *Reform*]

Dissenting Views

Inevitably, there were those who questioned the efficacy of such books at this time, especially among children. Was it psychological conditioning or brainwashing that made them so responsive?

'... It is strange that children have had to be helped in trouble of death - by Lewis. Is it that a previous fear of Heaven and Hell has been put in their minds? Minds that should not have to suffer adult fears, especially as so many people allow **fear** to dominate their lives ... Why should these little people have this fear put into them in the first place? Why should we try to tell them of horrors that might come? Living is difficult enough; in fact, some people have said never to fear dying as we are in Hell here. I sometimes think if we could tell them more that "Love is all - nothing else matters."' [YOLANDE, *Reform*]

'The Celestial City'

One respondent didn't think Lewis quite got the perspective right. She had just heard that her husband was suffering from a life-threatening heart condition; in fact, it transpired that she was nearer the point of bereavement than she could possibly have realised. Nevertheless, she wrote,

'Near the end of *Surprised by Joy* he writes that as we near the "City" (Celestial City) the signposts aren't close together anymore! He suggests disappointment regarding this "fact." We disagree with Lewis about this - the signposts are **still** close together - they're just different. We worship often with elderly people and we sense that they talk and sing of "signposts" as they minister to family folks and neighbours.' [ZENA, USA, personal contact]

VII
BRIDGING GAPS

Influence, Insight and Lasting Debts

"'The farther up and the farther in you go, the bigger everything gets. The inside is larger than the outside."'[H]

Up to this point, aside from the criticisms and critiques, we have dealt largely with the responses of active personal faith - stories of faith commitment or spiritual support, not all clearly defined but generally with a positive religious element, 'orthodox' or otherwise.

LEWIS AS A ROLE MODEL

However, Lewis was first and foremost, an academic, and we have caught glimpses of the man about his business at the university. He was not a theologian in the academic sense of the word, but an apologist for Christianity. Then there were his countless unseen friends and followers, including some to whom he provided a role model of some kind ...

'C. S. Lewis more than any other writer of the twentieth century has influenced my life, shaped my spirituality and been the model for my own writing.' [ESTHER, *The Bulletin of the New York C. S. Lewis Society*]

'The clarity and limpidity (I think that is the word one ought to use) of his writing was also, I am sure, of no mean assistance to one called to express himself clearly in preaching and on paper. So whatever of his ('religious') writing I have been able to lay hands on through the years, I have read with stimulating pleasure.

Lewis was a "Barnabas" to me, an edifier, a builder, and I needed (and still think the Church needed) that kind of ministry in war-time and in subsequent years.'

[PATRICK, *Reform*]

Living by Standards

One respondent's enthusiasm ranged from the man to his message to his morality. Sharing something of her life-story she spoke of 'letting Lewis down' even though he had never let her down. Though their lives were so different she saw in Lewis a model of humanity which she seemed to latch on to, perhaps in a shadowy way of that with which some Catholics looked to Mary the Mother as their role model. She elaborated on this, just a hint critically, and then reached the major area of his influence.

'... His attitude to contraception (non-committal) helped a young R.C. couple accept that it might not always be sinful. Abortion was not an issue in his day, but his undoubted rejection of it inspired me to "fight" the pre-choice movement for twenty years. But I still haven't got to the crux of the matter. Did Lewis inspire me? Yes in every positive way. Did he ever fail me? Never. Did I ever fail him? Massively. He wrote an essay called "We have no right to happiness." When I fell in love, Anna Karenina-style, I could have rejected Lewis' uncompromising NO, this is **not on**. But that would have meant to lose the values I had lived by, for all my adult life. I chose to go on setting these values as my model for life. I was not possibly strong enough to follow them, I broke a husband's heart, left my kids and damned my soul to hell (temporarily at least), but I never gave up these values. Through it all I never excused myself, never gave myself permission to be happy ... Neither my husband nor myself succeeded in committing suicide, an eventuality Lewis mentions in that essay on happiness, and other writings, as the work of the devil. My husband remarried happily, my children coped and grew up, and in the end I married the man I had no right to be happy with, and we are, always, very happy. The Church has forgiven us, my first husband has not ... It would have been easier to feel "permissive" and blame it on our parents, like Mark in *That Hideous Strength*; it would have been better to have resisted temptation altogether, but Lewis' standards still seem valid, even though I didn't live up to them ...' [WANDA, Bermuda, *The Universe*]

Mixed Messages

Lewis' general stance has also gained him many enemies, for he was, first and foremost - and certainly in his later days - a Professor of

English, and permeating his whole outlook, a philosopher. It caused one respondent to remark,

'...This plain ordinary man (reminds me of some of my farming friends) smoking his pipe and befriending his students did not appear like someone who could influence the minds of unknown readers.' [WINIFRED, *Reform*]

And another, more pointedly,

'The value I gained in adolescence from the fact that a noted English scholar (by reputation, at least) was a practising Christian and demonstrated by his example that self-examination and the pursuit of religious truth were worthwhile exercises for a modern intellectual, was ultimately undermined by the apparently limited depth of his self-examination and his failure to find a life that was fully integrated with his beliefs, and by the fact that his intellectual searching stopped once he had taken in orthodox theology, and from then on his mind was devoted to selective learning and ingenious logic-chopping to confirm conclusions he had already reached. There was no progress forward; no growth in faith. The parallel with his blunt but un-self-challenging literary criticism was inescapable.' [GLYN, *The Friend*]

In all his roles he has had something to offer and inculcated a debt to someone. His sphere of influence has stretched well beyond the boundaries of Oxbridge.

Dynamic Duo

Not Lewis only, but J. B. Phillips held a special place for one respondent, largely because he had known him personally through the Scout camps he had organised as a young curate.

'... I well remember his great influence on those boys (and on me!) - his daring riding on his motor bike and his stories in, I think, *The Boys' Own Paper* and *Chums* which he used to dash off in the evenings round the camp fire. Later his translations of the Gospels and St. Paul's Letters were a great help to me, and countless others, in our spiritual life and understanding of the Word.

I often think of them as "Lewis and Phillips" - a sort of spiritual equivalent of "M and S" - having a good product to sell, well-presented, for the benefit of millions of "customers"!

I thank God for the lives of these two Christians, one of whom I knew personally, the other only through his written and spoken words.' [NIGEL, *Reform*]

PARAMETERS OF INFLUENCE

'**All** Lewis' books have influenced me,' was the response of one reader, and it was a fact that whereas some readers could home in on specific books or even extracts, others were wide-ranging, sometimes having difficulty in separating fiction from non-fiction in their attempts to pinpoint areas of most influence. They do, however, provide an indication of the incredible way in which Lewis has permeated lives and implanted himself on people's consciousness (not to mention their sub-conscious).

One respondent sent a postcard indicating that the answer to my question was contained in the books he himself had written. Lewis, he said, had had 'a vast influence' on his life, 'first in his books, then as teacher and friend.' He then named two books familiar to me, adding that in one of these were Lewis' letters to him, 'deepening his influence.'

'Over My Shoulder'

There was a ready response from those who wanted to talk about the way in which Lewis had influenced their thinking, whether in general or in literary terms.

'I have read many of C. S. Lewis' non-fictional works, and also *Till We Have Faces*, the science-fiction trilogy and the Narnia books. The Narnia books have almost been a sort of personal "bible" for me in the past, and have influenced my outlook on life possibly more deeply than anything else I've read. They also formed my literary tastes for fantasy, allowing me to enjoy Tolkien, Ursula Le Guin and others.' [AARON, *Catholic Herald*]

'Lewis' first influence on my life came from his scholarly writings, particularly *The Discarded Image*. The second influence came from his *The Four Loves*. More recently I have been influenced by the Narnia Chronicles and by *The Screwtape Letters*.' [NORBERT, USA, *Christianity and Literature*]

In a further letter he expanded on this.

'... I was assigned several of his books (I remember particularly *The Allegory of Love* and *A Preface to "Paradise Lost"*) in graduate school ... and came to realise that although I knew him only through his books he was more one of my teachers in the field of Mediaeval and Renaissance studies than any of my actual teachers. He really touched me and continues to touch and teach me through his "presence" and through his believability. Later, in my own teaching, I was influenced in similar ways by his *The Discarded Image*. In all of these books, and in most others of his, I can hear his "voice" right over my shoulder.'

Moral Awakenings ...

'I open my copy of *The Screwtape Letters*, and there on the flyleaf is written "Londonderry, 1945" and immediately I am transported back to those hectic, insecure, highly coloured days towards the end of the Second World War.

I had been stationed at ..... where I was happy, but by June we heard that the Base was to close down, and we would all be separated and drafted to different Bases. A friend persuaded me to go to Church. The text for the sermon was "Only be thou strong, and very courageous." That hit me between the eyes. It had never before occurred to me that anybody, or anything, could say to me, "be not afraid, neither be thou dismayed," could offer some kind of comfort in my disintegrating world.

When we were drafted, to a horrible camp near Londonderry, my friend came with me, though not for long - she was sent [elsewhere]. But before she left, she introduced me to the Chaplain, and she also said, "You ought to go and buy *The Screwtape Letters*, I think you'd find it interesting."

So, on a free afternoon, I got on the bus from camp and went to Londonderry and bought *The Screwtape Letters* - the first of the countless religious books I was to buy in subsequent years. When I opened it, it struck me like a searing light - I had never before really thought that it much mattered how I behaved to other people, that it would make a difference, as long as I got what I wanted from life. I suppose *The Screwtape Letters* awakened my sleeping conscience.

I couldn't afford any other books for years. When I could, I bought C. S. Lewis, and C. S. Lewis, and all of C. S. Lewis, and he was my guide through all the difficulties of adjusting to civilian life and working out a career.' [FREDA, *Woman and Home*]

As a sixth-former one respondent had read *The Pilgrim's Regress* without explanatory notes. He concluded that the 'Little Brown girls' were an allusion to the temptation in the wilderness, adding the aside, 'That was something that wouldn't have got past the censor a time or two.' He went on,

'I remember that in the early part of the book because this is where he is sorting himself out and the brown girls become a very living presence. All the time ... you have this incisive thought of C. S. Lewis who gets into things so well and helps you to understand them.' [CEDRIC, personal contact]

One response came in the form of a brief three-point summary of those theological motifs which had most significance for him:

'1.*The Screwtape Letters*: Items of personal significance:

a] I was convinced St. Paul is correct: there is spiritual warfare. I chose to join the fight.

b] Screwtape presented counter-examples for daily behaviour maybe I don't know what to do, but I can at least eliminate what **not to do**.

2. *The Lion, the Witch and the Wardrobe*: Item: Atonement for Sin; Sacrifice of Guiltless for a guilty traitor (Deep Magic and Deeper Magic - the Deeper from before time ever began). We sinners are guilty traitors (read what Encyclopaedia Britannica says about the penalties for traitors) who deserve treatment of traitors. A willing Substitute who gives His life can ransom guilty, sinning traitor[s]. (If appropriated by guilty ones.)

3. *That Hideous Strength:*

a] Moral absolutes do exist.

b] Desiring to belong to "the" Inner Ring is a dubious and possibly vile goal.' [DEAN, *Bulletin of the New York C. S. Lewis Society*]

'The Eternal Fountain'

Not everyone who reads and appreciates *A Grief Observed* does so following bereavement. One respondent sent me a very moving account of his encounter with this book and the heights and depths to which that encounter subsequently led him ...

'During the fall of 1977, I wandered into a bookstore in York, Pennsylvania and began looking through *A Grief Observed.* The book was so powerful I stood in the store for over two hours until I finished it. Lewis chose to end his work with the following quotation: *"Poi si torno' all' eterna fontana."* My initial sense was that this was simply another example of a scholar's use of foreign phrases that most ordinary readers don't understand. I therefore ignored the phrase and went on, with a sense that I had encountered a most wonderful and provocative work, one that I incorporated into my course immediately.

Two years later a curious coincidence occurred which began a wonderful series of related events. A colleague of mine gave me a copy of *A Severe Mercy* by Sheldon Vanauken, which I devoured very quickly. In one of Lewis' letters to Vanauken, he suggests that he "read the *Paradiso* ... Note the moment at which Beatrice turns her eyes away from Dante 'to the eternal fountain' and Dante is quite content." I immediately made the connection with *A Grief Observed*; I was amazed that the translation of that line came to me in such a fortuitous manner **by Lewis himself**. Since that time I have become very interested in Dante, and I am now teaching for the ninth year a senior elective on *The Divine Comedy*. This poem has been a great eye-opener for me, and, in a sense, I have Lewis to thank for that.

In 1984 a final curious thing happened which tied a nice knot around all of this for me. I was in a bookstore near our school and I came across C. S. Lewis' *Letters to Children*. A woman who was looking over my shoulder at the time said that when she was a little girl she received a letter from C. S. Lewis. After convincing her that I wasn't a "pick-up" artist, I told her that I would love to see that letter. A few months went by, but eventually we made contact; the letter was a wonderful thing to see **and** hold. Lewis did not just write a short, impersonal note. It was a "real" letter directed to the concerns of that young girl. When I noticed the date of the letter I was especially touched and impressed. It was dated July 22nd 1960, four days after Joy Davidman's funeral. Lewis had the kindness of heart to write to a strange ten-year-old girl ... at such a very painful time in his life; when I told the woman about the context of her letter, she was moved to tears. Lewis and she now have a very special bond, and I feel especially blessed to have been a witness to such a wonderful chain of connections. A friend of mine once told me that coincidences are God's way of remaining anonymous; I think God just blew his cover!' [JACKSON, USA]

The Enchanting World of Narnia

'I was eight years old when I discovered the enchanting world of Narnia - along with Tolkien's Middle-earth and the world of Mary Norton's *The Borrowers* - as my class teachers read *The Lion, the Witch and the Wardrobe* to us. By the age of eleven, I'd read all seven Narnian Chronicles, and because the Gospel was explained to me at a very early age, I perfectly understood the rich symbolism running through the stories. Aslan is probably the most splendid and convincing literary presentation of Jesus in the whole of children's literature; "not a tame lion," always there but not always tangible, wild, real, gloriously alive, infinitely wise and understanding, rich in compassion (and humour), old beyond time, and yet anchored in a three-dimensional world, Narnia - and, of course, transcending Narnia's barriers as he does every other world's. You can't bargain with Aslan, but he is always your friend.

The entire Christian story is presented in the Narnian Chronicles, from the Cross (Aslan's death and resurrection) to the Anti-Christ and Judgment Day (*The Last Battle*); from Creation (*The Magician's Nephew*) to the end of time.

As a former librarian, I consider Lewis' Narnian Chronicles as masterpieces of children's fantasy: the "other-world" he creates is magical and convincing, spiced with a lot of fun as well as darkness, vividly imaginative, and beautifully unforced in its parallels with Christian truth. No other Christian writer has done it as well as Lewis so naturally, and with such style. The eccentric Oxford don proved to be a formidable children's storyteller.' [IMOGEN, *Church of England Newspaper*]

Narnia, she said, had enormously affected her 'imaginative capabilities' and even though she was now an adult who enjoyed adult novels,

'there are still moments when I enjoy a quick trip back into Narnia.'

'I wouldn't say that reading C. S. Lewis has changed my life. I'm not even certain if my thoughts and beliefs would be any different if I had not read any of his books. As they have been part of my development it is impossible to tell. However, I am sure that his stories have given the right "feelings" to my beliefs and given me the pictures that my imagination needs.' [OLWEN, *The Universe*]

Bridging the Gap

'I think Lewis' books supplied a very real lack when I was about ten years old as they bridged the gap between "fairytales" and "baby books" which children of that age were too proud to be interested in, and books written exclusively for adults, with only adults as heroes or heroines. That was what made me enjoy them - the fact that the heroes/heroines were both male and female and they were my age. I could identify with them and the stories were not too incredible.

Lewis' works in general have certainly influenced me, but they are so interwoven that it may be impossible for me to say how his fiction has affected me. *Perelandra* is my favourite, probably because Milton is my academic speciality.' [XAVIER, *Christianity and Literature*]

'It's difficult to say just what influence a particular book has had on one's beliefs. In fact, it's rather difficult to say what influence anything has had. I am convinced that Christianity is right, but it's difficult to say what led me to that conviction. When you stand in the centre of the maze (to borrow an image from Chesterton), it is often hard to remember exactly how you got there.

The Screwtape Letters impressed me enormously; above all, I think, by its common sense. I've never been any good at apologetics. I can't argue convincingly for Christianity (or for anything else). In this book I found a writer who could. He was doing it in the mirror, so to speak: presenting the arguments supposedly from the other side. (That may be why he took such a dislike to the book.) Time after time he was hitting the nail exactly on the head. And he wrote so well. Not, I think, as well as Chesterton at his best, but very well indeed. (I think, too, that most of Chesterton's apologetics consisted of demolishing the arguments of the other side. Lewis, in this book and in others, presented the arguments **for** belief as well as against unbelief.)

We seem to be living in an age that has substituted feeling for thought. Time after time I read an attack on Christianity that seems to present no arguments at all; I am left with the impression that I could do a much better job myself. All the writer seems to be saying is that he isn't interested, which he seems to regard as an argument. A while back I read something by a militant feminist, supporting the idea that God should be regarded as female, but adding "I don't see why we need a personal God at all." It isn't a question of what we need. It's a question of what is true. When we recite the Creed, we don't begin by saying "The following suppositions appeal to me." We say "I believe."

Lewis had no use for the subjective approach. As he saw it, the Christian dogma was the truth. The fact that the prevailing climate of opinion (much more, I think, in Britain than in the USA) does not accept it makes no difference to the fact that it's true. As he tells us in *Surprised by Joy,* he didn't become a Christian because the idea appealed to him. He did so, with the utmost reluctance, because he came to accept that it was true ...' [ORVILLE, *Literary Review*]

'... *Surprised by Joy* is such a clear illustration of how unsafe it is to be a humanist, when God has so many ways of breaking through that shallow philosophy, with the massive and solid reality of His Kingdom.' [BEVIS, Brazil, *Christian Newsworld*]

Some people needed intellectual stimulus to quantify their faith while others raised the matter of the relationship (or gap) between science and religion.

The Cuckoo of Science

Although I had stressed that I was interested in Lewis' fiction, nevertheless letters still came in bearing witness to insights and influences from the non-fiction. For one respondent, *Miracles* was extremely important,

'... because it described how most people picture life today, as thorough-going Naturalists. They believe in Cause and Effect, in a closed system. The cuckoo of science ejecting the remains of Christianity in the nest, and I came to see that that was the reason for the real situation in the Church today ... also ... that this could be one of the causes of the depressed people in our society. As Dr. Carl Jung said, a one-sided science is barbaric, and that the religions are the psychotherapies of mankind. I then knew where revival would come from when people understood these things.

Lewis ... shows clearly that the Naturalist, in not being able to stand outside nature, is in a poor position to judge it. I realised that the vast majority around me think they are able to do this. Hence anything goes ... I realised that Christianity in England might now be a lonely matter but any talk of anything from humanism being superior was the non-recognition of the dark side of man. What we had witnessed in Germany in this century meant nothing to the humanist.

It has made me realise that Christianity has need of thinkers who will not fudge the issues. Lewis shows that evolution by itself can give no reason for the development of rational thinking. As Dr. Albert Schweitzer put it, "Evolution is not going with the natural current but against it." These two minds are agreed on this point. It shows that science must have faith to sustain it.

I have no doubt that that book, *Miracles*, has had a considerable influence on me.' [JACOB, *The Local Preacher's Magazine*]

'Alternative Physics'

'... I have a considerable interest in Lewis, particularly in regard to his views as to the relationship between the individual and the state. However, the point on which I thought I would write to you relates to something I have never seen touched upon in any critical writing about him. That is, what I call, for lack of a better term, his "alternative physics" as described on pp.108-9 in the Pan edition of *Out of the Silent Planet*, and on pp.84-88 of the Fontana edition of *The Dark Tower*. As a science fiction freelance editor ... I am familiar with such formulations in science fiction itself. However, with a few notable exceptions, these are written by authors with strong secular views. Equally, Christian writers seem practically never to venture out upon such waters, and Lewis is remarkable in the way in which he seems able to combine, in these notions, both imagination and logic. Imagination, after all, is not such a rare quality. Only the very rare thinker, such as Lewis or Carroll, is able to produce concepts which strike the reader as being both imaginative and commonsensical. The explanation of the physical world set out by Augray, one that any child could grasp, seems far more logical and **likely** than the ones we are customarily given!' [HAROLD, *Writers' News*]

'What I can say is that my mind has received much of his imagery and I frequently remember incidents and scenes from his books ...

It is likely that a consciousness I have of there being levels of reality beyond my physical perception owed much to my long acquaintance with the fiction and allegory of C. S. Lewis. This has had a profound influence on my perspective, particularly in relation to Theology ...' [PRESTON, *Gradlink*]

INSIGHT, INSPIRATION AND IMAGINATION

The word 'imagination' is a cross-cultural one and has already featured in a number of responses quoted under the 'influential' heading. Similarly, many of the truths highlighted as specific influences could be termed 'insights.' Why, then, separate the two? Answer: largely because that is the way in which respondents address the question.

Imagination is a faculty one respondent regretted was not adequately employed today. It is the root from which all creativity springs. Without an imagination that will project and see the end product, no creative artist could even begin. How he or she continues is a matter of individuality.

Without doubt Lewis was a man with a keen imagination. As already noted, according to one respondent he was even credited by reviewers with inventing the plot on which *Perelandra* is based!

One respondent, in referring to the inspiration received by Lewis from both Chesterton and Tolkien, observed, 'I see both of these also as God's smugglers.' [BERNARD, *The Universe*]

This could be seen as another way of describing those 'watchful dragons' Walter Hooper wrote of.[32] This was the genius which so captivated - and, one could say, ensnared - many readers.

One respondent's children had been 'caught up' in the Narnia stories -

'but more than that - I believe they have helped to elucidate for them some of the mysteries of the Christian faith.' [EVELYN, *Christian Woman*]

A Rite of Passage

'As a child I was no great reader, but I do seem to have read and I think re-read the Narnia stories. I associate with them that longing which grows stronger as you near the end of them - wishing the books were longer. I have often wished Lewis would have written more Narnia stories so there was more to delve into although perhaps limitation adds to value. And, in any case, I have never been disappointed in reading them, in experiencing them, however many times I go to them. I find them as moving today as I did twenty years ago. I suppose I am fairly emotional by nature although there can be few passages I have read in literature that I would find as hard to get through reading out loud than many a Narnia tale!

Over many years I have turned back to the Narnia books - despite the many unread books on the shelf - at times when I have wanted to read something that will somehow be a positive experience yet not just "light" or fanciful. Lewis seems so in touch with imagination and yet so in touch with reality as well. The two seem to come together in the Narnian books and he has such a way of getting you to understand something, to feel something, to know just what he means by a picture or even just by a few words.

The books have been very important in giving me insight into the Christian faith I have long held to - they have helped me to understand aspects of the Christian experience and to reach deeper down into my feelings as well as intellect at times.

... Lots of ... pictures come to mind; ... one I can remember reminding my children of is where (in *The Horse and His Boy* ...) Aslan reminds one child that he only gets to know his own story not his companions' - we sometimes are more interested in how others get on than our responsibility to get on with what we have been given to do. It even sometimes reminds me when telling my daughter off not to do it in front of the other one or similar! ...' [KINGSLEY, *Gradlink*]

In speaking of 'insights' in what area are we working? Inevitably, again, the religious.

'*Mere Christianity* and the Narnia series ... have been particularly helpful to me in my Christian life in that they explain deep truths about God in a devastatingly simple way.' [MALCOLM, *Gradlink*]

'I was a grammar school teenager at the time. Most of my contemporaries, particularly in the science set, were in process of losing the religious faith they had been brought up in (a few, but only a few, had been brought up as atheists). Through God's grace, I was able to keep mine. But that grace was very much given to me through the above [Lewis' books]. I don't think I convinced anyone, but the arguments of *Broadcast Talks* helped me to defend my corner as one of the small minority of Christians in our sixth form arguments. The combination of common sense and intellectual force in C. S. Lewis robbed the arguments of the other side of power to influence me. Meanwhile, the imaginative tour-de-force of *The Screwtape Letters* was a great help in making the idea of the supernatural believable, and for that matter, a help in resisting temptation.' [KEVIN, *The Universe*]

Christianity 'just as it is'

'I am a Christian and Bible college student and have received enormous benefit, both academically and personally, from C. S. Lewis' writings, in particular *Mere Christianity, The Screwtape Letters, Screwtape Proposes a Toast, The Great Divorce* and *The Problem of Pain.*

I have read other books by him, but the above writings, I found to be outstanding.

Being an academic he was able to communicate theological concepts and truth in a way that was profound yet simple ...

I do not agree with all of his interpretation of Christian doctrine, but basically he has endeavoured to present Christianity "just as it is."

I have recommended some of his books to other Christians who have also enjoyed his work, although some find him a little too "deep." Most Bible students usually find his literature recommended in their bibliography.' [GRETA, *Woman and Home*]

Read it Again

'If I remember rightly the death of Aslan was particularly moving, one of those moments in reading when you come to a standstill and have to read the passage again - surprising for an adult believing he was reading a story for children. Possibly it is because the parallel with the events of the crucifixion is so close and the gentleness of Aslan as he talks to Lucy and Susan shows us an aspect of Jesus we tend to overlook. He is so accessible as they bury their hands in the sea of fur and what follows is so appalling and so unjust. I think the story helped to deepen my understanding of the original.' [VAUGHAN, *Renewal*]

For one respondent, however, it was Lewis' apologetics that provided the impetus - apologetics built with the bricks of imagination.

Opening the Door

'I was brought up in a family where one was baptised and confirmed because it was the "done thing," not because it meant anything. We even went to church occasionally at Easter, but not Christmas which would no doubt have been most inconvenient! My father had a great admiration for things Jewish, because of their emphasis on education, and had in fact read the whole of the Old Testament; though as this was in the army it may have been because there was nothing else to read. I certainly never read the Bible myself, the KJV being somewhat daunting for a teenager, but I did have some sort of awareness of God. But my parents' semi-scientific approach to things like the impossibility of miracles, resurrection, etc. meant that I was more deist than Christian.

When I was in boarding school ... at the age of seventeen, a member of staff offered to take the senior boarders to a series of talks at the Cathedral on *The Screwtape Letters*. I went because any escape from the confines was most welcome. I do not suppose I would go as far as to say that C. S. Lewis changed my life but he opened a door to a whole new world.

I had never realised that one could associate humour with religion, and that they went so well together. I had not even known that there was such a thing as apologetics: that there were logical answers that did not just take refuge in blind faith or an appeal to the Bible. For years the only theology I read was C. S. Lewis. Through him I gradually learned that the Bible was to be trusted. Now I look back and it seems a weird thing to say, but then he was a constant reassurance that belief was the only sensible and logical way to go. It actually was not until I was twenty-four that I really became a Christian: I wanted my newborn baby daughter baptised and had to face up to the fact that it could not possibly be important for her if it was not for me.

Later, as a parent I discovered the Narnia books which my children, now in their late teens, still read. They were brought up in a Christian family and did not find it hard to make their own individual commitments. I think I probably resisted to the end, much heartened by Lewis' own confession that he awoke to find himself the most reluctant Christian in existence. I'd never known before that people felt like that or that they were prepared to admit it. I suspect I feared most superstitiously that God would not take kindly to the fact that people were searching for Him. The churches and school Scripture teachers seemed to take it for granted that everyone took it all for granted, and kept suitably and restrainedly quiet about it.

Years later when I came across Peter's comment in John's Gospel, "Where else can we go?" it reminded me very strongly of Lewis: this is the way it was meant to be, there is nothing else, you cannot fly in the face of fact and logic and plain common sense. I've read most of Lewis' books but not very recently - there are so many others that seem more to meet my current needs. But for a questioning high school and uni student that matter of fact "this is the truth" approach worked wonders.' [ENID, Australia, *Renewal*]

Waking up

'When at college from 1943/9 I found his writings, especially *The Screwtape Letters, Broadcast Talks, The Four Loves, The Problem of Pain*, etc., with their brilliant clarity and logic a great help during that time when many students find their faith tested in debate and argument, and during that period when everything that one believes in comes under attack.'

This respondent then went on to outline some experiences to which he related *Miracles* and the Space Trilogy, then continued ...

'... As if that was not enough to owe to C. S. Lewis, I have managed to collect almost all the writings of George MacDonald and read them. I know why Lewis hardly wrote a book without quoting him. Someone has described reading C. S. Lewis as like "opening the windows in a stuffy room and letting in the air and the light." I would describe reading George MacDonald as like "throwing the doors wide open and walking out into the fresh air." This is pictured well with Anodos at the beginning of *Phantastes*. Some have described this as a dream. I would describe it, and I believe C. S. Lewis would too, as waking up!' [NATHAN, *Reform*]

Not logic alone

'I read the three books [the trilogy] one after the other over a period of a few weeks. As with *Screwtape*, they gave powerful emotional and imaginative support to the idea of the supernatural and miraculous in everyday life. They have had an enduring influence on me.' [KEVIN, *The Universe*]

One respondent came to C. S. Lewis via *Out of the Silent Planet*, loaned to her by a friend who knew she was a devotee of science fiction. The work, she said, 'delighted' her.

'It is fully comparable in imaginative power with the early H. G. Wells, but with an added humanity or "hnauness."' [LAVINIA, *The Universe*]

She also tried an experiment outlined by Lewis - a direct challenge to the imagination.

'I found *Broadcast Talks* and read in the introduction a challenge to any open-minded reader to perform the experiment of sitting quietly and patiently and asking God to manifest Himself. It worked, as no doubt Lewis knew it would, for anyone truly disinterested - and I think I was.'

This led off on a mystical tangent which was eventually 'tipped in favour of Christianity by Dorothy Sayers' play, *The Man Born to be King*. This in turn led to *The Screwtape Letters, The Great Divorce* and *The Pilgrim's Regress.'*

Sometimes the experience is found in the sheer joy of reading and the avenues of imagination to which it leads.

THEOLOGICAL AND SPIRITUAL PERSPECTIVES

'... this man has been my main Christian influence, and has brought me very close to what I feel is the real meaning of life as a Christian in this world.' [ROSEMARY, *Catholic Herald*]

'Seeing Things Differently'

'You mention particularly the fiction and, interestingly, I feel I've been more influenced personally by the fiction than by the theological and philosophical works - e.g. *The Problem of Pain*; much as I admire this and others. I have also read with great interest the autobiographical *Surprised by Joy* and *A Grief Observed*; and have been both intrigued and near-terrified by *The Screwtape Letters.* And *The Great Divorce* did make a strong impression - especially the underlying concept that hell does not require flames and brimstone, since the everlasting pursuit of earthly satisfactions would prove ultimately hellish.

The science-fiction trilogy (though I'm not sure that sci-fi is really an exact description of these books) provided ideas and images that have remained longer with me. But it is the seven Chronicles of Narnia which have provided the strongest and most lasting influences and impressions. And this despite my never having known these books in childhood - I must have been pretty well grown-up when they appeared (now rising sixty), and I got to know the stories when my own children were reading them in the late 1960s. We went right through the series in family reading-aloud sessions (my husband also became an addict), and since then I have re-read the stories many, many times. And having a very good memory I can claim to know the books extremely well. At different times, different ones have been my favourites; but there are bits that I love in all of them.

However, you ask specifically about "influence." It's hard to define this; but I'm aware that my ideas on, for example, Time and Eternity have been re-shaped. And certain ideas and images seem now to be, as it were, built into life. Take the description in *The Magician's Nephew* of the creation of Narnia, which is brought into being by Aslan's singing: I seldom hear the words in the Creed "Through Him all things were made" without thinking of it. Just as "Behold the Lamb of God" will recall the lamb on the shore of the sea of lilies, saying in its sweet voice "Come and have breakfast" ... Then Jill's forgetting to repeat Aslan's instructions (*The Silver Chair*) recalls the danger of neglecting regular prayers - even "formula" ones. And *The Last Battle* is full of evocative scenes such as: the representation of the Last Judgment; the dwarves, blind to Heaven being all about them; the reward of the "good pagan" ("Every good thing is done for me.").

Lots more vividly symbolic passages and images - and in all the books. And one of the most important points, to my mind, is that the stories in no way depend on the reader's being aware of these allegorical meanings. For that matter, maybe other people see things differently anyhow!' [EDNA, *Catholic Herald*]

A Biblical Parody

'I first became interested in C. S. Lewis in 1986, when at the age of twenty-six I had just become a Christian. My first Lewis book was *The Silver Chair* given to me as a birthday present by a non-Christian friend ... He explained to me that in reading the Chronicles of Narnia this was an unusual place to start but he made no apologies for his choice of gift as this book was his particular favourite.

Instantly I liked Lewis and immediately drew parallels in style with another of my favourite writers - Tolkien (Much later I discovered that both Tolkien and Lewis were members of the "Inklings" - this explained similarities in style.)

I embarked on a quest to buy and read all of the Chronicles of Narnia and this I did, reading the books in the popular order of *The Magician's Nephew* through to *The Last Battle*. Later on I discovered that the books had not been written in this sequence.

The most influential and inspiring books for me have been *The Magician's Nephew, The Lion, the Witch and the Wardrobe* and *The Last Battle*. For me these three books are a parody of the Bible - beginning with Aslan's song of creation through to his sacrifice so as to save others who did not deserve it, through to the end of time and his judgment. In *The Last Battle* the poor donkey who was forced to dress as Aslan is a picture of deception that probably exists nowadays in the world with the New Age Movement. I have always seen Aslan as a "Christlike" figure, e.g. at the time of his resurrection in *The Lion, the Witch and the Wardrobe* he spoke of a deeper magic that the Queen did not know about. Lewis goes on to follow this theme in *The Screwtape Letters* when the old devil says, "If only we knew what the enemy's purpose is."' [INGRAM]

Influential Texts

Another respondent shared a number of snippets which had had a great influence on her, such as the idea of God's caring for us all through our lives [Psalm 139], paralleled in *The Horse and His Boy* [p.139, Puffin], and the idea that God is trying to contact us, but can only get to us if we will hear.

'Oh Aslan,' said she 'it was kind of you to come.'

'I have been here all the time,' said he, 'but you have just made me visible!'[B] [GERALDINE, *Reform*]

The Problem of Evil

'Recently a friend lent me *The Screwtape Letters* and I found it not only hilarious but also very pointed. I suppose I am a little too interested in the problem of evil - I firmly believe, for example, in a personal devil. If we were naughty as children my mother would say, "You've got the Old Nick on your back."

And here was this writer explaining how Senior Devils train Junior Devils - far more convincing than any theological argument.' [LEO, *The Friend*]

'I first read Lewis' science-fiction trilogy when I was fourteen, as they were on a list of books recommended by our English teacher, who also taught us scripture. The one which impressed me most vividly was *Perelandra*. I had grown up in New Zealand with an overly sheltered background, and it was only at this time that I became really aware of the extent of evil in the world, and was trying to come to grips with the problems and questions this awareness raised. Looking back now, I would say that the book crystallised my concepts of good and evil. It helped me to see the world situation, and that of every person including my own, as part of a cosmic struggle between what St. Paul called "principalities and powers." It also convinced me that it is not a struggle in which we are helpless pawns or mere spectators, nor are we alone in the fight against evil, because God is with us and the ultimate victory lies with Him. What is important is that we each have a part He has given us to play in this struggle, and it is for us to make a conscious choice for good, aware however dimly that more depends on us than we can see at present, and that the lives of others are bound up with our choice. God is not simply an optional extra for people who happen to find religion a cosy security-blanket!' [TAMARA, *The Universe*]

'Lastingly formative'

'I have admired his theological works from the years they were first published ... but what has been the most formative for my understanding of the Christian Faith has been his teaching on the meaning of Eternal Life, i.e. **zoe**, which I first read in 1946 in the publication *Beyond Personality*. It lit up for me, as well as for others to whom I have tried to explain it, the Gospel of St. John, especially the discourse on the Bread of Life.

The same book's teaching on the Trinity has also been lastingly formative on me ... the idea of God being beyond personality; that we should not back away from likening God to human nature as if that were too coarse an image, but rather should think of Him as being even more human than human nature as we know it, not less than personal but even more so: "If you know how to give good gifts to your children, how much more ..." This aspect was reinforced in the book *Miracles*.' [WESLEY, *Renewal*]

To substantiate his point, he enclosed a page from *Beyond Personality*,

Part I, 'Making and Begetting.'

'... in his book called *Miracles*, very good in the chapter called "The Grand Miracle" around page 30 (Fontana), where he hints at immortality, but of course does not tell us how to achieve it. This is one of the mysteries to which I have already referred and for which the answer lies open to the four winds in the life of Jesus, especially John 3:1-8 and Matthew 5-8 ... [KIRK, *The Friend*]

Narnia as Primer

A primary school teacher had found some episodes in Narnia 'particularly significant' and she had also used them in school assemblies. She listed these and explained why.

1. In *Prince Caspian* the children are going through a wood and are unsure of the way. Lucy sees Aslan who shows her the way, but the others don't believe her. This is an example of the need to believe a person who normally tells the truth and is reliable - or at least to think he/she **might** be right. Also, Lucy **could** have followed Aslan alone, and one ought to have the courage of one's convictions but often does not. Finally, Aslan gives Lucy another chance [pages 110-133].
2. In *The Voyage of the "Dawn Treader"* when Lucy reads the Magician's book, she finds out what her friends are saying about her and Aslan says, "*No one is ever told **what would have happened.***"

So often one wishes one had done or not done something and all one can do is to go on from where one is. Also Aslan says, "*I have been here all the time but you have just made me visible.*" That is a profound thought about God/Jesus/Holy Spirit [pages 133-137].
3. In *The Silver Chair*, when the witch tries to make the children and Puddleglum believe there is no sun and no Narnia, Puddleglum says, "*Suppose we **have** only dreamed and made up those things ... I'm going to stand by the play-world, I'm on Aslan's side even if there isn't any Aslan to lead it. I'm going to live as a Narnian even if there isn't any Narnia.*" That is the most significant of all to me. Instead of bothering about trying to prove the existence of God, etc. one just has to get on and **live** as much in accordance with the teaching of Jesus as one can. I **try** to live as if the Gospel stories are true even though I'm agnostic about the Resurrection. I find this passage in *The Silver Chair* extremely helpful [pages 156-157].
4. [In *The Horse and His Boy*] Aslan says ... that one isn't supposed to know someone else's story. Lucy asks what will happen to someone and that is the answer. I find this a help when wanting to ask "why does God let such and such happen to So and So?"
5. In *The Last Battle* I find the illustration of the dwarves sitting in the stable thinking that the feast they are given is just old roots, etc. significant. People can be so

determined not to believe something that they close their minds and **cannot** believe [pages 132-135].' [VERITY, *The Friend*]

Speaking through Imagination

'... If you will allow me to speak on a more personal basis, I think that God uses this sort of book quite a lot (!) when He wants to tell me something. I have also read the *Dragon King* trilogy by Stephen Lawhead. That also made me think twice about a few things. I think God speaks to me very much through my imagination. These books seem to get through my emotions and I don't laugh them off as make believe as I think other people might do. I remember that C. S. Lewis said ... that he was drawn towards Christianity by Tolkien's (or Barfield's) comment that it was God that gave the imagination to the novelist and so every novel has its root in God ...' [RAYMOND, *Baptist Times*]

Beginning with 'Screwtape'

An American respondent wrote about the way in which Lewis' books had influenced some of the major vocational decisions in her life, and especially that of her husband ...

'When 'way back in 1945, we read *The Screwtape Letters* and then *The Great Divorce*, we began to feel that we had found in Lewis a true mentor. Naturally, we read *Out of the Silent Planet, Perelandra* and *That Hideous Strength.* One by one after that, we bought his books as they came to our bookstores. Not only did Lewis become a profound influence on our spiritual lives, he became the key factor in my husband's ... career decision.

Like most young people in the days when we knew World War II was ending, Ford and I were facing an uncertain but exciting future. Atlanta, Georgia, where we lived was rapidly becoming the commercial hub of the South. Career opportunities for young adults were opening up in all businesses and industries. A growing, forward-looking bank was especially interested in Ford whose business experience ... they felt qualified him to run their expanding factoring department. There was an excellent future in it.

At the same time, the combined influence of Lewis and of a friend, an Episcopal priest his own age, elicited from Ford a confession that for a year he had been battling his desire to enter the priesthood. It was out of the question, he thought. How could a thirty-year-old man with a wife and child give up his livelihood to spend the necessary three years in the seminary? However, as Lewis deepened his (Ford's) yearning, the pressure of the bankers was forcing a decision.

As for me, I had followed my early training to be ambitious for myself as well as my husband. I had a rewarding, even glamorous, job as a broadcaster ... But my values, too, thanks to Lewis, were undergoing deep changes which enabled me to recognise Ford's wish as harbinger of a true vocation. We began talking, scribbling and figuring, sometimes far into the night. When we were through, we felt that with my salary and the sale of our house we should be able to pay our way through the seminary years. We never doubted God's help in this.

In the summer of '49, Ford ... graduated from the ... Theological Seminary, was ordained an Episcopal priest and was known henceforward as "Father ... " He turned into a thoughtful, hard-working, compassionate, and faithful priest, beloved by many. He was also a good husband and father. Our family grew to three children who, not surprisingly grew up on the Narnia tales. Over the years I wouldn't be able to count the times Ford quoted Lewis in sermons and in classes of instruction, or how many parishioners he interested in reading those books which change lives. In retrospect, I can't imagine our lives without Lewis' work. After Ford died in March of 1989, *A Grief Observed* helped me. ...' [FAITH, USA, *Bulletin of the New York C. S. Lewis Society*]

Insights and Influences

One respondent, declaring that 'C. S. Lewis was the author who has most influenced my life,' wrote of her time working as a junior dietician in a city hospital. She and two colleagues were members at a well-known city centre church and attended serious study sessions there.

'It was at this time that I started reading *Mere Christianity* which gave me a sure foundation for my developing faith. Also, *The Four Loves*, which gave me inspiration and insight into the four aspects of human love, especially agapë and eros. I also recall listening to his broadcasts, at this time and discussing him with my mother, probably at holiday times.

The Problem of Pain helped to rationalise and to gain an in-depth study of the problems faced by our patients. His philosophy has also helped me to cope with the effects of a fractured skull sustained in Snowdonia in 1966.

The Screwtape Letters certainly proved to be an amusing attack on the wiles of the devil!

... It is certainly true to say that reading the books of C. S. Lewis has broadened my understanding of the Christian way of life and answered many philosophical questions as they arose.' [JOSEPHINE, FCW Newsletter]

The Feeling Intellect

'I am not terribly academic and emotional reactions, "the feeling of things," tend to leave a much deeper impression than facts or actual arguments. Facts, details of stories, etc. I forget very easily.' [OLWEN, *The Universe*]

Speaking of the 'tremendous impression' made on her by the Narnia books, another respondent went into detail.

'Lewis' portrayal of Aslan, to me is a far better way of thinking of a loving God than anything I have encountered - the "feeling" is just right for me.

Similarly his conception of the creation and the last day (of Narnia) suit my emotions and imagination much more than the bald accounts in the Bible.' [KIT, *Woman and Home*]

In Love with Narnia

'... in particular I love the Narnia series. I first read them as a young adult in the early sixties and have since read the series through many times. Each time I gain something more from the underlying theme and even now the final paragraph of the final book sends a shiver down my spine and I don't think I could read it aloud without my voice breaking! I have read one or two of the books to junior school age children whom I have taught and my own four children have also read them, the two boys seeming to be more attracted to them than the girls, strangely enough. I do so applaud the author's desire to put over the Christian message without putting people off and in creating Aslan I feel he has managed to accomplish this. If Christian attitudes and attributes can "sneak in at the back door" so to speak, I'm all for it.

I first read Lewis' science fiction trilogy in my teens and thoroughly enjoyed them, too, the last one the least, I must admit - but maybe it had as much or even more of a message for the days in which it was written than the other two! The space travel appealed to me and I can still read these books with great enjoyment - and their message was not lost on me either.

I could honestly say that those nine books I have mentioned have contributed to the way I have tried to live my life.' [BRIDGET, *The Methodist Recorder*]

Behind the Fiction

One respondent made the point that Lewis influenced him more to read general books than to read religious ones. Much influenced by

Brethren, who had 'certain reservations' about some of Lewis' books, he found that Lewis

'... fitted in with the type of book I, myself, was reading at the time. I certainly considered him, even then, much more thought-provoking than the generality of Christian "Testimonial" paperbacks.

... Perhaps the thing I like best ... is discovering some of the ideas behind the fiction. In the published lectures he seems to repeat certain ideas again and again, but in the stories they are given flesh and bones. Such as the idea of the Inner Ring.

... I had become a Christian when a teenager. So I read C. S. Lewis' theology books because they were easier than proper theology but more thought-provoking than the average evangelical paperback. In fact you can find one of his ideas in almost every religious paperback published these days, at least any I've read. He influenced me more to read general books than to read religious books.' [FINLAY, *Success*]

LEWIS' WORLD VIEW

A number of respondents looked beyond themselves and their own narrow worlds and commented on Lewis' wider sphere of activity.

Other Dimensions

Expressing adverse reaction to 'this frighteningly up-to-date' book, *That Hideous Strength,* one respondent wrote,

'When I hear of new abominable advances in so-called medical technology, I recall that book.

I am prone to ponder on other worlds like ours, in other universes - has God needed to redeem them? We can't be the only ones whirling away in space.' [ROSEMARY, *Catholic Herald*]

'In a time when too many were succumbing to the attractions of profit and development at the expense of nature he used his gift for writing to expose these values as shallow and ugly.' [GEMMA, *Woman and Home*]

To stress her point she refers to Eustace's conversation with Aslan in which, to Eustace's assertion that, 'A star is a huge ball of flaming gas,' the Lion replies that that is 'only what it is made of.' She comments,

'This is the great strength and beauty of his character and all his work, the ability to accept and understand that there are other dimensions to the world, that we as humans are not the pivot around which the universe revolves, and that science alone cannot solve the riddles of existence, but rather we need the entire range of human qualities - logic, sensitivity, emotion, intelligence and so on, otherwise we will lose ourselves in our own cleverness.'

In Need of Metaphor

'... the way Lewis' fiction has primarily influenced me is that it places me inside his world view in a way the non-fiction cannot (except for perhaps *Surprised by Joy*). This is not to imply that his fiction is didactic or illusory. Instead, I find his fiction clarifying. For me the experience of Shasta meeting the Lion in the fog ... is far more powerful than any single passage in *Mere Christianity*. Like Lewis, I am one who needs metaphor for understanding. In Lewis' fiction, his metaphors are freed from the restraints of the essay form and I ride across the world, but not an unreal world. That ride is always back into the labyrinths of human nature as it is. Lewis never romanticises human nature but he places it in its context as a product of the Fall. He subtly teaches us to return to being creatures.

The second most important thing about Lewis' fiction is that there too, we find joy. In fact we find it experienced like our own experience. This was almost the most important aspect for me. My childhood experiences, especially about joy, were extremely similar to Lewis' in their spiritual quality. When I read *Surprised by Joy* I felt as if I were reading my own autobiography in spite of the differences of half a century and a continent between us. I too was that little boy, bookish and frightened, smitten by joy in my inner life and poorly adjusted to school in my outer life. Lewis was and is clearly a soul-mate. The fiction has the same quality as *Surprised by Joy*. The triumph of the inner life over the social imbalance of the outer life seems a dominant theme in Lewis' fiction as well as in my own life.

The Narnia tales in themselves were influential in my youth. I discovered the Space Trilogy and *Till We Have Faces* later. For me Lewis' fiction is full of sanity, of truth.' [NYALL, USA, *Christianity and Literature*]

Through Darkness to Joy

Picking up the theme of joy another story pointed up a different kind of encounter with death and demonstrated how one of Lewis' books,

Surprised by Joy, enabled the reader to come through the darkest period of his life.

'The earlier sections of the book appealed to me because of the central notion of Joy, which reaffirmed the value of those experiences that, though rare, give our lives at least a subjective meaning. It was, however, the last few chapters that hit me with the strength of something like revelation.

In a few short chapters Lewis synthesises an argument drawn from other writers and his own experience that is clear, lucid, inescapable and for me powerfully convincing:

That the experience of Joy, which is all that gives meaning to our lives, is a yearning for something outside ourselves, that it is impossible to experience and at the same time be aware of experiencing Joy, so that the most important things about our life are, as Wittgenstein concluded, not susceptible to our language and, as Lewis himself suggests, not susceptible to our understanding. The notion that we do not know reality, but that the "utterly real" or Absolute is the root of our existence and that Absolute might just as well be termed Eros.

In a few short pages the fallaciousness of my atheistic and materialistic assumptions - assumptions I had ceased to be aware I was making so deeply ingrained had they become - became obvious. I was now a theist ...

A theist and a genuine agnostic - seeking knowledge of the God I must now believe not only exists, but is almost certainly the only thing that really does exist.

Thus, then, Lewis has deeply affected my life and I am deeply grateful to him.' [BYRON, *Catholic Herald*]

LASTING DEBTS

At this stage in such an enquiry, when many responses have been scrutinised, dissected, compartmentalised in one way or another, can any new note possibly be sounded? Has not all that can be said been said? Perhaps not.

A Desire to Believe

'... I gave my heart to Jesus as a child of nine, but drifted away during teenage and early twenties. I married and had two small children, and when taking my elder son to nursery school I met a young woman who lent me a book by Oswald J. Smith which brought me to a true repentance and infilling of the Spirit. I had quite a struggle to make this commitment, and I was lent *The Screwtape Letters* which showed me the work of the enemy. This has never ceased to be a blessing to me, and I do find that many Christians are quite unaware of the spiritual forces with which we contend. On speaking to my husband about my commitment I was surprised to find that he was an agnostic. (I had always supposed that everyone had a belief in God even if they never spoke of it.)

We had a very happy marriage, but I had always been inclined to agree to go along with my husband's wishes, and we both realised, as I told him that I must now put God first in my life, that things might become more difficult.

My husband wanted to believe, but just felt that he couldn't. However, eventually I persuaded him to go into ... Cathedral, and ask God (if there was one) to help him.

At the very moment he prayed that prayer I was given the answer - get C. S. Lewis' book called *Broadcast Talks*. In God's wonderful way this enabled my husband to believe, and needless to say we then bought *Christian Behaviour* and *Beyond Personality*. Seven months after my own commitment, my husband became a Christian and was used by God in many ways especially with teenage boys.

Needless to say, our bookcase contains many of C. S. Lewis' books. ... I shall never cease to be grateful for the wonderful way God blessed us through C. S. Lewis.' [KAROLYN, *Renewal*]

Not the Head Only

'I have felt for many years that I ought to put down on paper something about my great debt to him and this is a good opportunity.

I graduated in Theology ... in 1960 ... I had loved every minute of the course but left ... with my degree and teaching certificate but no real belief in Christianity - it had been academic - and I was faced with teaching Religious Instruction in a secondary school thinking that this detached, academic approach would be enough, just another school subject to prepare children for their "O" and "A" levels. God, however, had other ideas. The Chaplain (Anglican) ... had suggested I read C. S. Lewis but he was always rather despised by the lecturers as a writer who in "popularising" theology was not to be taken seriously. I later came across English graduates who felt he was not a proper English scholar because of his "popular" Christian writings. Therefore I did not take the Chaplain's advice, until, in my first year of teaching, the gulf between my own lack of faith and consequent lifestyle, and the matter of my subject began to worry me. My head of department said, "Read C. S. Lewis and Charles Williams" - so I did.

I began with *Mere Christianity* and *Miracles* and was struck as if by lightning with the realisation that I had not previously really known what Christianity was all about. The clarity of his style and thought bowled me over. In *Surprised by Joy* I recognised those moments which for me, too, had seemed to be the most significant without realising what they signified.

I discovered the Narnia books and the novels of Charles Williams and *The Lord of the Rings* all at about the same time, and shall never forget the sense of being on the brink of a new world. I am sure now that God was using these writers to try to get through all the barriers I had set up against Him. What the Narnia books and later the three "scientific" books did, I think, was to open up a world in which goodness was real, and the supernatural was real, and life presented many more possibilities than previously imagined. C. S. Lewis himself describes it as the "baptism of the imagination" when he read George MacDonald. That is precisely what happened to me, but without the will-power to change my way of living. That and the Church came much later (as in *The Pilgrim's Regress*) but the process was without doubt begun and accompanied for most of the way by the writings of C. S. Lewis. When I heard the news of his death on the same day as the assassination of John Kennedy I felt bereft of a personal friend, as I'm sure many others did.

... I have tried to compress into a couple of pages the experience of many years but it has helped me to acknowledge in a small way all that I owe him. I have, of course, encouraged others to read him - friends and pupils - over the years, and have reread the books many times. Recently I reread *Till We Have Faces* and I think really appreciated it for the first time, and I think the best allegory is *The Great Divorce* whose images have helped me in teaching about heaven and hell.' [HARRIET, *Gradlink*]

Providing the Tools

'I cannot point to any one event or experience. I have no dramatic testimony of how C. S. [Lewis] helped me through some spiritual crisis. It seems that I have nothing to tell you.

Yet, as I think back, I realise something of the debt of gratitude I owe to the man. I do not - and never have done - believe everything he said or agree with all his ideas. But his ideas have consistently proved useful, both for my own spiritual growth, and for helping others. He has helped provide me with tools that I continue to use and develop long after I have forgotten their source.

The images and illustrations he used, both in his novels and also in his collected talks and essays have been repeatedly used. The simplicity and clarity of his writing has formed a model of effective communication.' [BARRY, *Reform*]

A Father in Faith

However, one might look at the general nature of some of these debts.

'Like many people, I owe a great debt to C. S. Lewis for making God and the way to Him vivid and real.' [SOPHIA, *The Universe*]

'I am convinced that if C. S. Lewis had not kept his foot in the door for me during those years, I would have given up hope and might (who knows) have lost my chance. Maybe not - God has many ways of working; but in fact for me He worked largely through C. S. Lewis, and though I never met him I think of him as my "father in faith." My debt to him is incalculable and I am grateful to you for this opportunity of acknowledging it.' [KATHRYN, *Catholic Herald*]

'Yes - of all the men I thank God for - C. S. Lewis heads the list ...' [PERCY, *Harvester*]

Lewis is spoken of with 'respect,' tremendous enthusiasm ...

'God shall have the glory for anything good I have done, but C. S. Lewis deserves my gratitude for turning me round to the right path. Praise God for him.' [HUNTER, *Renewal*]

Realism ...

'Reading his books restored me as an orthodox Christian and I am grateful to God for raising up C. S. Lewis. What he has done for me I am quite sure he has done for thousands of others.' [LESLIE]

And is continuing to be so ...

'Yours for ever searching and finding, always thanking God for His servant C. S. Lewis. It has been useful writing this thanks.' [MARK, *The Friend*]

Perhaps a note from one of the academic respondents fittingly rounds off the enquiry.

He wrote that some years previously he had produced a paper for a series entitled 'What would you say to students if this were your last lecture' ...

'The essay was inspired principally by a single remark of Aslan to Aravis in *The Horse and His Boy*: "Child," said the Lion, "I am telling you your story, not hers. No one is told any story but their own." When I read that the whole of the so-called ego-centric predicament fell into place. The post-modernists have found nothing new. This is typical of my experience of Lewis. Such is the debt.' [GRANT, *Christianity and Literature*]

CONCLUSION

"The term is over: the holidays have begun. The dream is ended: this is the morning."[1]

The question that now has to be asked is, has the thesis I put forward at the beginning of this book been substantiated? - i.e. is it an indisputable fact that Lewis' fiction has influenced individual lives - even dramatically changed their direction?

The answer, I believe, is neither 'yes' nor 'no.' Once bring the human element into the academic and that is inevitable. I began the enquiry with a supposition - that I would be enabled to find dynamic stories to slot into the category of each book and that the whole could be very neatly packaged and presented. It did not take long to realise that that was not possible: I was dealing with human emotions and experiences and they cannot be reduced to mere formulae. Only when I was able to accept that this was not the road to go down did I begin to be able to process what I had received, but even when the first unwieldy draft had been produced there seemed a long way to go before any reasonable coherence could be achieved.

A second unforeseen factor was the eventual strength of the negative responses. After the shock waves of receiving the two major ones had died down, I realised that my original intention of referring to these in an appendix was untenable. Even without the publication of A. N. Wilson's biography, which heightened awareness of the black spots, there was a thread of unrest running through many - even enthusiastic pro-Lewis responses - which could not be ignored.

Yet neither could the fact that for each negative assertion there was always a positive one to set alongside it. However, to have pointed this up (as I did in one of my earlier versions) would immediately have been to 'load the dice' and this I did not wish to do. It is my belief that books should be left to speak for themselves. So, too, should respondents to enquiries. I had already been taken to task by a handful of correspondents for drawing conclusions they did not agree with.

So, from the appendices, the criticisms - all of them - were moved to a more prominent position and the judgment as to how many of their arguments are countered in the subsequent testimonials is left to the reader.

Inevitably in a project of this kind, a lot of editing and editing-in has to take place but I trust that I have remained true to the original in every case, even when severe cutting was necessary. I have endeavoured to reduce editorial comment to a minimum, though just occasionally the urge to insert an aside was irresistible. It is there to link, to group, to summarise and occasionally to correct. In a few instances, as with the unforeseen academic responses, I have felt it necessary to ask questions which, though done honestly, I hope have been without offence - I think Lewis himself might have done as much. For the rest, the respondents have spoken for themselves. It may be that by my doing this people who are pro-Lewis will have been annoyed at mere suggestions, or those who are anti-Lewis feel that their case is minimalised; or that non-Christians feel that the religious element has gone over the top while the committed fundamentalists feel offended by the direction some responses have come from or are going to. These, however, are facts, and I have done nothing to disturb the balance. A statistical breakdown of the responses should convince the sceptics on those points. The major outcome of these very mixed directions only really showed itself when the book as a whole was complete: the difficulty of categorising it since it is not wholly general nor can it truthfully be described as 'religious.' For that reason alone, several enthusiastic publishers declined to take it under their wings!

So what, then, is the final conclusion to be drawn from this enquiry? That, yes, the writings of C. S. Lewis have made a tremendous impact on lives, in both religious and secular spheres. But no, people for the most part are independent thinking beings and do not put their names to statements they are not also prepared to consider critically.

One thing has been made abundantly clear. The good things these books have achieved far outweigh the fears lurking in the minds of his accusers. True enough, Lewis set many of his stories against a Graeco-Roman background, in a middle-class society and academically elite environment - because that was what he knew, and the premise to 'write what you know' holds as good for him as for the rest of us.

Just one omission did surprise me. There were plenty of people ready to voice anti-occult opinion, yet while comments on Lewis' lifestyle and his denigration of those who did not think as he did were made in passing, not one overt response appeared from someone like me - teetotal, non-smoking vegetarian: the kind of person C. S. Lewis himself had no time for and would have sent up at the first opportunity as being socially inept. That omission confirms one thing, as did the few responses received from gay Christians: they, like me, are able to see beyond the man to his message, and that is the way he would have wanted it to be, and the way it should be - and, I am firmly convinced, the way it will continue to be.

EPILOGUE

To conclude on a high note, there follows a selection of the cogent statements that have jumped off the page as I read. No form of identification is appended since they seem to me to echo the thoughts held by the majority of respondents - including some of Lewis' keenest critics.

Firstly, however, a salutary note about Lewis' younger readers ...

'We should not underestimate the spirituality of children ... The seeds are sown in the younger years and blossom later when conditions are favourable.'

*****

'I came across some other books (*Out of the Silent Planet* and *Perelandra,* if I remember aright) in the mobile libraries that visited the troops. They were all refreshing waters to a very thirsty soul.'

'I read *That Hideous Strength* and it was like a burst of sunshine on a bleak winter scene.'

'Everything is contrived in a way but some is art concealing art while other is art getting in the way of art.'

'... And lastly in the fiction side, there is *Screwtape,* which for me is a sort of half-way house between his theology and his story telling. It always makes me roar with its absurdity and precision of understanding. I was very struck one time by the idea of fear, that we are afraid of many mutually exclusive things and that the first step to overcoming fear is to realise they can't all actually happen to us.'

'... a 'taste of the other.' The essentially indescribable cannot be conveyed by allegory let alone in terms of everyday life; for me, "Narnia" succeeds.'

'We shared the entire set of tales of Narnia as a community a few years ago when we read them aloud in the refectory during dinnertime, as is our monastic custom, and we were glad to think that others have, like us, derived much that is of lasting spiritual benefit from them.'

'When pregnant with my first child, I returned to the tales of Narnia and read them with renewed intensity, I don't know why. They steadied me with their timeless sense of rightness.'

'*Mere Christianity* and the Narnia series ... have been particularly helpful to me in my Christian life in that they explain deep truths about God in a devastatingly simple way.'

'But the nub of his importance is his ability to translate his highbrow theology into very simple terms.'

'Certainly "Joy" is something that comes quite out of the blue and is gone - but we know we've experienced it - a glimpse of heaven.'

'I suppose C. S. Lewis' most enduring legacy to me is still the feeling, deep in the roots of my mind, that there is something very magical about a closed door which I have not yet opened.'

'... a good friend from college and I used to reflect together on our mutual enjoyment and encouragement as derived from his works; together we hypothesized that the Lord still has this master composing new writings to encourage, entertain and edify when we all join him in the Lord's presence.'

'Perhaps one of the reasons I have fallen away is the hagiographical turn Lewis studies have taken. I do think Lewis would want us to "go farther up and farther in." While there was so much that he thought through ... he also presented provocative paths that he did not have the time to pursue that we could pursue. This to me would be the greatest tribute of all.'

And finally ...

'His non-fiction and fiction are woven from the same cloth, and his non-fiction so laced with metaphor, and his fiction done in an essayist's narrative voice, that we might have a hard time strictly dividing the two.'

With the utmost conviction I can say, we did!

A PERSONAL POSTSCRIPT

Only when I had completed the above did I feel that something was missing. I began on a personal note, and in order to be true to myself and my own conscience, that seemed to be the way I should end.

I am not, to quote one respondent, 'a Lewis nut' - and for that reason perhaps I have been enabled to view the responses more objectively. Furthermore, I ask, could a 'Lewis nut' have asked - and answered - the questions without bias?

This will surprise some respondents, against whose negative remarks I initially defended Lewis. It may surprise even more to know that Wilson's much criticised biography left me unmoved - depressed, in fact; so much so that when I had finished it, at 10.0 p.m. one evening shortly after its publication, I promptly spent the next three hours immersed in Douglas Gresham's *Lenten Lands*, which redressed the balance and proved to be a much more palatable book: I commend it.

The truth lies in re-reading more openly than previously, and in a socially changed climate. Then, I was looking for the theological examples. Then, too, I was more open to **what** I was reading, and it is here that I have to say that the accusations of blasphemy and particularly of racial prejudice should not lightly be dismissed: they are indeed there - blatantly. The logical defence is that Lewis was using the language and concepts of his time - but that was no excuse for not having the Christian interpretation and the possibility of ambiguity in mind. The irony is that the very people who condemn Lewis' social setting also tell us that we must 'address the present age' in our own writing. It imposes the question, what will they be saying of **us** in fifty years' time? We can, however, take much courage from Lewis' success in sneaking past the 'watchful dragons' - who today have become even more menacing - and at least in that, be unafraid to follow his example.

Of those I received, I don't think any story moved me so much as that of 'Eustacia Clarinda' because, as she identified with Eustace Clarence

Scrubb, so I identified with my respondent in so many instances of her childhood. Thus, from an initial, this is far too long, I moved to dare to include much more, mainly on the grounds of self-indulgence but also, because I believe that there are many other people out there still living in the wake of complex childhoods and maybe they, too, will find identity with some aspect of Eustace's portrayal - or, as I did, affinity with the writer.

Quite recently the statement was made that it is not children themselves who buy Narnia books today but adults who buy for them. Lewis, it was felt, did not have direct appeal, was too difficult for today's children. While I have no statistics to verify this either way, evidence both here and in my past experience in retailing would suggest to me a 50/50 split. Television has encouraged children to spend pocket money and book tokens on the books as has reading one book in school which has led to the voluntary purchase or present requests for others. This would seem to be borne out by the respondents who first read Lewis as a child or in school. The question might well form the basis of a future student's dissertation enquiry.

As stated in the text, one item sent to me during my enquiry was the postcard of the Narnia window at Headington Quarry Church. At the time it was numbered and filed away. Nine months into attempting to market the manuscript I thought of it as a possibility for the cover. I then began to look for a suitable portrait of Lewis for the flyleaf and visited the National Portrait Gallery, returned home and happened upon the photograph I had taken on my visit to Oxford in 1998 - and the symbolism became apparent: Lewis, over thirty years after his death, still speaking, even from the grave, to new generations of children, still inspiring, angering, provoking controversy - and still leading people to begin their own stories of faith in the Living God.

Moving On

He's a hard act to follow, but I have been asked more than once who are Lewis' successors. Many suggestions from people's experiences are included above. I would add two more:

To follow the Chronicles of Narnia - the Pangur Ban books by Fay Sampson (published by Lion);

To follow the Space Trilogy, especially *That Hideous Strength* - *Night of the Wolf* and *Nightfall*, by Christopher Bryan (also published by Lion, though possibly no longer in print).

And to assess the way in which evil is at work in society, in every age and time, then go to William Golding, and with the addition of human frailty, a penchant for seeing from a child's perspective and the macabre extreme to which human fear and desire can go, many of the novels of Beryl Bainbridge. I say this, not to detract from Lewis but because we all need to move on and widen our horizons and these are just a few more of the horizons I have found it profitable to look towards.

Patricia Batstone

APPENDIX I

Notes on the Fictional Works of C. S. Lewis

THE PILGRIM'S REGRESS

The Pilgrim's Regress is in essence the story of Lewis' own philosophical search for God - God equated with a severe landlord, with an indescribable longing and with the realisation of Joy. Lewis subtitles it 'An Allegorical Apology for Christianity, Reason and Romanticism.'

It is presented as a drama in which John, a boy living in Puritania, has the wonderful experience of seeing an island which arouses a feeling in him of utter Joy, and he spends the rest of his life seeking to have this experience over again - just as Lewis himself did following what he described as a childhood feeling of 'Northernness' or *seinsucht* at the sight of the Castleraegh Hills from his nursery window. He doesn't realise the identity of the Joy he seeks and travels far and wide, meeting hazards and people of all kinds - people who are allegorical representations of the religions of paganism and superstition as well as his own base self, the various dogmas and doctrines of the institutional Church and schools of thought, courts Wisdom, keeps company with Vertue, sojourns with History, and is imprisoned by the Spirit of the Age and released by Reason, spending time with the Sensible and the Humanist and a myriad shades of theological opinion, all jostling for position. In the end, when he permits Mother Kirk to lead him, he arrives back where he started - to open his eyes and find - God. Until he had undertaken this journey and reached its conclusion, he could not have known what he wanted.

The story is vividly told. It is a story, in some senses, of self-abandonment, of 'letting go and letting God' - though using the imagery as he does, it can be read by anyone on many levels - and be enjoyed as pure fiction by those who do not understand it all. Because many critics did not understand the symbolism in the first edition, subsequent editions have contained explanatory notes by Lewis which form sub-headings to each chapter.

THE GREAT DIVORCE

The Great Divorce has been described as both an allegory and a theological fantasy. Lewis calls it a dream in which he finds himself at a bus stop in a Grey Town. People come and go from the queue and when they eventually board the illuminated bus he finds himself transported out of the expanding greyness into a bright light, eventually arriving at a place taken to be the 'holiday zone' of Heaven, all light and bright - yet solid underfoot, and all in it so heavy that one of the Ghosts (for that is what the passengers are) cannot even carry an apple back to the bus.

In this place he meets a variety of people, some solid, some transparent, all obviously dead, most of the transparent people being encouraged, in their embarrassment, to take the journey towards the mountain where they will become more solid. There are a few surprises - the High Church Bishop who rejects heaven, and Sarah Smith, the poor mother-figure from Golders Green who appears to be one of the saints; famous people, rejected lovers, grasping mothers - all are there, fighting against their new state.

Then Lewis meets a Guide, George MacDonald, the writer and divine who had most influenced him, who answers his questions, explains a theology of salvation and tells Lewis all about what is happening. When it comes to departure time a lot of people opt to return to the Grey Town, the midway point between heaven and hell. Lewis himself wakes up in rather a state.

Again, the idea is not original, but culled from the old Catholic idea of the 'Refrigerium,' a period of intermission or place of rest or holiday, from hell, based on a translation of an old seventeenth century Parisian missal (now lost) by Jeremy Taylor.

THE SCREWTAPE LETTERS

Described as both 'theological fantasy' and 'satire,' *The Screwtape Letters* is an 'infernal correspondence' of thirty-one letters between a senior devil, Screwtape, and a junior devil, Wormwood, who has been assigned to care for a young man, the Patient, with instructions to shield him from contact with 'the Enemy' at all costs, and to obtain his soul for Our Father Below. Unfortunately, he does not succeed in his task very well and the young man becomes a Christian and, worse still, dies, still in his youth, with the realisation of Satan's presence as clear to him at that moment as the sight of God Himself. This leaves Wormwood, to all intents and purposes, a diabolical failure.

On the surface the book is humorous, but this hides the real thrust - the showing up of the way in which the devil works and the accompanying warning about being on guard against his every wile - the 'psychology of temptation.' At the same time it makes clear Lewis' position on the Nature of God.

The book was first published as a series of letters in *The Guardian* (not to be confused with the daily newspaper). In his preface to the book Lewis warns against the big mistake of taking the devil too seriously. He later confessed that writing this drained him, giving him a kind of 'spiritual cramp' because of the necessity to appear to embrace the upturning of every moral value he held dear.

Sequel to *The Screwtape Letters* and in some editions published with it, is

Screwtape Proposes a Toast – an address by Screwtape given at the annual dinner of the Tempters Training College for Young Devils. The 'dinner' had consisted of human souls - though not very tasty ones, by all accounts.

This 'lecture' traces the social and religious history of the last two centuries which have led to the unprecedented state of abundance of souls they currently enjoy. A few respondents referred to this in passing, but none highlighted it, presumably because it is not considered in the same league as its predecessor.

OUT OF THE SILENT PLANET

This is the first volume in what has come to be known as Lewis' 'Space [or 'cosmic'] Trilogy.' It begins very conventionally with the hero, Elwin Ransom (a philologist), on a walking holiday, being side-tracked by the mother of a retarded youth to help rescue him from the big house on the other side of a fence. The owner turns out to be Dick Devine, an old school colleague and enemy, who is now charming to him, introducing him to his friend, Weston, a physicist.

All too soon he finds himself imprisoned by them and shipped off in Weston's spacecraft to Mars - or Malacandra - where he encounters a series of other beings: sorns (scientists), hrossa (the creative artists) and pfifltriggi (the 'worker bees' of the planet) - all three working together assisted by 'eldila', ('guardian angels'), glow-worm creatures identifiable only as bright lights. All are governed by the Oyarsa, a figure or 'ruling essence' culled from Mediaeval cosmology, who remains invisible. Weston and Devine had assumed that these creatures needed a sacrifice and Ransom, rather than the youth (now freed) becomes it.

Instead, Ransom befriends some of the creatures and has numerous adventures with them until one of the hrossa is killed by his two vicious colleagues. This triggers a turn in relationships, for the action then concentrates on overcoming the 'Bent One' (evil) who killed the hrossa. Eventually they return to earth - Thulcandra, the Silent Planet - and Ransom concludes his adventures by turning up at a Cambridge pub, apparently unaware that he is stark naked.

It is a very descriptive story of an ideal society invaded by evil, and how they cope with it, yet not in any sense an overtly religious novel, though Lewis sees the idea of other planets as being 'good ground for "spiritual" adventures.' He was closely influenced by David Lindsay, J. B. S. Haldane, Olaf Stapledon, H. G. Wells and Jules Verne. At the time of its publication Lewis described it as 'an attack on scientism.'

PERELANDRA: VOYAGE TO VENUS

In this sequel to *Out of the Silent Planet* Ransom is again taken to outer space, this time willingly and to Venus. His spaceship is a coffin-shaped box from which he emerges 'piebald' because of his exposure to the sun.

He soon discovers that his role is to prevent the Adam and Eve of this new planet from falling as their earthly counterparts did, especially when he realises that the enemy, the serpent-equivalent, is none other than Weston, the 'Bent One' of *Out of the Silent Planet*, who becomes possessed by evil. The task is not easy, as the 'serpent' is flattering and persuasive. In the end Ransom has to take on the 'Un-man' Weston has become in order to free this new Eve and her husband from the grip of evil. He receives a serious wound to his heel in the struggle.

This book, too, is very descriptive, for from the moment Ransom steps on to Perelandra (Lewis' 'Old Solar' name for Venus) he is surrounded by luxurious foliage, luscious fruit and a mass of floating islands on which he is transported to the 'fixed land' on which no one is permitted to spend the night. He first meets Tinidril, the 'Green Lady' of the island (whose husband, Tor, is absent throughout the action) when he is on one of the fast moving islands and she, on another, momentarily mistakes him for her lost husband. A mental picture of the floating islands was the inspiration behind the story.

The final chapters of the book describe a great cosmic dance as the pair are united, with the Oyarsa and the spirits of the planets revealing themselves, and all coming together in an act of celebration. Ransom is absent from earth for a year.

THAT HIDEOUS STRENGTH

Lewis describes this in his preface as 'a "tall story" about devilry.' The Pan paperback is a much abbreviated version of the original. The story is set in a small provincial university, its chief protagonists a modern young couple, Mark and Jane Studdock, on the one hand, and the Community of St. Anne's, a commune where are Dr. Grace Ironwood, a Scottish pessimist named MacPhee, Mr. Fisher-King alias the Pendragon of Logres (alias Elwin Ransom), and as well as various other people a menagerie headed by Mr. Bultitude, a large bear. It is to this community that Jane escapes at the behest of her friends, Dr. and Mrs. Dimble, when it is realised that she is a visionary.

Conflict arises at the College when the Progressive Element headed by Lord Feverstone (who is none other than Dick Devine moved on apace) pushes the sale of Blagdon Wood to the National Institute of Co-ordinate Experiments (N.I.C.E., though anything but, for short), with which Feverstone is also connected. The two communities are bent on eliminating each other for at the heart of the conflict is the fact that buried in Blagdon Wood are the remains of Merlin the Arthurian magician, due at any time to rise again from his fifteen hundred years' sleep. He actually comes to before the N.I.C.E. wake up to the fact and attaches himself to St. Anne's, disguised as a tramp.

Mark becomes involved with the destructive 'inner ring' and finds it conflicts with his marriage and doesn't realise he is being used to try and get Jane into the clutches of the N.I.C.E. because through her dreams she knows too much of what is actually going on there. It also begins to conflict with some long-held principles and the crunch comes when he is told to trample on a picture of Christ and cannot bring himself to do it.

The N.I.C.E. are experimenting with the head and brain of an executed French scientist, Alcasan, and the eventual denouement is a very messy affair, especially when Mr. Bultitude runs amok in the laboratories. At the N.I.C.E. is an assortment of people including Fairy Hardcastle, a lesbian chief of police, Filostrato, an Italian physiologist, and Mr. Straik, a parson who mistakenly believes that the N.I.C.E. are poised to usher in the Kingdom of God. All claim the assistance of supernatural powers, not realising the evil origins of these 'macrobes.'

The ending reflects *Perelandra* with Venus paying a visit to St. Anne's and wreaking havoc of a different kind among humans and animals alike. Ransom is spirited back to Perelandra to be healed from the wound received in his struggle with the Un-man on his previous visit. Lewis was much influenced by Charles Williams when he wrote this book.

THE DARK TOWER AND OTHER STORIES

The Dark Tower is a fragment, an unfinished (barely begun) part of what was to have been the sequel to *Out of the Silent Planet.* It begins in Orfieu's study at Cambridge with Scudamour, his assistant, MacPhee (the sceptic of St. Anne's), Ransom, 'the pale man with the green shade over his distressed-looking eyes) and Lewis, the narrator. They are discussing bodily time-travel which, says Orfieu, is impossible. He is looking toward a machine that will '[do] to time what the telescope does to space' and the debate centres around this possibility - a debate before its time, since it touches, for instance, on the possibility of pre-birth memory which psychotherapy has now confirmed.

The conversation is leading to the introduction of his invention, the chronoscope, a large screen projected onto another time, not like a cinema screen but more real, like a window onto a tower darkly glowing in the moonlight, frequently obscured by cloud. They later recognise it as an unfinished version of the library at Cambridge.

They continue viewing by shifts for two weeks, and see a man in a room - a room with a pillar on top of which sits a many-bodied idol. And the man has a sting in his forehead which resembles a unicorn's horn - a poisoned sting, used to turn human victims into automata, 'jerkies,' who are employed in building the unfinished tower. The man turns and faces the 'audience,' performing a variety of obscene acts.

At the end of the two weeks Scudamour is planning a few days off when Camilla, his fiance visits him, but MacPhee suddenly realises that they are watching Scudamour's double - and Scudamour is sharing his pain, the pain of a growing sting. Matters come to a head when he sees his fiance's double about to be stung and he then throws himself at the screen to protect her, in so doing unconsciously changing places with the Stingingman who then escapes to wreak havoc in Cambridge while the real Camilla is doing likewise on the telephone.

Meanwhile, Scudamour is imprisoned in Othertime, mistaken for the Lord of the Dark Tower and the Unicorn of the Eastern Plain, and, he believes, actually in the company of the real Camilla. Unfortunately, the manuscript breaks off as he studies Othertime scientific experiments in the library, so how he gets back to This-time (it is made clear that he does) remains for ever a mystery.

But the book itself is a mystery. The story goes that it was rescued by Walter Hooper from a bonfire days after Lewis' death, but that of all the Inklings, the group of friends who met round Lewis at the Eagle and Child public house or in Lewis' rooms and shared their writing progress, only one at first recollected it ever being read to them. That story and the explanatory note in the book are plausible enough, but for some reason best known to herself, Kathryn Lindskoog, an American academic and former acquaintance of Lewis, decided to scrutinise the story and concluded that C. S. Lewis did not write it but that it was all a big hoax on the part of Walter Hooper. Some of her own arguments, published as *The C. S. Lewis Hoax*, were equally plausible, though they generally relied on the opinions of 'experts.' The long-drawn out affair did nothing to help the health of either Hooper or Kathryn Lindskoog and eventually, after some retraction, faded off the scene, leaving a distinctly nasty taste.

The Dark Tower is published in a volume containing a number of short stories, only one of which, 'The Shoddy Lands,' is referred to by a respondent. The tone of the story and its familiar academic setting are those of *The Dark Tower.* It is other-worldly insofar as it involves a brief instance of a dull man being able to read the mind of an even more dull woman. Of the other stories, 'The Man Born Blind' is most poignant - the story of a man who had just received his sight, yet could appreciate nothing about him because no one had explained to him the concept of light. 'Ministering Angels' is a fun-piece about a space-crew on a three-year mission to Mars suddenly being sent, for their psychological well-being, two very diverse women companions! 'Forms of Things Unknown' is also a space story, but this time weird and set on the Moon. Three missions have already ended in disaster with the astronauts cut off in the midst of their first report to earth. Everything hinges on the fourth man discovering the truth and overcoming whatever adversity lurks there.

The final piece, 'After Ten Years,' is the opening of what was to have been a novel about the last years of Helen of Troy but Lewis died before he could finish it.

TILL WE HAVE FACES

Described as 'a myth retold,' the story is set in the barbarous kingdom of Glome where the King brings in a Greek tutor, Lysias, nicknamed the Fox, to educate his daughters, Orual, Redival and Psyche, their half-sister whose mother died at her birth and whom Orual has brought up and loves intensely. Their idyll is shattered when King Trom discovers that Redival has been having an affair with a soldier and at the same time lets Orual know how ugly she is. From that point Orual dons a veil, eventually creating an illusion that really she is beautiful.

The most beautiful sister, Psyche, is, by demand of the priest, sacrificed to the gods to save their country from famine. So, once hailed as a goddess, Psyche is now condemned to death, accursed, leaving the heartbroken Orual to follow her sister's progress and discover that she is apparently alive and has become the wife of the god, but when she encourages her to defy the ban on seeing him Psyche is banished to wander the earth alone - and Orual continues to search for her when she has eventually become Queen and secured her country. She proves to be a good queen but only when she is eventually forced to strip the veil from her face and stand naked before the gods' accusations does she encounter Psyche again and receive the gift of true beauty.

What might be called the sub-plot (though not an isolated one) is the struggle between the old religion (represented by Ungit, the block of granite that is the god-image) and the new philosophy of the Greeks as taught by the Fox. Orual is convinced that the god of the Grey Mountain, son of Ungit, hates her. It is also a story of love - plumbing the depths of genuine out-going love and selfish possessive love, and of the heartache each causes another by misunderstanding. Redival is a symbol of Eros, earthy, but so is Orual's own unacknowledged love for Bardia which only his wife perceives.

The storyline is not original to Lewis. He reworked it from Apuleius' myth *The Golden Ass*, based on the legend of Cupid and Psyche, and Christianised it. It was both his favourite book and his 'worst flop.' He wrote it in 1955 while the then Joy Gresham was still married and staying with the brothers, and she assisted in the editing.

It is, for all the ugliness necessary to its portrayal, a beautiful story with an infinite conclusion to Orual's question to the deity: 'You are yourself the answer.'

THE CHRONICLES OF NARNIA

This is the over-all title given to the seven books which comprise the adventures of a group of children in a land beyond this one, in some 'other time,' where the Great Lion, Aslan, is the saviour figure who calls in the earth-children when extra help is needed for the beleaguered Narnia.

The background and context are decidedly mediaeval, though the England from which the children depart each time resembles that of the 1940s/50s, the period when Lewis was writing. The one exception is *The Magician's Nephew*, where the action begins in Edwardian London.

There is dispute over the ordering of the Chronicles. *The Lion, the Witch and the Wardrobe* was the first to be written, originally intended as a one-off but it proved so popular that the author wrote another, and another - and was then challenged to write a book that explained the origins of Narnia - hence, *The Magician's Nephew*.

In ***The Magician's Nephew*** two children Digory Kirke and Polly Plummer, are forced into the strange land by their eccentric Uncle Andrew who has been experimenting with magic rings left to him by an equally eccentric aunt. Then they meet the wicked Queen Jadis whom Digory unleashes by disobeying an injunction not to strike an ancient bell. She brings evil to the newborn land while Uncle Andrew can only think of financial implications. Scared of the Lion, he throws a metal bar at him but it hits the ground and begins to grow into a lamppost identical to that from which it had been wrenched back in London.

The animals in Narnia talk, among them being a cab-horse, Strawberry, spirited into Narnia by Uncle Andrew's magic. Given wings, he eventually flies Digory to an orchard to pick a special apple that will heal his mother of a serious illness. He takes this back home to her and then plants the core which grows into a tree. When, years later, the tree falls in a thunderstorm, he uses the wood to construct a wardrobe.

The action now switches to ***The Lion, the Witch and the Wardrobe***, for into the wardrobe come the four Pevensie children, wartime evacuees, playing hide and seek in Digory (now Professor) Kirke's house. Lucy, the youngest, hides in a wardrobe, but pushing her way through a pile of fur coats she finds herself in a strange country, completely snowbound, and in the midst stands a Victorian lamppost. She meets a faun who takes her home to tea and tells her about a wicked witch casting a spell to keep the country permanently in winter. No one believes Lucy's story except the Professor. Edmund is the most scathing but he finds his way into Narnia alone, meeting, not the faun but the White Witch, who charms him with Turkish Delight and elicits the information about Lucy from him. He promises to get the others to come and meet her.

Eventually they all get into Narnia and meet Mr. and Mrs. Beaver and finally Aslan, whose coming causes the snow to begin to melt. The witch holds Edmund prisoner and Aslan and she do a deal in which he allows himself to be killed in Edmund's place, much to the distress of Susan and Lucy. However, he comes back to life, the spring arrives and the witch is outwitted. The children become kings and queens in Narnia in fulfilment of an old legend.

The action of ***The Horse and His Boy*** takes place during their reign and involves a boy named Shasta, rescued from a drifting boat by a fisherman, and his talking horse named Bree. He runs away from the fisherman and meets up with Aravis who, with her horse Hwin, is escaping from an arranged marriage. They are both travelling towards Narnia where they hope they will be free. Also involved is Corin, a young prince who is identical to Shasta, who turns out to be his long-lost twin brother and heir to the throne of Archenland. In a variety of guises, Aslan accompanies Shasta and Aravis until they all reach their destination, as well as their destiny, and so live (relatively) happily ever after.

Prince Caspian introduces the first of the Narnian kings, deposed by a despotic uncle, and the four children are called to Narnia to help Caspian reclaim his throne, assisted by an assortment of animals, a badger named Trufflehunter, a dwarf named Trumpkin and a larger than life mouse named Reepicheep, together with Dr. Cornelius, his tutor. The enemies include Nikabrik, a dwarf, and the Telmarines, a pirate race from earth who are eventually sent back there.

Reepicheep turns up again in ***The Voyage of the 'Dawn Treader.'*** This time Lucy and Edmund, with their obnoxious cousin, Eustace, find themselves drawn into a picture of an old sailing ship. They are to go with Caspian and rescue seven lost lords who had been banished by his wicked uncle during the time of *Prince Caspian*. Their adventures take them to Dark Islands, among giants and invisible oddities named Dufflepuds. Eustace has a life-changing encounter with Aslan when he finds himself metamorphosed into a dragon and Lucy learns a few hard lessons before she can help the Dufflepuds become visible. At the end Caspian meets the daughter of Ramandu, a retired star, and while Reepicheep sails happily to the End of the World, Caspian returns home with his new queen.

Caspian and his wife have a son, Rilian, and he is the focus of the sixth Chronicle, ***The Silver Chair***. This time it is Eustace and a girl from the experimental school he attends, Jill Pole, who are pulled into Narnia while escaping punishment. The first thing Jill does is to accidentally push Eustace over a cliff but Aslan saves him and then makes her remember three signs which they must follow to reach the place where he is held prisoner. She immediately forgets and this leads them into some frightening situations, including almost being the contents of a pie at the Castle of the the Giants of Harfang. They meet up with Puddleglum, a Marsh-wiggle whose pessimism is a great leveller in the situation and eventually they find the prince and are able to set him free and overcome the wicked witch.

By the time of ***The Last Battle*** it is Rilian's son, Tirian, who is in need of help - this time to outwit an evil ape Shift, who has made Puzzle, an innocent donkey, dress up as Aslan to fool the people that he has returned. He is aided by Ginger the cat and seeks to treaty with invading Calormene forces who slay talking animals, which is forbidden in Narnia.

Shift tries to persuade everyone that Tash (the Calormene god) and Aslan are one and the same god and names him Tashlan, but he is horrified when the real Tash turns up. Central to the action has been the stable in which the bogus Aslan was kept and Shift starts throwing people into the stable where Aslan is supposed to be, but they meet Tash instead. However, the real Aslan is there for his followers and also accepts Emeth, a sincere but misguided follower of Tash, positing a hint of universalism in the religious content of the book. Only the Dwarves fail to find salvation because they cannot see with the eyes of faith.

The children don't want to go back to England and are delighted when they are told they needn't, for this is the end of Narnia and now they will go to a better place where they will know Aslan in a new light - for they have been involved in a train crash and all are dead - Polly, Digory, Peter, Lucy, Edmund, as well as Eustace and Jill. Only Susan has escaped because, they are told, she has grown up and is no longer a friend of Narnia.

APPENDIX 2

A
Age Groupings of Respondents

Group	Number	%
Over 60	58	27
41 – 60	58	27
26 – 40	18	8
Under 25	11	5
Not Given	73	33
Total	*218*	*100*

Gender Balance

	Number	%
Male	84	39
Female	133	61
Not Known	1	-
Total	*218*	*100*

B
Participating Publications

	Number	No. of Responses	%
Denominational Publications			
Seventh Day Adventist	1	1	
Roman Catholic	2	30	
Church of England	1	6	
Brethren	2	4	
Baptist	1	2	
Methodist	3	8	
United Reformed	1	14	
Quaker	1	17	37
General Christian	5	35	
Education/Christian	1	1	
Christian Literary	4	10	21
Small Press Literary	3	7	
Major Literary	2	9	7
Academic Literary	1	12	
Academic – Graduate	1	9	9
General Magazines/Newspapers	6	40	18
C.S.L. Journals	3	6	
Not stated	-	8	
Personal contacts	-	3	8
Totals	*38*	*222**	*100*

• The discrepancy between this figure and the number of respondents is due to several people citing more than one publication.

C
Fiction Cited by Respondents

ADULT BOOKS

Title	Number	%
Great Divorce	23	12
Pilgrim's Regress	16	8
Screwtape Letters	55	28
Out of the Silent Planet	24	13
Perelandra (Voyage to Venus)	22	11
That Hideous Strength	23	12
(The Space Trilogy – General)	14	7
The Dark Tower	4	2
Till We Have Faces	13	7
Totals	*194*	*100*

CHILDREN'S BOOKS

Title	Number	%
The Chronicles of Narnia	87	53
The Magician's Nephew	7	4
The Lion, the Witch and the Wardrobe	29	18
The Horse and His Boy	4	2
Prince Caspian	1	1
The Voyage of the 'Dawn Treader'	7	4
The Silver Chair	9	5
The Last Battle	21	13
Totals	*165*	*100*

SUMMARY

	Number	%
Adult Fiction	194	49
Children's Fiction	165	42
Non-Fiction	37	9
Totals	*396*	*100*

REFERENCES

1 These were the days before inclusive language was obligatory.
2 'Shadow into Substance: Education and Identity in the Fantasy of C. S. Lewis and J. R. R. Tolkien,' p.4
3 Mythcon II Proceedings, 1976
4 The actual date of his death was 22nd November 1963, the same day as both President John Kennedy and Aldous Huxley died, Lewis being the last of the three.
5 *C. S. Lewis: A Biography*, 1990
6 Hodder and Stoughton, 1985
7 Sub-titled 'Religion and Fantasy in the Writing of C. S. Lewis, Charles Williams and J. R. R. Tolkien'
8 'Dogma and the Universe'
9 'Myth Became Fact'
10 *Laws* 923A
11 'Christ and the Christ Figure in American Fiction' in *New Theology,* Vol.2, 1965, pp. 297-316
12 Reference to Walter Hooper: *Past Watchful Dragons*
13 Malacandra
14 Sydney Carter adapted this from an Urdu song.
15 The references to the respective Bishops do not, of course, refer to the present incumbents!
16 Obituary, *The Daily Telegraph*, 3.3.92
17 *ibid*
18 Spring 1994, Vol.2, Issue 1
19 By Sheldon Vanauken
20 This area will be considered in greater depth in Part IV
21 This was from a series in *The Independent*, c.1990, 'Stirred by rumours of immortality' by Andrew Walker, Director of the C. S. Lewis Centre.
22 'Snobberies, Sneers and Narnia,' *Books for Keeps*, No. 83, November 1993
23 'The poet of longing and the lost boy,' 24.2.90
24 Book written by Hilda Lewis.
25 *Screwtape Among Friends* - with Apologies to C. S. Lewis by Ann Owen
26 Charisma Records, CD5401
27 *Methodist Hymn Book*, No. 452
28 This account was written in August 1992

29 'The Shoddy Lands' in *The Dark Tower and Other Stories*. In the story the woman is referred to as Peggy.

30 See Chapter 12. The Marsh-wiggle uttered the sentiments in a final confrontation with the Queen of Underland.

31 Page numbers quoted are from the Faber paperback edition, reprinted 1990.

32 *Past Watchful Dragons*

Quotations from The Chronicles of Narnia used as chapter headings are from the Puffin editions, as follows:

A *The Horse and His Boy* - 1965 [1976], p.170
B *The Voyage of the 'Dawn Treader'* - 1965 [1975], p.136
C *The Magician's Nephew* - 1963 [1979], p.94
D *The Silver Chair* - 1965 [1979], p.28
E *The Silver Chair* - 1965 [1979], pp.144-5
F *The Silver Chair* - 1965 [1979], pp.200-201
G *The Silver Chair* - 1965 [1979], p.203
H *The Last Battle* - 1964 [1975], p.162
I *Last Battle* - 1964 [1975], p.165

BIBLIOGRAPHY

A
Books by C. S. Lewis

[Listed alphabetically within groups]

Note: Unless stated otherwise, all books in print are published by Harper Collins and, where applicable, are edited by Walter Hooper. An ISBN number indicates that the book was in print at the time of going to press.

FICTION

The Chronicles of Narnia [complete set 0006-27494-3; omnibus 0006-75386-1]; *The Complete Chronicles of Narnia,* Centenary edition, [0-00-185713-4]; *The Magician's Nephew* [0006-71667-9]; *The Lion, the Witch and the Wardrobe* [0006-71663-6]; *The Horse and His Boy,* [0006-71660-0]; *Prince Caspian* [0006-71664-4]; *TheVoyage of the 'Dawn Treader'* [0006-71665-2]; *The Silver Chair* [0006-71668-7]; *The Last Battle* [0006-71669-5 and 000-674036-7]

Cosmic Trilogy, The (incorporating *Out of the Silent Planet, Perelandra* and *That Hideous Strength*) [Pan Books, 0330-31374-6]

The Dark Tower and Other Stories [000-628084-6]
The Great Divorce [000-628056-0]
The Pilgrim's Regress [000-628055-2]
The Screwtape Letters, [000-628060-9]
Screwtape Proposes a Toast [000-628061-7]
Till We Have Faces [000-628059-5]

* *in the following sections denotes books referred to by respondents.*

JUVENILIA

Boxen: The Imaginary World of the Young C. S. Lewis

POETRY

Narrative Poems [including 'Dymer'] [0006-27837-X]
Poems [including 'Poems' and 'Spirits in Bondage'] [000-627833-7]

AUTOBIOGRAPHICAL

All My Road Before Me: The Diaries of C. S. Lewis, 1922-27 [0006-27645-8]
* *A Grief Observed* - Faber and Faber [0571-06624-0] [1995 edition has a foreword by Douglas Gresham]
* *Surprised by Joy: The Shape of My Early Life* [000-628083-8]

LETTERS

* *Letters to an American Lady,* Ed. Clyde S. Kilby [Eerdmans, 0802-81428-X]
* *Letters to Children,* Eds. Lyle W. Dorsett and Marjorie Lampe Mead
Letters of C. S. Lewis and Don Giovanni Calabria: A Study on Friendship
* *Letters of C. S. Lewis* - edited, with Memoir, by Warren H. Lewis
* *They Stand Together: Letters to Arthur Greeves, 1914-63*

ANTHOLOGIES, DAILY READINGS AND GIFT BOOKS

* *The Business of Heaven,* Daily Readings from C. S. Lewis [000-6266398]
A C. S. Lewis Reader
The Joyful Christian: 127 Readings from C. S. Lewis [Foreword by Henry William Griffin]
A Mind Awake: An Anthology of C. S. Lewis [ed. Clyde S. Kilby]
Readings for Reflection and Meditation (formerly *Daily Readings with C. S. Lewis*) [0006-27921-X]
The Wisdom of C. S. Lewis, Brian Sibley [Lion 1997, 0-7459-3932-5]
C. S. Lewis on - Faith [000-628074-9]; *Grief* [000-628077-3]; *Joy* [000-628076-5]; *Love* [000-628075-7]
C. S. Lewis Journal [Eagle Publishing, Guildford, 0-86347-192-7]

ESSAYS - General and Religious

Christian Reunion and Other Essays [0006-27494-3]

Compelling Reason: Essays on Ethics and Belief [000-628090-0]
* *Fernseed and Elephants and Other Essays on Christianity* [000-628082-X]
* *First and Second Things: Essays on Theology and Ethics*
God in the Dock: Essays on Theology [000-628088-9]
Of This and Other Worlds [successor to *Of Other Worlds*]
Present Concerns [0006-27023-9]
* *They Asked for a Paper: Papers and Addresses* [Geoffrey Bles]
Timeless at Heart: Essays on Theology
* *The Weight of Glory, and Other Addresses*
The World's Last Night and Other Essays

LITERATURE AND EDUCATION

* *The Abolition of Man* - Reflections on Education with Special Reference to the Teaching of English in the Upper forms of Schools - Riddell Memorial Lectures, 1943 [0006-25198-6]
* *The Allegory of Love: A Study in Mediaeval Tradition* [Oxford, 0192-81220-3]
Arthurian Torso - containing the Postumous Fragment of *The Figure of Arthur* by Charles Williams and a Commentary on the Arthurian Poems of Charles Williams
* *TheDiscarded Image* - An Introduction to Mediaeval and Renaissance Literature [Cambridge, 0521-47735-2]
English Literature in the Sixteenth Century, excluding Drama [Oxford History of English Literature, Vol.III, reprinted as *Poetry and Prose in the Sixteenth Century,* 0198-12231-4]
An Experiment in Criticism [Cambridge, 0521-05553-9]
The Personal Heresy: A Controversy [with E. M. Tillyard]
* *A Preface to 'Paradise Lost'*: the Ballard Matthews Lectures, delivered at University College, North Wales, 1941
Selected Literary Essays
Spenser's Images of Life, edited Alastair Fowler
Studies in Mediaeval and Renaissance Literature [Cambridge, 0521-29701-X]
Studies in Words [Cambridge, 0521-39831-2]

RELIGION

Christian Reflections [000-628091-9]
* *The Four Loves* [000-628089-7]
* *Letters to Malcolm: Chiefly on Prayer* [now *Prayer: Letters to Malcolm,* 000-628057-9]
* *Mere Christianity* (incorporating **Broadcast Talks, *Christian Behaviour* and **Beyond Personality)* [000-628093-5]
* *Miracles: A Preliminary Study* [000-628094-3]

* *The Problem of Pain* [000-628093-5]
* *Reflections on the Psalms* [000-628092-7]

Selected Books - Omnibus containing *The Four Loves, Mere Christianity, The Problem of Pain, Prayer: Letters to Malcolm, Reflections on the Psalms, The Pilgrim's Regress, The Screwtape Lertters, Screwtape Proposes a Toast, Till We Have Faces, The Great Divorce, Surprised by Joy* and *Miracles* [000-628133-8]

B
Select Bibliography – General Books

[Listed alphabetically by author]

+ denotes book mentioned in the text

ADEY, Lionel - *C. S. Lewis, Writer, Dreamer and Mentor* [Eerdmans, 1998, 0-8028-4203-8]
CARPENTER, Humphrey - +*The Inklings* [0261-10347-4]
COMO, James T. - *C. S. Lewis at the Breakfast Table and Other Reminiscences*
GIBB, Jocelyn - *Light on C. S. Lewis*
GIBSON, Evan K. - *C. S. Lewis: Spinner of Tales*
GOFFAR, Janine - *C. S. Lewis Index: Rumours from the Sculptor's Shop* [Solway, 1998, 1-900507-57-9]
GORMLEY, Beatrice - *C. S. Lewis: Christian and Storyteller* [Eerdmans, 1998, 0-8028-5069-3]
GREEN. R. L./HOOPER, Walter - *C. S. Lewis: A. Biography*
GRESHAM, Douglas - +*Lenten Lands: My Childhood with Joy Davidman and C. S. Lewis* [0006-27495-1]
GRIFFIN, William - *C. S. Lewis: The Authentic Voice*
HART, Dabney Adams - *Through an Open Door: A New Look at C. S. Lewis* [University of Alabama Press]
HOOPER, Walter - *C. S. Lewis: A Companion and Guide* [0006-27800-0]
+*Past Watchful Dragons*
KILBY, Clyde S./GILBERT, Douglas - *C. S. Lewis: Images of His World*
LEWIS, W. H. - *Brothers and Friends: Diaries of Major Warren Lewis* [Ed. Clyde S. Kilby and Marjorie Lampe Mead]
LINDSKOOG, Kathryn - +*The C. S. Lewis Hoax*

MACDONALD, George - +*Phantastes: A Faerie Romance* [Eerdmans, 0-8028-60605]
PAYNE, Leanne - +*Real Presence: The Holy Spirit in the Works of C. S. Lewis*
SAYER, George - +*Jack: C. S. Lewis and His Times* [Hodder & Stoughton, 0340-69068-2]
SCHAKEL, Peter - *Reading with the Heart: The Way into Narnia*
SCHOFIELD, Stephen [Ed] - *In Search of C. S. Lewis* [Bridge Publishing, U.S., 08882-70544-X]
SIBLEY, Brian - +*Shadowlands: The Story of C. S. Lewis and Joy Davidman* [Hodder & Stoughton, 0340-70979-4]
URANG, Gunnar - +*Shadows of Heaven: Religion and Fantasy in the Writings of C. S. Lewis, Charles Williams and J. R. R. Tolkien*
VANAUKEN, Sheldon - +*A Severe Mercy* [also sequel: *Under the Mercy*]
WALKER, Andrew/PATRICK, James - *Rumours of Heaven: Essays in Celebration of C. S. Lewis* (formerly *A Christian for All Christians: Essays in Honour of C. S. Lewis)* [Eagle Publishing, 1998, 0-86347-250-8]
WALSH, Chad - *The Literary Legacy of C. S. Lewis*
WILSON, A. N. - +*C. S. Lewis: A Biography* [0006-54428-2]

Unpublished Ph.D Thesis:

BATSTONE, Patricia - +'Shadow into Substance: Education and Identity in the Fantasy of C. S. Lewis and J. R. R. Tolkien' - University of Exeter, 1987 [available on microfilm]

See also Dissertation Abstracts for scholarly works on Lewis and his writings.

INDEX

A: Lewis Books Cited

Please note that many pages contain more than one reference. A figure in brackets indicates that the title is inferred. Essays, stories and poems are indicated by plain type.

B: Characters Cited

Characters are referred to by the name by which they are most commonly referred. Where one character is known by several names all entries are included together. Numbers in brackets indicate that presence is inferred but unnamed.

C: Respondents Quoted

Respondents are identified by the names allocated which, as far as is known, bear no resemblance whatsoever to the real names of any persons contributing to this study.

Secondary persons referred to, those involved in the Pilot Study and those not directly quoted are not included. A number in brackets indicates a back reference. In the majority of cases the page referred to is that on which the name actually appears.

D. *Miscellaneous References*

This list includes journals and newspapers through which responses were received and these are indicated by an asterisk.* Each page may contain more than one reference.

THE AUTHOR

PATRICIA BATSTONE obtained degrees at Hull (Theology and Education) and Exeter (Religious Education/Literature). Her doctoral thesis (1987) was entitled 'Shadow into Substance: Education and Identity in the Fantasy of C. S. Lewis and J. R. R. Tolkien.' In 1988 she participated in a Symposium at Mercer University, Atlanta to mark the twenty-fifth anniversary of Lewis' death. Following that she contributed a paper on 'Education and Identity in Modern Fantasy' to a volume in the series 'Aspects of Education' published by the University of Hull - *Religion and the Creative Arts* (edited by D. H. Webster, 1989). She became a Methodist Local Preacher in 1964 and has, until recently, been a correspondence tutor with the Methodist Open Learning Centre.

A member of the Society of Women Writers and Journalists and of the Association of Christian Writers, Patricia Batstone is also a freelance writer and editor who has worked for a number of organisations and small press publications and is a regular contributor to many more. She has published a number of books, mainly poetry and devotional. A resource book for preachers and others, *Prayers for Worship*, was published by Moorley's of Derby in Autumn 1997.

Cottage Books is the imprint usually used by this author/publisher in producing small press books which are largely non-profit or sold for charity. *In Debt to C. S. Lewis* is not published within this category.

BY THE SAME AUTHOR

Prayers for Worship

Moorley's Print and Publishing, Ilkeston, Derby.

Poetry:

Messages of Devon
Farewell to Wincolmlee
A World of Love

Religious:

Aspects of the Sermon
Time and the Gospel
Occult: The Hidden Dangers
Letters to the Editor
Memo to God
Still Dancing
Candles in the Darkness

Miscellaneous:

Adhering to the Rules
Stand Up and Be Counted!

U.K. Action Publications:

Something to Rhyme About
(Co-Editor with Daphne Ayles)
Fish-Cakes and Fantasy
(The 1996 Winterton Memorial Lecture)